# His Own Worst

## 40 Fantastic Years

## The Autobiography

### Triggering Trolls, Mocking the Afflicted @ Fingering Fart Heads

# ALEX BELFIELD

Published by Belfield Book Company

**Mush Manor**
**Tattyfilarious Lane**
**Likiend**
**Cockfosters**
**AB1 VOR**
**Bangkok**

alexbelfield.com

*Special Thanks To:*

**Big Boned Jean** – Manuscript Mule & Common Law Assistant
**Dame Jan** – Tippy-Tappy Typist
**Network Nick** – SVoR Tech Wizard
**Angel Tigger** – Proof Reading
**Al & Mr A** – Head of Legal Blame
**Dolittle and Diddleum** - Legal
**Tim C** – Dotting 'i's' and Crossing 't's'

All trademarks and brand names are trademarks or registered trademarks of the respective owners and their use herein does not imply any association or endorsement by any third party.

Alex Belfield asserts the moral right to be identified as the author of this work.

All rights reserved. No part of this publication may be reproduced, stored in a retrieval system or transmitted in any form or by any means, electronic, mechanical, photocopying, recording or otherwise without prior written permission from the author.

ISBN - 978-1-918006-10-0

Copyright © 2025 - Alex Belfield

## **Dedication**

*I dedicate this book to my Mum, Dad, Sister, Nephew, God Sons, Beloved Friends, Miss Doddy, Absent Friends, My man sausage admirers with palatial jelly wobblers and <u>YOU</u>.*

*Yes - YOU! my SVoR friends and family who collectively have saved my life and made my dreams come true.*

*I especially thank all of the trolls, medicated mentals and haters in their mother's back bedroom for paying their good earned dole or PIP money reading about my blessed life I blame care in the community.*

## **NO REFUNDS!**

*A huge thanks to my PA and hug monster Big Boned Jean who has visited every shithole slammer in Britain to collect these books page by page. Huge credit to Delicious Dame Jan for transcribing my incomprehensible, illegible and shambolic scribbles. I'm indebted to tech wizard Network Nick who kept SVoR alive. And finally, huge thanks to my producers James N, Hayden and James B for their solidarity.*

*I hope you like my epistles……..*

## **You're all Diamonds!**

*I would not be alive without the collective love and kindness.*

## Contents

About the author .................................................. 6

Preface: His Own Worst Enema ............................................. 8

Introduction.................................................................. 9

Chapter 1  Maverick or Muppet? ...........................................20

Chapter 2  Looking Inside ME...............................................51

Chapter 3  Puberty, Clearasil, Choir, Showbiz & The USA..........95

Chapter 4  Belfield at the Beeb – Radio Ga Ga......................119

Chapter 5  Hakuna Matata .................................................156

Chapter 6  A New Century Dawns!........................................186

Chapter 7  Millennium Madness...........................................220

Chapter 8  London, My Big Break and High Court! .................277

Chapter 9  The Calm After The Shitstorms...........................319

Chapter 10  Man Up! Grown Up............................................344

Chapter 11  ITV, London & Becoming a Loose Woman ...........390

Chapter 12  The Circle of Life.............................................403

The Titles that Didn't Make it! ...........................................428

Don't miss the other books in the series:...........................429

## About the author

Alex Belfield is the UK's most notorious convicted talker! He's been entertaining the nation - WITHOUT fear, alarm or distress – for 30 years as of 2024!

Alex is a comedian, entertainer, journalist, and sex symbol for the visually impaired. He has worked for 80+ radio stations around the world and has toured the UK extensively since the age of fourteen.

His books were all handwritten and edited whilst in prison at HMP Lincoln, HMP Stocken, HMP Five Wells, HMP Erlestoke and HMP Fosse Way between 2022 and 2025. Alex did not use a tippy-tappy or a ghost writer – just a pen, paper and a lot of brain power over 33 months! What you read here is warts and all. No airs and graces. It's not 'nice' – it's a series of memoires of over 40 years of a media mogul's life and the establishments finely choreographed witch hunt to 'close him down.'

Alex is arguably YouTube's most successful UK reviewer, theatre critic and investigative journalist. His influence made him the #1 target by the far-left mafia. In 2020 he shot to fame with 'The Voice of Reason' – his no holds barred YouTube chat show where he amassed 500,000,000 hits and he was selling out theatres across the UK.

Alex Belfield is a broadcaster and entertainer who in 2020 became the UK's biggest YouTube news satirist with 500,000,000 views. He sold out two UK tours from Glasgow to Bournemouth via his spiritual home in Blackpool. After 15 years at the BBC, he became the nonce factory's #1 whistle blower writing for the Mail, Sun and Mirror.

In 2022 Alex was sentenced to 5.5 years for 'Stalking' people he hadn't met, been near, threatened or in two cases didn't even know – under a new 'on-line' [s]talking law. It all started with an anonymous email from a BBC employee who wanted to 'close him down.' The BBC presented the entire witch hunt to the police.

Officials at the MOJ calculated him to be a 0.17% risk. Alex's stretch cost the tax payer £150,000 and £3 million in legal fees. This political prisoner didn't qualify for any rehabilitation due to his almost zero risk to the public. HMP unlawfully prevented his progress to an open prison.

Alex wrote his six books, including this, whilst pleasuring his majesty So, enjoy Alex's scribbles written whilst held hostage by the state. If you spot a mistake in this epistle, keep it to yourself – Alex is no Stephen Hawking!

To the thousands of fans who have kept Alex's heart and soul alive during his kidnapping - this book is dedicated to you.

## Preface: His Own Worst Enema

I'm no shrinking violet. If I've got something to say, I slap it on the table. I'm proud not to like woke, lefty, nonbinary, gender fluid radical left lunatics who want to destroy the very fabric of our once Great Britain by believing men can have a cervix.

Being proud of your prejudices is seemingly an arrestable (and an imprisonable) offence post Covid – but why? I've never given offence – if you take it, that's your problem. "You can't say that!" Why not? Why has our fundamental human right to breathe and talk been so eroded leaving us all walking on egg shells like lemmings avoiding attack?

This autobiography is the story of a little boy who from a very early age had a walk-in mouth. All he really wanted to do was make people laugh. For forty-two years it went swimmingly as Alex Belfield worked around the world as a radio DJ, theatre critic and comedian.

Alex Belfield is his own worst enema. He's still proud and prejudiced – and what is wrong with that hey?

This pit estate lad was jailed and gagged for five and a half years for words. Find out what led to him becoming a convicted talker after four decades as one of the UK's most talked about entertainers.

# Introduction

From my very first day in show business, I encountered the most peculiar, weird and creepy people who need two hands to wipe their arsehole and a mirror to find its location. This may explain why I end up getting fired or walking out of almost every single radio job I've ever had before losing the will to live and having a dirty protest in the studio LIVE on-air. Why me? How do these people find me? Why are there so many weird dysfunctional whack jobs in entertainment? It's a brutal pissing contest of one-upmanship and smoke and mirrors.

It's 5pm on 25th December 2022 and I'm onboard HMS Stockings, Pleasuring His Majesty in the arse end of Leicestershire. I gave it this name as it feels like a shitty cruise ship which you can't get off – YET. Good Lord, it's the Bigman's birthday so we mustn't take this hostage situation seriously. In comparison to Jesus, my 'punishment' is nothing, but I hope my second coming will be equally as spectacular! The book you're about to read is my life story (which sadly for some isn't over yet!). It is not particularly exceptional, shocking or outrageous and goes up to the birth of the 'Voice of Reason' and the knock on the door from the corrupt NPM = Nottingham Police Mafia. They're currently in 'Special measures' – as most of the cuntstables I met are <u>VERY</u> special!!! Never trust the bizzies, they're worse mobsters than the goons at the nonce factory!!!

Despite my luck and success working around the world in America, Spain, Germany, Nairobi and even the arse end of

Swansea – it's come at a huge personal toll! In fact, the ultimate price = PRISON! I wasn't incarcerated for violence, drugs or sex - no, I was silenced in my prime having amassed 500,000,000 hits on YouTube over a new and mysterious online offence created especially for me and manufactured and orchestrated by the evil BBC and CPS = Corrupt Persecution Service. It was an institutional led heist to hold me hostage to keep me quiet to protect the venality of the British establishment. Words are my tools of the trade - some words seem to touch a nerve when powerful and rich people are involved, especially words like fraud, liar and nonce! Words took away my freedom and gave me the opportunity to write 100,000's of words for these six books. For that I'm eternally grateful.

After an anonymous email was published to 'close him down' by a BBC person (and all the evidence given by the evil BBC to the police), a connected group of people choreographed my three-year sabbatical in the hoosegow. Four people were not believed and two were given a conviction of stalking WITHOUT fear, alarm or distress.

Since being a political prisoner, the BBC's highest paid news paedo – Huw Edwards has been convicted. I think my investigative journalism touched a nerve in showbiz – the exclusive trade of all of my accusers. This is my story of how I built my 'act' and life – a blessed life surrounded by incredible people taking me to places I could only have dreamt of from my tiny bedroom next to Gedling pit in Nottingham. I've never had a proper job, but I lived my life 100% and had a dream thirty-year career with my punters on-air and on stage who I adore!

Is being principled, having pride and an inner fight for justice a benefit or a curse? It's been a crazy life and I've loved every gig, job and encounter - but I ended up being taught a palatial lesson. This book is forty years of a man on a mission; to entertain, to expose and to tell the <u>truth</u>! I don't believe in compromise. Why should I change who I am to pacify bottom sniffing arse bandits, powerful and wealthy megalomaniacs and civil servant robots with no experience or brains who have an axe to grind? I did it my way – their way is riddled in dullness – a far worse crime than anything I'll ever commit! I've mastered the art of triggering trolls and fingering crooked arseholes!

This book is about solidarity, fortitude, love, work, ups and downs, hirings and firings and my incredible life story of sheer tenacity and determination standing up to management, institutions and protected paedos, bullies and fake charlatans. These are the only qualifications you seemingly need to survive showbiz. This book would never have been written if my life hadn't been put on pause by the biggest criminal stitch-up in showbiz history! I'm far too lazy to do this in the real world. This book has saved my life and sanity - 100% distraction. Even now I'm a lucky lad! Thank you HMP for the opportunity.

As I sit here in my con cabin with a wall full of love and hope in front of me, I can't help but count my incredible blessings.

Perhaps an odd thing to say when my saboteurs have closed me down and the state is holding me captive? My career has been insane but through it all I have had more fun, joy and love around me than most humans can dream of in a lifetime. I've never taken 'the biz' or my bosses seriously. I was cautious, contemptuous and unimpressed by the foolishness of this dopey world. From day one I watched, mocked and ridiculed.......leading to a lot of paranoia from a lot of my creeps and conniving devious colleagues. I've been so lucky to do what I want to do – when I want to do it. You could say I'm my own worst enema and an enema of the state for obvious reasons – FOR NOW! But they can't stop the clock. They can just turn the lock. That will end. I WILL be back!

I've now found my new normal at this holiday camp for the bonkers, bewildered, crackers, evil and disenfranchised. It's identical to BBC Broadcasting House when you think about it – just with fewer untrustworthy criminals. It's HMPontins for pilchards who want three meals a day and a free Xbox to play with to stop themselves from self-harming. My heart is like a volcano missing, loving and thinking about the angels in my life. So, to avoid ANY bitterness or anger, I'm writing to you! This experience as a secret investigative journalist exposing the imbeciles running HMP has underscored how incredibly lucky I am to have this unique access and opportunity. The only way to cope and survive this nightmare is to see it as a job – that's all. I haven't had a second off since being in the clink. I'm an author at forty-two years of age! Surrounded by plant pots, wet wipes, breadbins and fart heads as my co-stars. I'm always the optimist. I <u>never</u> give into bullies. Pint half full of vodka and diet cherry coke hey?

Hopefully by the end of these epistles you'll realise there's two Belfields - the public entertainer and the very caring, private and loving family man that helps out if someone needs a hand up or hand out. 'Special people' like medicated trolls and the establishment mafia seem incapable of recognising this.

Look, the world and life are not fair. Nowhere is it written good people always win and prosper over dark forces. Nowhere in the great libraries of New York, London or Paris does it say you're entitled to happiness, success or even freedom! HOWEVER, I am blessed to be surrounded by so many good souls and angels that have stuck by me 100%. I thrive off people. They've been my oxygen for my entire life. I'm dead without my punters near and far. I've paid the ultimate price for 'my truth' (as Meghan would say) – well it seems post Covid that some people are more entitled to <u>the</u> truth than others. I will never surrender to liars and if this five-and-a-half-year staycation doesn't cement my courage and resilience NOTHING will! For thirty years, I've had to fight for every single gig I've got and lost. My tenacity is still un-rocked! I will not be intimidated by money, power or self-important wallies!

From a diddy, big boned, plain looking ginger lad dragged up on a pit estate in Nottingham with a distinctly less than average micro penis to an infamous and notorious gobshite with a £1Million YouTube empire by forty-two, this is MY LIFE – warts, boils, rashes, verrucas and ALL! Magic Mike Live, rocket science or gynaecology was not my calling - waffle was! I want a PhD in gobshiting!!!

If you're looking for a book of tittle tattle, self-flagellation or self-pity - you've come to the wrong place. We've all read Russell Brand's *My Booky Wook* rammed with every carnal confession. We all know airing your dirty laundry is a very costly exercise in this woke, virtue signalling and nonbinary pernicious world. Everyone knows that gingers with half an inch and a dozen wrinkles can't get a portion anyway so no one in their right mind would shag a strawberry blonde – ask Chris Evans!

This is MY LIFE. I hope you like it! I'm boring, there's no sex, drugs and rock and roll here – only digs, mockery and sausage rolls! You won't be reading about those I've had the one, two buckle my shoe with. They're currently in therapy and witness protection. It was just a lot of moaning, groaning, regret, damp patches, apologising and huffing and puffing anyway! I've got the receipts and reviews to prove it. This is my life done my way - no matter the profound consequences. I don't need to tell you about shagging Su Pollard, Ann Widdecombe or Susan Boyle to sell books - not my style, that's classless and a cheap gag far beneath my high-brow standards! Oy vey mush, this is awkward and we're only twenty pages in!

When you lose your freedom, you are stripped of everything materially. Money, houses, cars, 5* hotels and holidays become irrelevant. Honestly, I promise you, I haven't missed them one bit. Incarceration makes you find out <u>exactly</u> who you are. Trust me an arse hole wouldn't last two minutes in the slammer. The conscience will eat you alive. All that is left is the clarity of your own head and sanity. I can see myself from a hundred miles away – and always did. I've done a lot of introspection (with the help of a mirror). I like who I am and love what I've created – a life with no regrets. Why? Why? Why? Because of the people surrounding me. Heroes are a testament to your character.

Thank God I was born in 1980 – a good thirty years before the social media bullshit began. My self-worth is defined by the company I keep – not the affirmation from my creepy peers with likes on Insta for pictures of their supper. It's woeful. I hate group think and passive aggression from lefties. I REFUSE (even now) to conform to the mincy media. My prejudices are thought out and an opinion I'm entitled to no matter how much heckling! Sadly, these days this makes you a pariah and a target by the cuckoo crowd and the radical left who have only one default position of pack mentality which is to close you down!

Most people in life want to be accepted. Most people want to be loved, popular and fit in a pack. I've never given two facks about this. I just wanted to be me from being a small boy. But why such clarity? Where did this inner strength, insight and I guess confidence come from? I wanted to be totally sincere and 100%

true to myself. Authenticity is gold dust to me. 99% of media showbiz dopes are complete deep fakes. The AI .gov mouthpieces worked from behind by the establishment and their captors……not my style. My strategy for life wasn't intentional. I didn't know I did it - I was too busy to worry about such self-indulgent psychobabble. I just thrived on words and music – they were my Heroin from being four years old. I loved to learn…..just not at school. BORING! Melody was my crack cocaine. Language and conversation were my heart and soul. The greatest people I've ever met are unique and completely individual. They create their own success and don't follow the sheeple. I thrive in their presence. Their uniqueness sets my brain on fire and their bravery to be unparalleled is only to be admired! The thing I'm most proud of is that I've had the chance to meet so many of my heroes and incredible souls and legends who define the above. If I could just be 1% like them, I'd make it! I was able to learn from the very best, which is a remarkable good fortune, windfall and life blessing!

My biggest failing is my inner sense of truth and injustice. I cannot stand liars, cheats and the insincere. This sums up <u>almost</u> everyone I've ever met in show business. It is indeed a '<u>game</u>' where perception (for most) outweighs reality and who they truly are. Ask Phillip Schofield and Huw Edwards! Don't get me wrong, I've found some of the most incredible friends (and loyal confidants) in the world on my travels, but it's like discovering a needle in a gaystack! Less is more. An entire thirty-year career to find about twenty diamonds. That'll do. I'm a big believer in quality over quantity…...just like in the bedroom! Anyone who truly believes they have more friends than fingers and toes is a liar, delusionist and should be sectioned! You have to sort the wheat from the chaff in an instant. If you take away the creepy NONCES in showbiz you're down to 50%. If you remove those highly medicated, bipolar, bisexual or bifocal narcistic numpties you're down to 2% and the rest of them are currently dead or cancelled. Not exactly rich pickings, is it? You take my point? These are official Government statistics from the ONS by the way. I tell you no lies.

Let me be clear. TV, radio, newspapers and live entertainment attracts some of the most weird, creepy, dysfunctional, classless, unstable, bizarre and truly bonkers/mentally ill dopes imaginable. This isn't just 'stars,' I'm talking PRs, managers and all egotists in front and behind the camera. What comes with the lunacy (on very rare occasions) is genius – or just massively annoying pains in the arse who you avoid like the plague. I swear to God there's more unhinged medicated and addicted Mogadons per capita in showbiz than parliament! Seriously, it they're not rug munchers, haemorrhoid harassers or transformers – they're sticking Ketamine up their chimney pipe. So, the art of success and sanity is learning a sixth sense of who to avoid! Pick and choose wisely. Max Clifford once told me his job is 99% protection and 1% promotion. If they can't better you, they'll set out to destroy you …… after feeding their grandma to the lions! May Max rest in pieces! This man knew EXACTLY where the bodies were buried! He was literally the gatekeeper, bodyguard and protector to entertainment industry which let's face it isn't exactly renowned for its class, credibility or good intentions towards women, children and the vulnerable. Having said all that, I've met so many life-long friends who I would trust with my life. I'd love you to meet some of them on my long and winding road to forty....

My way of dealing with the business (known as show) is very simple – utter contempt! My derision has never been greater, especially since Covid. Who can we trust? Certainly not the 'news' or politicians. It's not just the BBC and twirlies we need to be wary of - it's now police cuntstables, Clown Court and now the utterly broken and dangerous HMP. Disdain in our post lockdown two-tier world doesn't come anymore screaming than my ludicrous new (made up) conviction – if I were a paedo like Huw Edwards I'd be at home now enjoying my BBC millions protected from scrutiny or scorn under mental 'elf! So often in my life I find myself saying 'you couldn't make it up' or 'you couldn't write this' – well, now I will! I've got plenty of time to do it – two years nine months to be precise…...unfortunately for them!

This autobiography was inspired by Stormy Daniels who assured me that there is no better rehabilitation than opening yourself up wide to your punters. It was either six books or my own fetish OnlyFans page – no one needs to see my ginger gentleman parts, so, it's time for me to open and poke around pandora's box on the secret world of the UK's only credible, loved and trusted Voice of Reason. Strap yourself in! It's a rocky road. See what happens when I bent over backwards for showbiz for forty years and ended up being rogered senseless and banged up for boohoo hurty words.

And so, it began…….

# Chapter 1

## Maverick or Muppet?

On Monday 14th January 1980 Alex Aloysius Cornelius Obofour Xavier Vanessa Belfield was born without a fuss in the wee small hours. You never recover from being a caesarean baby – when I get out of the car, I still use the sunroof! I was so ugly that when my mother saw the afterbirth, she thought she'd had twins. My midwife was so appalled by the sight of me she put tinted glass on my incubator. My dad couldn't stand the sight of me so he put shutters on my pram. When he took me to Skegness, all the children crowded around my pushchair – they thought it was a mobile Punch and Judy Show. We were so poor I was six years old before I realised Sheba and Pedigree Chum were not bougie baby food for vegan whippersnappers.

You don't know how lucky you are until your life stops and you're able to reflect and look back on how blessed you've been. Trust me, nothing gives you a wake-up call like being in prison to reconcile your true character and who you really are inside! I've been stood over a metaphorical mirror with my binoculars for thirty months trying to open myself up for you to peruse my inner sanctum! OK, full disclosure, I'm not being coy, my career thrives on drama and talkability. The energy I create on-air and on stage is what 'feeds the beast' and keeps me relevant, topical and of course the fascination of the mentals. You cannot be controversial or edgy without making yourself a target. This is entirely intentional and always was – even as a boy at school. I NEVER wanted to be nice and liked. I want to be honest! So, what is it that made me the most disgraced, controversial and hated enema of the media, theatre and establishment in 2020? Let me try and explain in this substantial and girthy epistle....

When you have a 'real' life none of the 'media' noise matters. I couldn't care less what is written about me or gossiped about over the water cooler. All I care about is that my loved ones and my audience are OK and entertained. Everything else is chicken shit, malarkey and of zero interest. You cannot take showbiz seriously. It's just dress up and words. Only an imbecile or medicated mincing Mary would think tittle tattle and the opinion of others has any impact on what really matters. You need this leveller, or you'd end up like so many catching the bouquet at your own funeral. Your life will only end up in one direction! Seriously, it's brutal. If you believe your Instagram hype – you're finished. It's all about your foundation and grounding...... I've never been on Instagram BTW – Gingers are banned. I should start a protest.

My family are amazing. They have no interest in this world of showing or spouting off or indeed talking shite. I'm just Alex. They've lived it all and care even less about notoriety. There's no room for a bighead or airs and graces in our house – I'm too busy emptying the dishwasher. 'Their' Alex isn't anything like the intentionally misleading hype. It's a job, it's a show – my beloveds are all that matters and they will be here long after YouTube has finally been bribed or blackmailed into closing me down or the government have sent me to Auschwitz. Being defined by your box office is a vacuous and empty existence which only ends in tears. I do this job because I LOVE IT. I was born to entertain. So many fall for the ego. I never turned my nose up at any gig – no matter how small. Work is work. My dad worked his arse off all day for a show fee. From fourteen years old when I did my first paid gig, I <u>never</u> believed I was too good for any gig of any size if people had the grace to book me? Nothing good comes from the champers or an after-show party. Red carpets are the devil for the soul. I'll pass thanks! I rather be on Schindler's List than the Mingler's List! I've never been interested in the very reason for which most luvvies come into this game. As you know, I'm very sneery about those who go to the opening of an envelope simply to be seen. I believe it to be the definition of insanity. I'd rather be in my kitchen with a fisted chicken, close friends and my Aunty Fanny than sipping champers with Christopher Biggins, Linda Robson, Bonnie Langford and the other free bevvy brigade (as cheery as these legends are).

My public life is exactly that and my private life will never be shown... until now. 'He's an enigma' BBC creeps would crow. Errr no, it's just I don't like you, trust you or want my open heart to be anywhere near you. Now put down the childcare catalogue and leave me alone!!! Colleagues HATED that I had no interest in drinks after work. Why would I? They're fake and boring. I want to get home to real people who I adore. I've never changed in thirty years. I was always the same from day one. <u>NOT</u> interested in schmoozing. This didn't make me popular with the players.

'He's aloof,' or 'he thinks he's better than us' – all correct allegations – GUILTY! Now do one, stick your head down the bog and pull the chain and let me get back to walking the dog!

The truth is that I live for my family and friends and always have from being tiny. It's a stifling curse of love and responsibility. Indeed, my duty. I only ever feel 100% me when surrounded by 'my' people. That's the way it should be right? Curiously I feel exactly the same at VoR. Completely authentic. I'm 100% me on the phone-in or on-stage ranting and raving. Sadly, social media encourages these no talent tosspots to create their fake hapless world or pretend phony-boloney. You can't find fame – it finds you. You never retire either……you just stop getting booked. None of this 'being seen' or 'good for the CV' crap actually works. The only strategy is longevity through TALENT. I'm proud I played the long game that way. Thirty years to be an overnight success ain't easy. It took a lot of practice to be this divisive!

The biggest achievement in life is to have a mum and dad who adore you and will do anything for you. I got lucky! I don't have abuse stories and I can't boohoo about a broken home. A small appendage and a walk-in mouth are my only disabilities for which I get PIP and a blue badge. We have a proper unit of love – two parents, a sister and a family to inspire and encourage. I can't get enough of them. Even now I'm besotted by the ones who brought me up and have stuck around ever since. No pressure or expectation – just me. If I could be anywhere in the world, it would be around my table breaking bread. It wasn't always easy.

My mother wasn't sure about me to begin. She was seventeen months pregnant when she had me. She kept putting it off and putting it off. I now realise, more than ever, that to have a mum and dad who are so devoted to each other is the greatest and most special gift in life. It teaches you everything about integrity, unity and solidarity. It's now sadly exceptional and not the norm which is depressing. For my folks to still be together and besotted as they were fifty plus years ago is incredible. Utterly inspiring.

Life is full of ups and downs but we've been relatively lucky. Aside from the circle of life, we've not had too many tragedies and we've always stuck together regardless. For the first time in my adult life, I'm not able to be the glue for my wider family so when I get out of here there'll be a lot of catching up to do! You can't bank memories you can only make new ones – quickly! There's no denying some memories will have been stolen by this hostage situation in the hoosegow. All I've ever wanted is to be happy, sat around the table with simply fab food and a bottle of Pinot Noir. You see I'm a feeder. Gathering people together for dinner and breaking bread is magical to me.

I understand this is very old fashioned but it's all my gran's fault. Nana Lil was my hero. She was the most beautiful, uplifting, funny, inspiring and at times facetious and acid tongued woman I've ever met. For twenty plus years she made me who I am. It's basically all her fault! Blame her! She was my best mate. I adored the bones of her. Through my gran I spent a lot of time with silver tops and that's where my love for characters, language, fun, sarcasm and mockery came from as I watched quietly and took mental notes from being a toddler – prior to a whippersnapper. I learned more about interaction, teasing and getting laughs at the bingo in the community centre on Cavendish Road than all of the bullshit online courses on comedy put together. I've never done a course on anything by the way. University of life and <u>doing it</u> is the only way to master your craft. I just sat, observed and listened to <u>real</u> people having <u>real</u> argy-bargies. Verbal joust was intoxicating to me. It's delicious. It was like an orchestra to me! One day I dreamed of being the conductor!

My dad is the man I wish I could be. He's perfect. He's got the biggest heart of anyone I've ever met, always putting himself second and devoted to mum beyond my wildest comprehension. He has amazing generosity not only to provide for his family but most importantly he is loyal beyond words to anyone he loves. He's never let me down – he's never let any of us down. He worked his arse off all his life to provide, but was never really rewarded for his own talent, skill and dedication. A diesel engineer that was taken advantage of for fifty years by millionaire directors who didn't reward him for his selfless devotion and dedication. So humble, he declined promotions or even commission at the end of his career as a salesman. He wanted his brown packet each week to guarantee he could feed us greedy guts. He isn't confrontational, doesn't have a mean bone in his body and will never offend. Why can't I be like this? Blame his mother, Nana Lil! At eighty years young my old dad is the biggest hero of them all.

Mum and I are similar, straight talking, strong minded, spoilt but soft as grease deep down. I don't like the word stubborn but it might be true. Mum was quite unique in working all through my childhood so that I could become accustomed to the lifestyle to which I now enjoy. It wasn't easy in the eighties. I so admire her tenacity and sense of pride. She's a hero and ahead of her time. If you want something you work for it. Beautiful ethic. No credit cards or benefits – if you can't afford it, you don't have it. We're two peas in a pod and love our argy-bargies…. they're fun right? Ask Freud though, a mothers' bond will make or break you. I've never loved her more than now at seventy. She's the Queen of the family. Don't mess with the matriarch – she'll do anything for her pack. An inspiration. Fearless strength and fortitude. I wasn't a soft lad. Even as a kid I knew how to work mum from behind. She'd drag me around M&S or BHS to be tortured by lines of those hideous clothes. I'd deliberately get lost and eventually go to customer services to be found. 'Could the owner of a porky, ginger fat lad, collect it from till six.' The shame would instantly get mum out of the shop. No flies on me! A clout around the ear never did me any harm!

For all of my childhood I lived in the pit estate in Gedling, Nottingham - I'm still only a mile away. The late eighties were not fun economically and people suffered bigtime especially through the Thatcher/Scargill years. I was completely unaware. My sister and I were protected from 'the real world' and just loved being loved and just being kids. We were so lucky. No iPhone, puberty blockers or social media - back then you had to have an imagination......and that's when it started. The idea of 90+ genders would have had you sectioned. Now it gets you a Pride of Britain award.

Some dopey celebs claim to remember their conception in their autobiography. I can't even recall what I had for my breakfast. My earliest memories all involve events and people. All I ever cared about was family parties, gatherings and holidays. We didn't have Xbox and I certainly didn't want one. The magic of childhood for me always starts with Christmas. God, I love it. The campery and theatre of Christmas Eve and the excitement when Santa has emptied his sack all over my mother's front room carpet doesn't compare to the endless visitors popping in and out. Being around the table, the festive fayre and games – the pure joy, even at thirty-two (current age-ish) I still love it! For me the elation is now vicarious and has been for twenty years through the kids and even my audiences. It never gets old. I love Christmas movies, the music, but most importantly – the people. As you'll hear later, by my mid-twenties I performed fifty plus Christmas shows every year for nearly two decades dispatching my condiments of the season. It was exhausting but fun and pure joy. It filled my heart with happiness each year and it was magnificent from being a kid. I couldn't wait to put the tree up – in November if my mother would let me! Curiously in recent years mum has turned her palace into a grotto. You can see our house from space in December with all the flying reindeer and waving snowmen. I've always had a 'creative' mind. One year when I was about six, I thought I'd help mum and dad by giving them a lie in. I naturally wanted to get up at 5am and they – well didn't. Christmas is a LONG day, they were smart! Push it to 7am and limit the brain damage, clattering of pans and exhaustion. We didn't have hundreds of gifts but each one was special. I hate those slappers who appear on BBC Breakfast every December with piles and piles of wrapped boxes for little Tamika, Courtney and Leonardo. Shameful! We had traditions. At the end of the bed was a bulging sack with a selection box, gold coins and a real orange (that went in the bin). I preferred the Terry's chocolate version which to this day I believe is much healthier as it's fruit and bigger! All helps with the five a day! We also had those little squares of twenty wrapped Cadbury's in a small box. These were allowed to be opened (and half eaten) before the racket began. It kept me quiet ahead of Dad's butcher's pork pie and brown sauce breakfast. Nope, me neither!

I talked my sister into sneaking downstairs and opening our presents to save mum and dad the fuss – the best Christmas gift of all right? WRONG! Eventually, despite the military level planning, going down the old wooden hill in awkward silence on tip toes, mum smelt a rat. No flies on that one! She always slept with one eye open in case I was up to shenanigans. Alas, by the time she thundered down the stairs EVERY gift to everyone in the entire house was half opened and I, she and my sister had absolutely no idea who sent what to whom. She was pissed off bigtime! I can't remember whose fault it was, but my sis is three years older than me so <u>SHE</u> should have known better. Boy that was fun…...not for mum. By St. Swithin's Day mum forgave me. She was spitting feathers. She laughs now but she didn't then, face like a smacked arse all through the Queen's speech! For days mum claimed no one could work out what was what. Grow up, I don't think the whisky is for my sister! It was a <u>VERY</u> frosty lunch. It took a good two decades to find the funny. Biggest bollocking ever I can tell you! I was sent to my bedroom before Noel Edmonds had made a load of disabled kids dreams come true by sending them for a guided tour of the Jim'll Fix It studios by Huw Edwards. Ahhh – the good old days of the BBC! Dad couldn't give two shiny shites. He kept his gob shut though so as not to undermine mother - he's not daft! Old school parenting. Only one pair of trousers in our house. Happy Wife – Happy Life. There was no naughty step in my day, you just got a smack in the gob with a Vileda mop!

Christmas these days is a double-edged sword. I still love it so much and I go to great effort for the kids, but it's always tinged with pangs of sadness. Over the last decade I've lost so many heroes; Aunty Mary, Aunty Marge, Nana, Aunty Jill, Uncle Ken, Uncle Tom, Grandma, Grandad - all gone. That was seven visits I did for two decades until one by one they were taken away. Life isn't easy, is it? Those we treasure most eventually leave an empty chair at our beloved table. You put on a brave face but it's galling. I know so many of you will feel this way. If you don't you have never been loved. The build-up is amazing and exciting but the reality of the day is always bittersweet. I'm always mindful of this now with my phone-ins. For so many it can't be a 'Merry' or a 'Happy' Christmas. Wasn't I lucky though to have twenty years as a kid of magical 'movie like' Christmases followed by a career on the road sharing my gags and festive tunes touring? Same gags. Same songs. Same show. You can't change it. Piece of piss. Kerching! It's all about perspective. You have to see everything through a kid's eyes and then take a moment to remember absent friends. Nothing lasts forever – the hardest reality of being a grown up. Compassion and empathy leave you vulnerable especially at the 'most wonderful' time of the year!

We weren't rich, we weren't middle class, I didn't go to private school and university – but – I was so drenched in love and memories. Childhood was tough, especially competing with birthday parties. My mother could only afford a laundrette for my friends. It wasn't exactly a whacky warehouse – we'd just sit there and play pass the Persil! Even today at twenty-seven years old (shut your face) I love to reminisce about Christmases through a child's eyes back in the distinctly average place I grew up. What places like Gedling have is community – the best feeling in the world. We were all in the same boat – and it felt like the Titanic! Talking of ores, my slut of a sister Veronica (I call her Vera, leave the nickas off) is just like Gedling – everyone knows where it is, but nobody wants to go there! When you lose that energy and passion for silliness and 'special days' I think you might as well be dead! I love to plan and order far too much food so that everyone can enjoy on all celebration days. Thank Mary and Joseph for Ocado and Simply M&S - that's what Christmas is all about!

From being a tiny kid, I always loved music. It was my salvation from six years old. I had keyboard lessons (poor man's piano) and only now do I realise the struggle mum and dad must have had to find £9 every week for my sixty-minute lesson. I will never forget this pressure that I put on them without even knowing. I didn't think anything of it at the time. They didn't flinch but it must have been tough. Only now do I realise how selfish I was - £9 in 1987 was probably £50 today. How can I ever repay them? Thank God though that I've never brought shame on them.... like being thrown in prison, oh wait....

As a boy, music and the piano were my Manchester United. I'd never fantasised about going to Wembley, I just loved LIVE music and later comedy. It was enchanting to me. My dream was to one day own a baby grand piano and in 2019 my dream came true at thirty-nine! I don't like to rush. The salvation and joy this work of art gives me is immeasurable. Playing the piano is truly my passion, my life blood and it's my <u>best friend</u>. When anything bad happens, twenty minutes fingering my organ sorts everything out. It should be on the NHS. All negativity just disappears through those magic black and white keys. Stunning therapy. Music is such a gift when it comes into your life. It truly is the rhythm of life as it will/can mirror your mood immediately and be such a relief and strength at the toughest of times. I guess it's my religion. It's my 'spirit' - another world - unparalleled. I would give up everything before music. Having said that I wasn't a child prodigy. In fact, I've always been distinctly average at everything I love but what I lack in natural talent I make up for in pure tenacity and energy. I truly believe perseverance outweighs genius – it is the key to success. You only fail if you give up too soon! I also have my mum and dad's work ethic that you fight on and never give in. The reason for my LIVE, Celebrity Radio and YouTube success is that I work harder than anyone else. They're all ego driven and lazy. Not me! I work my arse off 24/7. Whilst everyone else is 'playing' I'm busy learning…..even today! Think about it, whilst most lads in jail get off their tits on Spice, shag a bent screw and polish their criminal tools whilst in the pokey I've worked my arse off writing six books. I could have watched TV all day but it's not me. I've no idea where this comes from.

I later realised all of my passions are connected. Music is about rhythm and dexterity. So is talking. Words have a beat too. The more you practise and craft language, the more mellifluous it sounds – exactly the same as music. Equally, editing of audio and video is identical – it's all about rhythm. How did I find this passion? I guess this infatuation found me. As a kid while my peers were pissing about with Sonic or Tetris – I was either listening to incredible communicators or being inspired by remarkable musicians. I loved to learn new words as a kid. I practised how to use them. Even today I have a thesaurus to hand and strive to learn one new word every single day. Vocal dexterity is at the very core of my three passions intertwined.

Music, words and comedy. You can't be funny without rhythm, timing and vocabulary. An incredible alchemy and synergy.

I suppose you could say I have always been misunderstood by those in authority who take themselves too seriously and are undermined by my word play. I seem to have a gift to immediately put people at ease. I also have the ability to make people feel exceptionally awkward! Pomposity and position mean nothing to me. I have always been bewildered by the notion of paid authority. How right I was? Long before the Post Office scandal, Police corruption and BBC lies I knew (and felt in my heart) that just because someone has a uniform or badge - respecting them per se is a complete fool's errand. The last few years has taught us that those in power and making the rules almost never follow their own rules and most are utterly corrupt. As you probably know by now, hypocrisy and sanctimony are the two pitiful characteristics that blow my mind and send me nuclear. I first began to ask 'why' at a very young age - to the disgust of those who wished to remain unaccountable. Those in authority always lose their shit at 'why' – but why? Because they don't have an answer for WHY? WHY? WHY?

You see in my head 'why' is the perfect question second only to 'what do you suggest I do'? This is my 'go to' reply in any argy-bargy with chopsy arse bandits. When a numpty refuses to play along and gives you a naff answer – cut to the chase, throw it back at them and simply ask, 'What do you suggest I do?' They almost never will be able to answer. They can't accuse you of being rude, it's the perfect passive aggressive conversation cul-de-sac for fart heads giving you the upper hand. All of my life's woes are because of 'why.' Why? – Because they're all liars, bullshitters and fakers caught out. At the BBC I would regularly ask bosses during meetings 'Why am I here?' If they couldn't answer, I'd stand up and leave immediately causing instant fury. This blows their minds as they can't argue. You're effectively saying 'why are you wasting my time dick head?' but they can't be offended as you've switcherooed the question to force them to give you the answer. It leaves suits incandescent with rage. If I'm needed here, I'll stay if not I'm off to watch Loose Women. They HATE this. Undermines them which makes them hate you! Good. Tarra! I'm off to leave the todger dodgers to it. NEXT!

Even as a chubby young ginger lad I had this inner voice to challenge and question imbeciles. It wasn't done to be naughty or in malice, I just had an inner horseshitometer even as a young boy. I was basically born fifty-five years old with the voice, sneer and condescension of Jeremy Paxman. The problem is that bosses don't like being made to look stupid. It makes you very unpopular with the arse covering box tickers but a hero to the masses. In school the teacher must have thought 'what an annoying little twat' yet the kids thought I was hysterical and a hero! Basically, what I'm saying is I viewed my logic as common sense, authority view this as being a clever dick, troublemaker and HUGE thorn in their side. Common sense ain't that common right?

My school years were not particularly memorable to me. All I ever wanted to do was rush home to be with the family and grow up to never return. I have never been smart or an academic so my belief is stick to what you know. I haven't got the patience for reading as I end up drifting off to something more fun like the piano, fridge or more recently Youporn. Snore. I love to listen and learn – audio (radio) was always my gateway to the world of knowledge. I equally think if you can't be the best don't bother. I don't enter competitions as I don't like losing. Who does? It's far smarter to hyper focus on what you're good at. Tenacity will then determine your destiny. I'll never enter a piano contest because I'll never win. You <u>have</u> to know your limitations. Seriously that sums me up, keep your nose out unless you're qualified and right! Fight until the death. My Nana instilled this profound integrity. I can't genuinely recall ever being wrong. Can't imagine how embarrassing and humiliating that must feel. This does take enormous courage, character and tremendous fortitude but comes at a large five-and-a-half-year price!

Not only was my personality peculiar (and putting me in the ilk of a 'one off') but I also looked, let's say, 'comedic.' As a little boy I was large. I suppose I was the original Little and Large. I didn't care about appearance. Even now I have great pride in polishing my turd, but I couldn't care less about a six pack or big arms. It never struck me as important. Beauty is for the thick, feeble and weak. A brilliant distraction from their lack of substance, depth and insight. I've rarely met any gym obsessed whippersnapper who I'm envious of. To me vanity is a huge turn off especially those birds with pouty lips and painted on bloody eyebrows - the real ones they shaved off – Why, Why, Why? What's that all about hey? I see no profit in looks, fancy jewellery, flash cars or sparkly teeth. I don't have any jewellery at all – including a watch. Not interested. Why would I parade a £10k Rolex in Sickdiq's Crapital so some twunt on a motorbike can nab it off me outside Harvey Nicks or Ann Summers? Thinking about it all of my heroes and those I truly admire are wolf ugly. I think being deeply unattractive is a fatuitous comedic device. I wish I was attractive, but no one respects beautiful people – ask Angela Rayner! You only need five minutes in a room with these people and you quickly realise that there is little else. They make my teeth itch. I'll pass. I love to shag a hot bird but eventually they speak and I'm as limp as a filleted lettuce leaf. I'll be me thank you. If beauty is skin deep, I think my face is inside out.

Kids can be cruel though. Jibes at twelve can be brutal and wounding. I had pimples at one point. It was so bad one day a blind chap touched my face and insisted it was the brail version of the Chinese takeaway menu. I used words/jokes to deflect from my deficiencies but that doesn't mean the occasional zinger doesn't sting. I think being 'picked on' does make you stronger. There's no question its character building and 100% makes you a better gobshite in later life. Also, it teaches you about the Achilles heel – to which I am a master. Being the butt of jokes is not nice - but it does make you think on your feet. I always had to be a step ahead. Ad-lib went from being my hobby to a killer defence mechanism. I would never win a physical fight as I can't stand blood and I have gorgeous knuckles. I'm told they're the sexiest thing about me, so we can't risk ruining them. With words I had the punch of Tyson and Bruno. That is still true today to the boohoo disdain of my hurty words lefty 'victims.' After a while it stops cock wombles and twat heads coming anywhere near you for fear of group humiliation. I've come to the conclusion that one of the many things show business can't stand about me is that I truly don't care what <u>ANYONE</u> thinks about me. I don't play by the rules and I don't want to. I never did for some reason. I've always been content in my own peaky skin. I LOVE being an outsider. I don't want to be on the seedy and creepy in-crowd of showbiz. They're mostly creepy, charmless and full of themselves! Add in the spectrum of neurodiverse awkwardness and you could start a conference on their handicapped delusions and dysfunctions. I'm serious, I couldn't give two facks whether I have the approval of people who are worthless to me. From school to now I've never changed.

I'm respectful to everyone but cross me and you'll see the vipers strike of my big gob. I don't have a violent bone in my body, but it does appear that not only does the pen appear mightier than the sword in 2020+, but, the cut of my jib wounds far worse than a jab in the mush. Ask the MP who punched a constituent thirteen times in the pie hole without consequences! I sort of enjoy not being liked – especially by annoying twats! Don't tell anyone but it's my favourite schtick and calling card. I believe this is where our world has gone bonkers and fully explains the plague of mental illness and 'anxiety' of a generation who only thrive and survive on the affirmation of people they've never met. Totally cuckoo. No wonder they're all on pills to get out of bed. Seven million officially depressed in the UK. They can't all listen to Vernon Kay on Radio 2! It's the definition of insanity. Balls to that, I've got too many things to do to waste time and head space on morons. I pity them and hate them in equal measure for being so dopey. I want to scream GROW UP!!! Get a life and get out of mine for the love of God!

So, I opt for real life is what I'm trying to say. Tangible hugs. Not vacuous re-tweets. I only respect the views of family and friends who have no agenda or vested interest either way. The protestations of those with skin in the game is worthless to me. Mind you, family can be a double-edged sword too. Sir Ken Dodd once told me; 'never ask family their opinion about you – because they'll tell you!' So true. Isn't life complicated?! I'm never bored. I jump out of bed in the morning looking forward to what the day holds for me. I find life so exciting. I'm a natural cynic but taking the piss lifts everyone's day. Getting a laugh is the most wonderful and magical thing on earth. I'm so proud that that is my job of thirty plus years! I mostly don't know why people find my take on life so funny. NOTHING is scripted, it's just straight out of the horse's mouth. If you don't get it, that's your problem. Clearly the lift doesn't go to the top floor. Not my problem dear!

From being a bairn, I instinctively migrated to silver tops and still do. I couldn't (and still can't) engage in 'banter' from 'yuffs.' What is 'banter?' – mindless inane chest pounding crap right? It's aggressive and often offensive, dressed up as 'fun.' Life is full of banterists. Pfft. Hideously aggressive bullies who can't link a sentence and use insults as weapons dressed up as jokes. It's all <u>very</u> passive aggressive. Not my cup of tea. I don't really do fun either if I'm honest. Well not in a traditional way. Seriously, I'm not working you from behind. I see everyone around me enjoying themselves getting off their tits on drugs and drunk to oblivion. Bugger that I'll stick as I am thank you Mavis! Nor do I want to be working class since Corbyn and Kia Cars Starlin infer you have to starve and freeze to death to qualify. My fun as you'll learn is being entertained, breaking bread together and travel. My fun and joys are mostly simple like nature, animals and music. The world is amazing. Walking is my favourite thing, that costs nothing. Watching TV with a loved one and mocking moronic celebs. I basically invented Gogglebox. Each to their own hey? I'm a hoot after two vodka's critiquing Naked Attraction. If you watch 'One Born Every Minute' I have stirrups, blue gloves and gas and air as props. I guess my blessing is knowing my own mind. None of this developed. Unusually I was born completely confident in my own convictions and always knew my path. Blessing or a curse? I guess you'll decide at the end of this epistle. What I do know is that most people don't know their opinion instantly. I do! Mind you, many don't know their arse from their elbow!

I wasn't really the class clown but I was always an entertainer. Contrary to my critic's steadfast beliefs, I only ever really want to get a cheap laugh and bring joy. At heart, despite the serious news content often broadcast, I'm always aiming to inspire and lift people. I try to offer a different perspective, that's all. Often my material is nuanced. Halfwits off their tits on Diazepam appear incapable of processing this simple objective. As I sit here surrounded by hundreds of letters, emails and cards from the VoR family the consistent line is 'we miss the laughs' – I do too, trust me! I'll cherish that as my ultimate legacy. What a compliment. I'm a clown. I'm a jester. The piss I do take!!! This ain't rocket science.

I was a funny child (visually). It couldn't have been worse if I was German with callipers, ambivilacious in the gentleman's area or a Guardian reader who sits sellotaped to the M25 for attention. Thank God we didn't have 96 genders back then. I'd have identified as a pain in the sphincter! Nonbinary my hairy white arse. Impossible. Grow up for Christ's sake! This millennial hocus-pocus bunkum is proper Betty Swollocks! I was always incredibly popular with some, a mystery to others and the rest who just didn't get it were threatened by my acid tongue and ignored me as they couldn't keep up. Jealousy has plagued my entire life - even at school. If you willingly and unashamedly stand out, the thickos, inadequate and feeble hate it - ironically, it's the same in radio and theatre! My dismissiveness blew their minds. Ah, my acid tongue – that reminds me of Kenneth Williams' autobiography. The problem with wit is that some choose to distort the sarcasm and intentionally be offended. I've never given offence in my life – <u>EVER</u>, I promise ya. Yet so many precious snowflakes appear to delight in seeking me out to take offence. BORING! Piss Off and shag a woketard root vegetable! Another disturbing post Covid phenomenon. You see the people I don't like I simply ignore. These days it feels like morons love to torture (only) themselves by forensically seeking out people they claim to despise, watching them obsessively and then moaning like a big girl's blouse that their angel like disposition can't cope. Snore. This has to be a mental disorder, right? Crackers! A condition for big babies who never had their arses smacked who thrive on competitive victimhood. This then leads to cancel culture – a game. A new Olympic sport. I'll talk about this later! Why do most of these pricks live in their mother's back bedroom? Why do they watch BBC Drag Race? Why do they either want to be in the West End in the med-yar or on radio? A creepy breed with very similar traits. Make's my inner thighs chafe with cringe, my tits tingle and my nuts shudder with embarrassment at their soulless existences. How did I find myself in these people's cesspit brains and inner sanctum? I'm a walking care in the community magnet for crackpots and cuckoo clocks.

Anyway, back to me. Is there any other?

I'm going to blame Nana Lil for my trappiness. I see no difference between Shakespeare and me - a man of few words like myself who entertained the masses and was best known for his Bottom. Lil Belfield couldn't care less. She was the best grandma in the world and her faith in me was boundless. If I said I wanted to be a brain surgeon or porn star she would have said 'of course you can!' In life you realise that there are two kinds of people, radiators or drains. Some give off endless warmth and others suck you dry and stink! My old gran didn't have a pot to piss in or a window to throw it out of – BUT – she had a heart of gold and wit bigger than her love for people and zest for life. She was an optimist despite a lot of adversity (it's nothing to do with your eyes). Her warmth was magnetic. I realised as a kid that people love an uplifting, positive and funny character. Her resilience was inspiring. How lucky was I to be blessed with this woman in my life? She had no ambition to be rich or 'successful' or indeed to be liked or a need for affirmation, but because of that <u>everyone</u> adored her and migrated towards her. Her unique personality, charm and wit made her hugely popular. I just wanted to be a chip off the old block. You need backbone to be 'you' though. It takes a <u>lot</u> of practice and determination. Nana lived in a council house with an outside toilet and no central heating. It didn't matter. She had her fire downstairs, a hot water bottle and never moaned. Frankly she knew no better. Kids today don't know they're born! The entitlement of this pathetic generation is sickening to me. Clueless. If only they could walk a day in their grandparent's shoes. I despair at the selfishness and lack of compassion, common sense, reality and empathy whippersnappers have. If they spent less time worrying about chopping their privates off and focused on being able to link a sentence maybe we wouldn't be in in this mess. In fifty years, we've lost all of our sense of community and worst of all – family!

What I (literally) adored about Nana was her natural commitment and devotion to those she loved. She had two sisters who she met every single day. Aunty Mary and Aunty Dorothy were her best friends. These were her lifeline five days a week. Every Wednesday we all met for dinner at 6pm sharp. I so looked forward to it with mum, dad, my sister, Uncle Ken and Nana. On Sundays it was even better as she alternated tea with Aunty Mary and the entire family got together for a buffet. I loved being with my uncle and auntie's kids. These are some of my happiest memories! The good old days......in the late eighties and nineties. At 6pm every Sunday the tins of corned beef and salmon, cheese salad, haslet, bread and butter, cake and trifle was laid out on the table which fed the entire family over three generations. The evening began with Jim Bowen's Bullseye at 5pm from Central TV, filmed in my hometown. Innnn Oneeee.... Who knew fifteen years later I would interview Tony Green and subsequently interview Jim Bowen many times until I recorded his final interview before he passed away. This is the astonishing thing about my life, I've met and often become friends with so many childhood heroes all watched at my Nana's growing up. The nineties were a great time on TV. I'd missed variety but at least comedy legends like Bowen, Monkhouse, Davidson, Davro, Conley and Barrymore had found a new home in light entertainment on quiz shows.

After tea we would watch a bit of Antiques Roadshow (snore) before playing cards. This is where I learned how to joust. My Uncle Derek was a powerhouse personality. I adored his confidence and cutting jabs to get a laugh. We later became very close and would go to the car boot together on Sundays simply to mock the shite people were selling for 20p. Derek was very funny and a man's man! They don't make 'em like that anymore. Soo commanding. I wanted to be that! His daughters were a lot older than me. Toni became my sister's and my babysitter and Tina later became a really close mate as she is today. I love the bones of her. We've had lovely times at dinner including in New York together. Over time I had a surreal take on life, born out of the daft and bonkers things 'real' people said and did. I saved all of this 'material' in my comedy Rolodex of content for later use. People fascinated me. Words and interaction were like a fireworks display. I loved and cherished those times. It was a weekly education. A brilliant lesson in love and community that has stood me well in life and show business. My Uncle Tat was the king of facetiousness, my Aunty Jean (who I adore) laughed at everything I said. My Aunty Jill was mother hen and the Queen of John Lewis who I adored. She taught me how to be prim and do things right. Nana and Aunty Mary lifted my heart with their infinite care and generosity. The atmosphere was intoxicating. I'd do anything to go back to that table in 1990.

Up until now I've not mentioned my sister. She's the complete opposite to me and has all of the diplomatic and empathetic qualities of my amazing parents. This, all be it unspoken, leaves me with a lot of guilt today. We're now the closest we've ever been but back then we were chalk and cheese. I've always adored her but we just didn't have anything in common as kids. We played until she became a teen and then I was just a massive pain in the arse – and an embarrassment. Despite our lives being so different only now do I truly feel our unbreakable bond. What my sister has done for me whilst I've been distracted Pleasuring His Majesty is unbelievable. Not only has she kept the family calm and together but she's also sorted out anything I've asked of her and kept my business alive. What an angel! It was no coincidence that a week before I was sentenced, she travelled all the way to Blackpool to see Hopkins and me on the North Pier. The love, unspoken for forty plus years, couldn't be more obvious. I'm so blessed to be so lucky with these lights in my life. We're not soppy in the North though. None of that 'I love you' bollocks – no, no, no. However. Since 'this situation' I say it a thousand times a day! Even as kids my folks gave short shrift to being mardy or soppy. You get a clout round your ear for falling off your bike and get a bit of mum's spit and a rub on your knee then get on with it.

I was the annoying younger brother who loved World Wrestling Federation (it all stemmed from Giant Haystacks in the eighties), aeroplanes and showing off. She was a quiet polite girl, hugely talented at art and all I did was continually pull focus and overshadow her – albeit unintentionally. It was never my intent to upstage anyone, but, in life this can and does happen by osmosis. We've never spoken about it but I genuinely pray she doesn't hold that against me. When your life is extraordinary by comparison to most it's hard not to be a distraction. Since my nephew was born, we've finally found common ground and spent amazing times together as a family. I cannot explain the joy babies bring to life. Anyone who doesn't like kids and animals is a weirdo creep and should be shot - their heart cannot be human and there has to be serious psychosis requiring urgent sectionable therapy! Children are the glue that connects people who believe they have nothing in common. They're the hope and untarnished future. BTW if you're offended by this then your soul is dead! The love and joy that Kaiden has brought to the Belfield's is indescribable. The fun times we've all had has enriched so many lives. Same with my god kids. Oh, to have a kiddie or doggy's innocence - inspiring.

So, in tribute to 'the good ole days,' I just love getting people together and at every possible opportunity. I make sure that my nephew has the joy of learning from amazing, DIFFERENT people in groups around the table. To be a rounded human you need a kaleidoscope of opinions, lifestyles and views. You cannot live in a bubble or you end up like that dreadful Greta Turdberg or hideous lefty Owen Jones. I shudder!!! Variety and different cultures and opinions is the spice of life.

Being me comes at a huge price for family and friends. The guilt I have for the worry and heartache I've caused those around me since being kidnapped by the state will haunt me forever. None of them deserved this horseshit. This is the only guilt in life, far outweighing the indignity of being surrounded by imbeciles in prison. Again, that reality check and huge awakening of love is indescribable. The strength others give you is electric. I'm a lucky boy. Of course, my lot don't care as long as I'm safe and well, they know my heart inside and out!

The problem with public life is that your family are unconsciously dragged in and powerless. It's a deal with the devil the second you seek public attention. I'm not naïve. They build you up to knock you down. It's a game. A sport that <u>every</u> star throughout time has had to play – ask Gino D'Acampo or Gregg Wallace. As you know the Mainstream Media (MSM) are disgraceful in editing the truth – ask President Trump. He's 100% correct that they spin <u>everything</u>. A good example was my conviction of 'Stalking <u>WITHOUT</u> fear, alarm or distress' was <u>NEVER</u> published or said anywhere……including in the court. To read complete bullshit about yourself is bad enough but it's ten times worse for those who instinctively want to protect you. They know it's fantasy and skullduggery for clickbait but they can't get involved. You cannot engage or react you just have to take it on the chin. It's not all glamour - ask Michael Barrymore, and John Leslie! You rise high but can be taken down overnight. This is why I'm so protective of my loved one's privacy. As my T-Shirts said, 'mind your own facking business.'

You have to remember the <u>noise</u> and whoop-de-doo is not 'real life.' This is entertainment for the mentals! You have to remember it's <u>all</u> tomorrow's fish and chip paper, from which the press just profit, daily, from misery. This is why I never wanted to be a news journalist. Imagine doing a job that gains from people's tragedy. The bigger the death toll or horrifying details the bigger the scoop. Absolutely shameful. I never lose sight of the reality and <u>humanity</u>. It's all just a big pile of constructed game and media hairy bollocks. All I know is that the blanket of love and support I've felt since this hideous stitch-up began is life changing! If you're reading this – thank you. I mean it. I truly love you and there's nothing you can do about it! No one could survive this level of disproportionate sabotage and hysteria alone.

For forty-two years I have been convinced that I would never have time to write a book and even if I did who would care? Well, it turns out that I've now got quite a lot of time on my hands as I'm sat here in cabin F27 in HMS Stockings! So, in some sick twist of fate your wish is my command! This is my life story up until I was so inconveniently and ungraciously visited by the NPM = Nottingham Police Mafia in 2020. That's the second book BTW! Little did I know there would be six books by the end of my £48,000 a year cruise paid for by you, the UK taxpayer around the shittiest hotels and asylums in the UK. Strap yourself in. It's forty fantastic but bonkers years!

My life has never been conventional, I have never been normal and never wanted to be. Life hasn't been easy though. One shithouse after the next but I never gave in! I laughed at all my dopey bosses and went on holiday, came back, got another gig and just carried on regardless. I've never been out of work in forty years. I've never had a problem with my punters or the public – it's always box-ticking Celia Imrie's with folders under their arms. Unlike most autobiographies these days this is not a sob story. I'm not looking for sympathy as I don't deserve it. I've never had a day's paid sickness, never boohooed for the doctor to give me anti-depressants and I've been blessed to wake up every day full of beans. When the chips are down, I pulled my socks up and carried on! Zero self-pity. I've always lived and travelled well and been lucky to be given opportunities that so many could only dream of. Maybe this explains the unimaginable amounts of jealously I've encountered from colleagues who haven't had such blessings or fun and believed closing me down would profit them. Maybe they should have been more dedicated and tried a little harder……...or just had matron up the meds.

Life is WAY too short and can't be taken seriously. Everyday I've loved, laughed and mocked the afflicted. You could say I'm my own worst enema! I will never change. It's not in my DNA to bow to brainwashing bullies or paymasters. I like me, who I am and what I stand for. I'm proud of what I've achieved. In the old days you'd be known as a 'one-off,' a character or an oddball. I know exactly who I am. I suppose one of my only regrets is that even now the heckle of he's a 'thicko without a degree from a pit estate in Nottingham' is still a cheap way for journalists, commentators and bitter losers to put me down. Do I care? Do I bollocks! My life's work is to trigger the lefty, woke, righteous, sanctimonious, supercilious pricks out of sheer contempt. I despise their arrogance and lunacy. They know it, which sends them loony toons and gives me license to be so scathing. Whilst they're 'stopping oil,' chopping their nob off or throwing paint over works of art whilst smelling like a fish monger's bucket - I'm tucked up in Trump's 5* Florida hotel thank you very much! You cannot intimidate me into conforming to this radical far left ideology. You're entitled to your (wrong) opinion – and I'm entitled to laugh at you! Each to their own!

I do admit that over the years I have tried to evolve and at the very least see myself on a foggy day from a hundred miles away. Self- awareness is at times traumatic as this mirror can really hurt. But I have always known from being a little boy exactly who and what I want to be - no matter how many numbskulls try and convince me otherwise. Finding and being yourself is the biggest struggle in life. Too many aspire to be popular and fit in. All I ever wanted was to be me and left alone to get on with it. My whole life people have tried to convince me to do it their way. No thanks, I'll stick to my way – regardless of the consequences. Introspection does mean we evolve, learn and grow but occasionally we can get it wrong. As of now, I'm confident I've never misjudged a nonce, fart head, corrupt civil serpant in public service – or indeed wrongly outed an inept or incompetent con artiste who is trying to convince me their shite don't stink. Exposing these scumbags is always liberating! The truth ALWAYS sets you free. History <u>will</u> vindicate all truthtellers, soothsayers and defenders of liberty and free speech.

## Chapter 2

## Looking Inside ME
## (with the help of a mirror)

I never found school terribly inspiring. I didn't fit the mould – story of my life. I remember going to 'careers' at fifteen and saying I wanted to be a comedian and she just laughed. Well, they're not laughing now! 'What about being a car mechanic?' I wonder how many other passionate, talented kids were immediately discouraged and gave up before they even started? A bit like prison, the BBC and vegans - I just found school flawed, pointless and a complete waste of time. OK, I know you have to learn but my school wasn't exactly Eton! Of course, in my day there was no ADHD and Autism – there were just little pricks in the corner diagnosed with being a pain in the arse. Algebra and woodwork all seemed an infantilised waste of time. I knew they couldn't teach me anything as I'd got my radio and music for that. I was steadfast in my future even at ten.

What terrified me, even in the 1990's, was the 'group think' mentality. If you thought out of the box you were a maverick and needed bringing down a peg or two. Over the next twenty years this unforgivable brainwashing and robot training went ballistic by evil Uni-trained teachers.

I never really liked the news to be honest. Two words – BORE RING! But talk radio (the format), even from a young age intrigued me – especially the controversial provocateurs like

James Whale, James Stannage, John Taynton and other lads who in the nineties weren't scared of having an opinion for fear of being arrested over a 'hate crime' – puke. They were mesmerising to me as performers. This was my genre. They were masters of theatre of the mind. All wordsmiths and kings of wind up. Word play to me was better than Alton Towers. Vocal gymnastics and the art of prank was intoxicating. Some were better than others but I loved how they captured their callers hook, line and sinker without them even noticing.

The art of 'wind up' is the BEST sport ever. Boy, I love it. You need to play stupid and be totally serene and calm - that's the key. As a kid I'd get CDs from America from stations like WCSX and obsessively learned what made 'it' funny. You say something provocative and wait with your fishing rod for some precious prissy reptile to kick off having totally missed the joke. It was like a pandora's box of silliness and entertainment. I'd got the toolbox of passion – now I needed the spanners, hammers and pliers to master the craft. You have to start young. This was identical to the piano. There's no shortcut. There's just hours upon hours of commitment! Repeat, repeat, practise, rehearse, practise and repeat for days, weeks, months on end. Talking the hind legs off a donkey is one thing, everyone does that in the pub, BUT would people tune into hear it? People get their own back. One day I had a letter shoved through the cat flap. I said, "Mum someone's written 'Alex Belfield is queer'!" She said, "you pronounce it 'esquire'!!!"

School just couldn't offer me any of this passion and devotion. It was all about conforming. Satirists are rebels – the exact opposite of compliant 'yes' men. School offered no spark, no free thinking, rebellion, passion and nothing creative. I found most teachers dull and boring. Even at eight I wanted to say, 'pep it up love, you've got your stage (and blackboard) so sell it for the love of God!' I was away with the fairies dreaming of showgirls in Vegas whilst Mr Johnson was explaining Pythagoras Theorem. You don't need fractions or algebra at Batley Varieties......pass me a red nose and size 26 shoes!

The downside of school is the bullies. I loved watching the peacocks and Mogadons vying for status. Often the loudest were the weakest - just the same in the pokey. The strongest were generally the most stupid. The similarities between playground bullies, BBC middle managers and police cuntstables is profound. Identical modus operandi. All about bravado bluster and volume distracting from the facts and their lack of intelligence. I'm very lucky being an enema/enigma. 99% of the bullies don't even know I exist as I'm not in their world. When they do take me on it's always in packs and when I bite back, they boohoo like a big spineless baby and claim I started it. Day one projection and deflection from being ten years old. I see these people coming now but back then I hadn't got the dexterity to slam them orally before they got in a first punch. In life you can't avoid the mentals who search for the weak. But usually these bottom lickers (and feeders) soon get bored and move on to their next victim. Ironically just like Twatter trolls, I've never met or interacted with a bully I'm jealous of. Weird that isn't it? Infinitely transparent that they're deficient in so many areas of life – mostly personal hygiene!

Back to the careers lesson, this meeting didn't end well for the toffee-nosed cow who tried to talk me out of going into show business. She said, 'go and do work experience,' I said, 'where? - I don't want to fix cars I want to fix planes.' Can you believe it, I ended up at London Heathrow Airport doing work experience with British Airways. I even spent one day working on Concorde – a dream come true. This was the first time I realised that very little about my life would be average or normal! A lad from a pit estate going to Heathrow when the rest of my class were stacking shelves in Tesco's trying to inspire their ambitions. This was the first ever lesson of taking advantage of a situation and not taking the easy option. I was always obsessed with aircraft. I had hundreds of postcards, model planes and airline gubbins. This to me was the coolest hobby on earth. As a kid I dreamed of spotting a Fokker 100 over Cockfosters. To me planes are like a fireworks display. They're amazing, defy gravity and take you somewhere better than where you've come from. Pure Magic. That week at Heathrow was a joy and opened my eyes at fifteen to the <u>REAL</u> world and how we're not all born equal! It's the survival of the fittest. Some clean the plane some fly the plane and others build it! Life choices my friends. Even today I marvel EVERY single time I see a plane fly over. I can't help but think of the technical miracle and all the stories of the excited hundreds on-board. Incredible to me on every level. I've often dreamed of doing a reality show on a Boeing 787 entitled 'Dreamliner Stories' – just interviewing people. Three hundred plus on board all with time to tell <u>their</u> story. Can you imagine the content?

Again, how lucky am I to have this unprecedented opportunity? This was my first awakening to 'if you don't ask you don't get?' Mum and Dad took me to London as a boy and it was life changing. We stayed at their dear friends Ben and Jane's house in Putney where the bridge over the Thames is the outer marker for the runway at Heathrow. Twice a day Concorde would begin to rumble after the skies had literally cleared at 10.30am (BA001) and 6.45pm. To my amazement this glorious, gracious, tiny and gorgeous bird would majestically and stunningly float past as it descended. What a wonderful British (and a tiny bit of French) invention! Some people like an Xbox, others ride horses, not me – not interested. I could re-live that electrifying feeling for the rest of my life of seeing Speedbird 1 fly over my head, spine tingling. When I worked on Concorde (for a day), I couldn't believe how small it was. Akin to my gentleman's area, what it lacked in size it made up for in speed, perfection and beauty!!! I was mesmerised. The wonder of the world encapsulated in one perfect dazzling work of art. Fifty years later it's never been bettered.

Did you know Concorde grew by seven inches when it was up? Seriously. Google it! (Fill in your own punchlines - mucky bastards!). So, you can see, unwittingly even as a kid I was always different…...which became very normal to my people.

However, to me it was just natural, I didn't think twice. It was perfect logic. I love planes so do work experience at British Airways – perfectly rational. I guess I was fearless. I never gave it a second thought. This has defined my entire life. No impulse just genuine passion. The lads at BA were brilliant, so encouraging. I must have been so annoying with my endless questions. I loved every second. Access ALL areas - best week ever! I loved to collect things as a whippersnapper. I was useless at drawing unlike my sister but I love art – colourful 'talking point' pieces - as my house attests. I collected mugs, badges, rubbers (not Johnny's) and later model aeroplanes as a lad. I still love my model of the Boeing 747-400 (best plane ever) and the hideous catastrophe Airbus A380 (blame Europe). That plane is just like Talk TV - doomed from take-off!

School trips were always exciting. Back in our day we didn't have health and safety, we just had Mrs Harrison doing a rough head count. If we lost a kid from special needs, she'd phone their parents and hope for the best. We had a local theme park down the road called American Adventure – it was like a shit Alton Towers but I loved it. I was never a fan of getting wet even as a kid, so the log flume had little attraction. I didn't like the roller-coasters, it made me nauseous just like Eurovision. The pirate ship was OK as long as I was in the middle and not on the end. Told you, I'm as fun as an inferno in a care home. For me the best days out were at RAF Waddington watching the fighter jets nearly crash or waiting at Netherfield Station for a steam train to pass every two years. I love trains too BTW, they are so elegant, fast and a huge tribute to our 'superior past.' The smell, sound and thundering approach is electrifying. I was in love with the Flying Scotsman as a kid. I'd go anywhere to see it pass and my Uncle Tat would let me know when one was due as he loved these triumphs of British engineering too. Tat loved cars too and drives an Aston Martin worth more than his house. I've never got that - I've had a Sportage lately as it's cheap, reliable and big enough to fit my gear and merch in. You wouldn't get many VoR T-shirts and mugs in my old Nissan Urinator…...although they're great for pissing about in! Planes were easier to enjoy rather than steam trains - few and far between in Nottingham. When I'm released from captivity, I want to do a load of those posh trips on the likes of the Orient Express or EMT to Skegness. My heaven!

One day Concorde flew into East Midlands Airport and I remember sitting on the road leading to the M1 littered with saddos like me waiting for this marvel to land. It was doing 'Bay of Biscay' sixty-minute pleasure flights for £999. Good Lord back then that was an impossible amount of money, these days I can piss that up the wall on the phone to the lawyers in twenty minutes! 'If only' – two of the most powerful words ever. I'd give up talking for a flight on Concorde. Aside from travel I loved food, even as a kid. Well, you don't get twelve stone by five years old eating lettuce. We didn't have a ton of money for restaurants but mum and dad cooked fresh every single night. I don't know how they juggled everything. Inspiring. I wasn't a picky kid but I knew good food from processed shite. I don't think a Turkey Twizzler has ever passed my lips. As a teen going to America was so exciting and ignited my passion for foreign flavours and believe it or not – fine dining! BBQ food was all new to us and my personal favourite. They're masters of the Texas grill. I'd much rather be dead than be a vegetarian. It's incredible that in my twenties, I ate like a king, and quickly became one of the most renowned food critics in Las Vegas. My YouTube video reviews would top Google akin to my theatre rants. In those days it used to be all seared Foie gras and steak tartar, but what I really love now is a Pork Belly, Lamb or Duck Roast with Parsnips, Yorkshires, Sweet Potatoes and Garden Peas. I don't do drugs or smoke - food is still my biggest passion. I always say to the current Mrs B that you shouldn't start your day without something warm inside you.

In the mid-1990s we did a school exchange with some kids in Alsace in Northern France. Now that was a culinary awakening. This blew my mind. For the first time I got to taste rich French cuisine. It was incredible. I went to a lad's house called Gilles. Shortly after he came to our house to complete the exchange – nothing gets past me. Blimey the trust involved – surely, they don't do this today? Gilles (pronounced 'Jille') was a very Parisian type of lad. Not exactly a bundle of joy but his family were lovely. At the end we went to a supermarket and I bought everything. I got so carried away and went £20 over budget – Gilles' father quietly paid. Such class. I wish I could repay him. I wasn't being greedy I just wanted my family to sample aioli, olives and charcuterie! Still three of my favourite things today that I'd never heard of in 1995. Christ, I hadn't even had a tin of Princes corned beef, let alone salami! I thought kalamatas was a euphemism for your knackers! This 'experiment' was an eye opener. I felt so sorry for him. I got off the bus in Alsace, he got off the train in Newark and ended up in a grubby pit estate that had long since seen better days. You couldn't 'level up' the incongruous difference unless you had the vision of Stevie Wonder. Totally different culture and a lot of language barriers, but I got through it. It opened up a new world of travel that I still thrive off. The fun on the bus there and back put me in mind of the pensioner's trips I'd go on to Skeggy with my Nana as a kid. Joyful community of excitement and fun. What's more fun than Bingo at 60MPH!

Our worlds are so small. I love to learn. I love to see how other people 'do it.' It's so exciting to step into other's cultures (don't tell the Ministry of Justice but I've even loved learning about their flawed and broken prison system as well!). Everything is intriguing to me. Endlessly fascinating to peep into different worlds. It never gets old. I guess this is the natural instinct and curiosity of a proper investigative journalist – a trade lost in hypocrisy and virtue signalling years ago. The world is so infinitely exciting. How lucky was I to be given these awakening opportunities to see the much bigger picture whilst so young? I have no idea how mum and dad afforded it. What must they have given up in order to afford £200 in the 1990s? How can I ever repay them? I'm eternally grateful for my horizons being widened.

Buddies, Bullies and Boobies

School for me was all about learning social skills and survival of the thickest. I wasn't exactly surrounded by geniuses who were likely to go on to Oxford or Cambridge (me included). However, I did make bonds with life-long friends I still love to this day. My primary school was in the heart of Gedling called Priory School. I truly can't remember anything before that in my mind's eye. There I met a dear friend called Kirsty who I lost touch with for a while until we were reunited at secondary school. Being a boy, I was always interested in young ladies but with my disability downstairs I was very naïve and I imagined it would be like chucking a chipolata up the Dartford tunnel. Kirsy lived next door to my Uncle Ken who was a football coach and coal board accountant. Ken and I had little in common for a very long time, but I admired him greatly. He was my dad's twin and Nana's son but they couldn't have been more different. He was clever and sporty – I was not! Kirsty lost her mum to cancer and it was for most of the kids at school a huge realisation that life was neither fair nor Disney. Heartbreaking. I'm so blessed that as I write to you both my parents are in fine health and are my living hope and angels. But I do worry about them every single day. To lose a parent before ten is beyond tragic. I remember one day calling Kirsty on my gran's 'old school phone' were you shoved your finger in the hole and turn the circle until twenty minutes later you were through. I'd never, as a kid spoken to anyone who had lost their mum and dad. How the hell did I know what to say? I tried.

One of the hardest things to 'master' as a broadcaster, especially on phone-in radio, is knowing how to react to heart-breaking situations sincerely. You cannot get it wrong! So many screw it up and never recover. The only way is experience. You have to be totally in sync with all three of the elements; brain – heart - mouth. The 'let's make great radio' gene far outweighs the true empathy required for heartbreaking situations. I hate those pretend TV radio DJ's who don't understand tone and the power of sincerity and put on that silly mincy voice – they're fooling no one. Kirsty and I became very close. By fourteen we went to comprehensive school together and my God had she blossomed – in more ways than one! Not everyone liked her, she did have her knockers……. It's no secret that I am still fascinated by jelly wobblers. Well, Miss Kirsty had the most impressive and delicious pair of milk jugs I'd ever seen. I'm talking double G's - for Golly Gosh!!! Freud would probably say that I was taken off the boobies too quick as a child as I'm still captivated by a decent pair of udders today. To me a fabulous pair of cans epitomises femininity. Miss K was voluptuous and looked like she'd been on the peanut and melon diet – the peanuts didn't work but… Put it this way, she'll never drown!!! I gave her two thumbs up! We remained very good friends for years reunited by my God kids twenty years later. My dearest bezzy, and angel, is Claire who I met much later during A-levels at Gedling Comprehensive. More about that diamond later. Gedling Comp was to education what Angela Rayner is to fashion, vocal dexterity and femininity. Pfft! Hopeless. No wonder I'm limp under the cap. Ironically another pal of mine was Jamie Bust – there's a comic irony there for sure!

His folks still write to me in the slammer. Other buddies are still close today. Dean was in the cool gang and kept his eye on me. He's such a hero that he even came to my sentencing at court and still pops in a lot to make sure the screws are behaving. 'You find out who your friends are' couldn't be more true. I never needed or worried about being popular but looking back I guess I was – without knowing it.

I always had pals like Carl, Scott, Adam, Jamie, Alex, Justin, Peter, Nick and David on hand, but honestly, I'd much rather be pottering between my karaoke machine and piano or up at my grans. I just couldn't be arsed with butch peacocking. My pals would often play Doctors and Nurses. Sadly, I was normally the ambulance driver. I could never be bothered with the brain dead six pack brigade. I envied their strength but pitied their inability to link a sentence. I can only remember one fight as a teenager – boxing wasn't for me. It might muck up my hair and risk injuring my face – my cash cow later in life. My model looks would define my mega success. No. No. I was a talker not a puncher! Being punched in the ring wasn't for me. A lot of that went on at the Beeb – I avoided it like anything with Jason Manford on TV. Not for me ta! I guess I just knew an argy-bargy was pointless. It's nice to be nice – and if they weren't I'd ignore them. If they persisted, I'd give them an upper cut of the best line I could clench from my filing cabinet of put downs nicked from Chubby or Bernard. I could see the pack mentality of school but it was all pretty moronic and rarely affected me. I genuinely was too busy in my own little world. I rose above 99% of shenanigans. The other 1% I put down to character building. For most I was an anomaly and invisible.

Since then, I've not changed. I'm just more of a curmudgeon and gammon but still feel twenty. Now, as an adult I just love dinner parties and fun with the family and kids. I was never a piss head (can't stand the hangovers) and I genuinely don't like shouting to be heard in noisy bars. I love a drink but I'd rather eat at a Morrisons café than chuck up after a night out. I can't stand clubs although by twenty I did find a few nice bars in Lace Market in Nottingham, where they were more likely to play REM than drug dealer gangster crap like you got on Radio 1. It's not the sticky floors or coke heads, I <u>hate</u> screaming and not hearing! I always seemed to know my place and it wasn't behind the bike sheds smoking. I can't stand smoking by the way! Have you ever kissed an ash tray? Not for me! Other than that, if you've got palatial mammaries and don't like Lambert and Butler, I'm your man! School creates your ultimate character. Childhood dictates your personality 100%. They reckon nearly all of our personality is developed by five years of age. I was very lucky to have such a good start – the rest was easy! I wasn't interested in school as it didn't connect or serve any purpose <u>for</u> <u>me</u>. I was not academic. I didn't care to remember or learn via robotic teachers who have never lived in the real world or done a proper job. I was street smart but knew nothing about history, maths or Shakespeare and cared even less. I didn't really respect the teachers as they didn't teach me anything I wanted to know about. It was all about getting to 3.30pm for me. It had to be done – but – I couldn't wait to leave........a bit like my course of antibiotics for that nasty rash.

Another of my 'blessed' pals in the Hooter's department, is my mate Laura. She lives in Tenerife now. I remember as a kid thinking she was one of the most naturally beautiful girls I'd ever seen. She can't get a big head as I hadn't been anywhere yet! Back then though she was the motherload of babes. She only lived two minutes away but she was way too cool, popular and in demand to make time for me. However, years later we also became great mates. So strange how we all grow up, well they did anyway, and end up back where we started. My dear friends created proper lives and families not silly skullduggery on the tippy-tappy. Kirsty has two beautiful daughters and a top husband and Laura is living her best life with her hard working and devoted dad to her two brill sons. I'm equally as proud of my BABY (grand piano) and my Doddy the Cockapoo whilst spending thirty years pissing about on the tippy-tappy and talking cack. My best friend ever Claire became my #1 hero and has been there throughout everything. Claire is the best mum ever and I'm totally in awe of her ability to juggle everything. Knowing yourself is the key to life. She's beyond authentic and appreciates exactly who I am. No one knows me better than this angel. Claire is the nicest, kindest, sweetest mother and person on earth. She gave birth to my two heroes, Sam and Oliver. These kids bring me more joy than words can express. Add that to my nephew Kaiden who is a chip off the old block. Kaiden is my best mate – well Doddy's his best mate actually. I love the blend and mix of my cracker's life. I get to live my perfect life on the road and be in the presence of all of these glorious souls.

Life is about choices. From ten years old I knew I'd be married to entertainment and show business which would afford me the opportunity to make <u>all</u> of my ambitions come true. I perform, make people laugh, piss off liars, cheats, out noncy fakes and most importantly get to travel the world in the process. I fulfilled my dream of constantly being surrounded by the biggest and best talent on the planet. This is my oxygen. A sincere and perfect balance I'd say!

<u>Kids Are Nuts</u>
In life success is relative. Some might think my proudest achievement is filling the Blackpool North Pier three times in a weekend or interviewing legends at the Palladium. This stuff is a hoot but momentary and more or less meaningless in the grand flotsam and jetsam of life. If you're defined by this guff, it and will leave you barren and empty. For me two of the biggest honours was being asked to be my best buddy Stewart's best man at his wedding – a wonderful and meaningful honour as well as being a God Father. When Sam was born, I was so proud. The cuteness of this buba was mind-blowing. I'm not really a baby person. Too much stinky bodily functions if I'm honest but toddlers are astonishing. The speed in which they learn is inspiring. Sam was the first baby I'd watch grow from day one. I took it seriously and saw him every second I could. Later Stewart, Giles (another long-time close friend) and my sister all

welcomed me into their unspeakably busy and exhausting parenting lives. It's not for me being part carer, part taxi driver and part UN peace keeper. I am able to get the best bits and bugger off home when I got bored. I win! I don't know how parents do it!

I do not have the time to be the Dad I'd want to be. You cannot commit to being a parent six months a year or three nights max. Most successful business men (and lady types) or pro entertainers pretend their working for their family. They're lying and frauds. Most living double lives. Two phones = two lives remember! They want their cake and eat it. I don't think that's fair. It does not sit well with me. I've seen a lot of examples where kids have paid the price. You have to know yourself. A child isn't an accessory. When Sam was born just like my darling sister's bundle of joy, I did everything I could – as often as I could and relished every second. My heart is on fire simply having 'that' feeling of pride, love and terror that you might break them.

One night I stayed over at Sam's parents Claire and John's and we got pissed, had a takeaway and played cards. Some of my happiest times ever! True friendship is intoxicating where you don't have to put on a fancy suit or do the act. I could just be me. Sam was about three so I offered to let his folks have a lie in and I'd get up and do the breakfast and dog walk. Marvellous, what could possibly go wrong? I was very excited to take the reins. Sam was a little chatterbox so I asked him what he wanted. Being the smartest kid on earth he asked for crunchy nut cornflakes and I thought nothing of it. Nor would his parents until that day. Until now he was restricted to Weetabix and Cornflakes. I didn't know. What's the difference? Like the ultimate Godfather that I am, I got him some water, milk and his cereal and we ate together. It was about 8am by now. We sat down and watched my beloved Fireman Sam from my childhood. God, I loved that cartoon. I was a big fan of 'Thomas the Tank' as well, but more about those long winter nights watching Tug TV in prison later.

The days of Rosie and Jim and Grotbags had gone. It was all Teletubbies and Pepper Pig these days. Suddenly Sam started to cough then choke. I nearly died myself in petrified horror. How would his incredible parents *ever* forgive me? After thirty seconds I shouted down his devoted dad John. Claire came down and immediately called 999. Sam was playing with his cars oblivious to the seriousness of his reaction. I felt the worst I'd EVER felt – worse than when Vanessa Feltz tried to dirty dance with me during the conga at the BBC Christmas Party. Awful. I took little Cotton the dog for a walk as the ambulance arrived. I'd done this. Entirely my fault. Can you imagine the shame? Worst still I didn't even know what I'd done. A mega fail - on 'my watch.' Godfather fail 101...or 999. Well, it turned out that Uncle Alex had unwittingly diagnosed Sam's unknown nut allergy. His throat swelled and the little diamond couldn't breathe. Now a teenager, I still beg for his forgiveness. All I wanted to do was give his parents their first lie in. I created a brewing tragedy - not exactly breakfast in bed. They've since thanked me for discovering the illness that could have been fatal if they hadn't called 999 and it had gone undiagnosed. Oy vey. Why me? When Sam's brother Oliver came along my heart couldn't be more full. He's the biggest and kindest sweetheart I've ever met. Love the bones of all these lads. It's a love unlike any other for a doting uncle. I'd do anything for them, just like Stewart's son Noah. Kids are the heartbeat of every household. More recently little Reggie has come into my life via a neighbour I truly adore. Anneka and Reggie have a tremendous place in my heart along with their incredible family who I adore. I'm so lucky to have the best of all worlds. I'd walk on hot coals for these bubas. So, would I like to have my own? I'll pass! Daddy to a cockapoo is more than enough commitment for me. I'm far too selfish and busy – it just wouldn't be fair. Sorry again Sam. One day I'll make it up to you Bigman! Knowing my luck with an afternoon tea including peanut butter on toast and an almond slice. I'm made up with the love, fun and laughter that the young 'uns bring. I'm a lucky chap.

So, school for me served little purpose. I couldn't fathom why you'd waste days or weeks learning things they knew you'd never need or use in 'real' life. Yet at the same time ignore so many vital things in life that were crucial like money, personality, linking a sentence, cooking and most importantly <u>ambition</u>. We're paying the price now with all the thicko dumbbells walking round like zombies taught by woke university millennial self-entitled nonbinary pricks blindly to go through life as if it owes them a living. Take me now! I truly only ever aspired to mediocrity academically. I didn't care. Then one day I had a lightbulb moment - comedy came into my life. Great comedians are wordsmiths and technicians of language. Funny peoples' brains are infinitely fascinating and their absurd view and perspective on the world is endlessly entertaining and fascinating. But how do they do it? This was far more interesting to me than English, Maths and Science. The masters are geniuses. On every level they're brilliant. This was my calling. I now needed to learn from the very best. This would take thousands of hours and I would dedicate the rest of my life to the art of getting a titter.

So now my stars had aligned, <u>WORDS</u> were the foundations of my passion for radio and comedy. Music was my literal heartbeat and gave me the safe footing for timing and <u>my</u> rhythm of life – laughs, fun and joy!

The final ingredient in the recipe of my life is silver tops. I told you about my Nana Lil – the biggest 'character' of them all. There was also my Grandad Ernie – a totally unique Captain of the family who stood proud over his five kids and ten grand kids. He was so confidant in who he was and the legacy he'd created. Two facks he couldn't give. This to me is an intoxicating human quality. I marvelled at how he held court and worked a room. Not dissimilar to Nana, he could be magnificently cutting but had a charm to pull it off with infinite warmth. None of my family were rich in pocket but in heart they were millionaires. This is winning at life! My entire life has been defined by much older inspirations who shaped every fibre of my being. I couldn't care less about the latest, coolest trend. I always wanted to be entertained, inspired and educated by those who had been there and done it and had a fabulous cut of the jib!

My first hero of significant was BBC Radio Nottingham legend Dennis McCarthy. I adored him. Every day he joined his radio family at 2pm sharp for decades. People didn't like him, they LOVED him! Addicted. Loyal. Utterly sincere. That's what I wanted, an authentic radio family and team. He was a family member to them and a piece of the furniture. I was fascinated how you create/develop and nurture that tremendous relationship! He taught me about that imaginary thread between you and the listener. Familiarity is the key. Give them what they want and be you. No lies or bullshitting, in fact they'll grow to love your imperfections and flaws more than your professionalism. You have to be 100% open and sincere – the hardest thing to be LIVE on-air. They'll catch you out BIGTIME if you're fake! He taught me about 'painting pictures' in the listeners minds. Having characters and most importantly – NEVER letting your audience down. It's a commitment! Be there. Turn up. All killer – no filler. It ain't rocket science, but it's VERY rare.

Radio is the most transparent of media. You can't hide four hours a day. You'll get caught out instantly. This is why I have no time for news journalists. They read the pieces of paper and keep their opinions to themselves. After that they should keep their sanctimonious traps shut! They don't have the inner honesty to be real and the introspection to be totally vulnerable. They're trained to be heartless. They revel in negativity – everything I

HATE! I've seen with my own eyes how journalists will cheer when the dead soldier is from their patch – so that they've got a scoop. Vile! That 'hardness' doesn't work with real people. It's unedifying, embarrassing, shameful and disgusting. There's little or no compassion or empathy whatsoever – the two keys to perfect radio. It's trained out of them. Watch Newsnight, Channel 4 News or The Today Programme if you don't believe me.

No one ever said they 'love' Naga Munchetty, Anal Rajan, Clive Myrie let alone Laura Kuntsberg. A breed of hyper-trained script reading robots and puppets who believe they're smarter and better than their audience and arrogantly ask questions but refuse to answer them themselves. You watch and learn from them – but would never love, enjoy or want to have a pint with them! Not my cup of tea at all. They're entirely removed from the public's heart. I truly believe it's the fact they have no wit or humour. They're taught to be totally devoid of ad-lib or 'the common touch.' They're not allowed to have an opinion, but we all know (sense) exactly what they think. There's no sincerity and therefore there's no bond. I would rather be dead than be regarded with such contempt. My sphincter is clenching just thinking about being in a room of these word reading, dead behind the eyes 'impartial' and 'non-political' (allegedly) public brainwashers. All I ever wanted people to say was 'he's one of us' or 'he's a breath of fresh air.' I never wanted awards or back slapping from some dopey group of incestuous geeky butt buddies who want you in 'their' club. I don't want to be in their 'gang!' Lord knows who is the 'leader' - ask Huw. I just wanted the public to think I'm me, real, a bit naughty, on their side, one of them and a top laugh and a good giggle. Credibility is defined by such qualities not a degree in pomposity and reading your editor's cleverly manipulated words. Autocue readers thrive on authority and blind reverence. They believe they 'inform and educate' – balls to that. I'd rather do nob gags. I'll stick to just being a low brow end of pier gobshite – the public love and trust that way more – now more than ever! All I want to do is give my punters a proper shaft of wit.

My infinite love for comedy was endless from a very, very young age. In fact, before I even knew it. My Uncle Derek and Tat were masters of 'banter' as they now call it during our weekly Sunday teas and especially whilst playing cards from 8pm – 9pm. Word play was mesmerising to me, a competitive sport, a thrilling game. Who had the best put down or zinger? Double entendres were alluringly hysterical and jokes were pure poetry. Puerile to some – delicious to me. The command comedians have is so powerful and in real life everyone wants to be around a clown - not a manic depressive. If you're offended by that – you're that lonely bore everyone avoids in the pub! Gagsters are raconteurs and conductors. The audience is their orchestra. It's a masterclass to see a funny man work a room. I say funny MAN as since Victoria Wood I haven't seen a WOMAN who can do it. Misogynist (another five years). #HateCrime-Call999. Look, there's a reason Peter Kay sells 18,000 tickets every night for a season at the O2. No one is paying £45 to see Victoria Derbyshire read an autocue!

One of my only ambitions – as far back as I can remember – is to get a laugh. Needy? Maybe. If that's my worst affliction, I'll take it. The most overwhelming blessing is being told 'we would cry with laughter…' This to me is like winning the World Cup. What an achievement! The roar of an audience is the most joyful noise on earth. But why, why, why? Why do people laugh? I had an amazing mentor who explained ……

Via Dennis McCarthy on Radio Nottingham, I became aware of a man called Ken Dodd. A mythical enigma whose stunning career spanned seven decades and will never be paralleled. Ironically starting his career in 1954 in Nottingham, no one in British history has come anywhere close to matching his achievements – or ticket sales as the UK's highest earning theatre headliner. One of the bestselling male singers of all time to 70 years selling out the biggest theatres until the very end at 90. How lucky was I that from being a teenager Doddy took me under his wing and taught me the good, bad and the very ugly of showbiz. To think twenty years later I'd be invited to his Knighthood afternoon tea opposite Buckingham Palace with his closest family and friends. I'll tell you more about Sir Ken throughout, but there's no denying he inspired, encouraged and literally crafted my career, personality and life. Oh, and encouraged my total disregard and contempt for most of the people I'd be forced to work with in this unhinged and creepy business.

You don't have to dig very deep in my show to see so many tried and tested comedic devices from decades of legends. I'm proud to honour them…....or plagiarise as some suggest. Remember, it's only nicked or old if you've heard it before! An old gag is like an old friend – you never forget them. I have never claimed I'm unique or original. No one I've ever met at the top of their game is either. So many have inspired me and I'm proud to keep their candle alight. The first thing Ken told me was LEARN, LEARN, LEARN! He read more than anyone I've ever met. So, I did. I spent more than ten years of my prime years from ten years of age watching every comedian I could find. Even ones I don't like. Identical to radio I've learned more from shit heads doing it badly than geniuses who were masters. I studied over and over again until I worked out why people loved them and what made them unique. Being beloved does not come easily. This is the gold dust I tried to discover. I'm talking thousands of hours watching videos and listening to radio comedy again and again for it to sink in. I genuinely believe akin to playing the piano, it's the only way to learn. Words, phrasing, delivery and constructing a thought or joke was my obsession. Fluidity of speech is of course the biggest obstacle. 'Recall' takes a lot of practice. Then, you have to find your own voice – that's the toughest of all disciplines in showbiz. You **HAVE** to be unique…....unless you're Joe Lycett pinching Julian Clary's entire act. How did I know to work at this? Divine intervention or too much time on my hands? It was osmosis – I have no idea how or why – I was just seemingly born to do it!

My favourite legends included Bob Monkhouse, Jimmy Tarbuck, (Lily) Paul O'Grady, Les Dawson, Frankie Howerd, Joan Rivers, Don Rickles, Barry Humphries and of course Doddy – the 'front cloth' comedians. All they need is a mic and a pin focus. Next were the legends of 'shock' like Roy Chubby Brown, Freddie Starr, Jethro, Bernard Manning and my pal Jim Davidson who I thought was the cleverest of them all in terms of storytelling. He could do adult filth on stage and then Saturday night Primetime TV or panto the next day. Genius. Well, he could until a lefty box ticker paid him £1m to leave the BBC and banished him from mainstream. Finally, one of the most important categories of comedian for me is the 'camp old tarts!' You can clearly see how Larry Grayson inspired my show characters like 'Tarquin the Producer' and my sister 'Vera' – he had 'slack Alice' and 'Pop it in Pete the postman' - all warm, loving, cosy and easy to poke fun at cast members. This stuff is familiar and is the element that softens my more edgy side. Texture, ebb and flow, light and shade and contrast are the key to longevity. This nuance takes a lot of repeat brain power and practice. It's a muscle that needs ninja training. The 1980s and 1990s contemporaries like Lenny Henry, Ben Elton and Eddie Izzard meant nothing to me. I'd rather watch Bobby Davro and Duncan Norvelle for proper woofers and comedy timing – not sneery, righteous, bitter, lefty cack. Ben recently impressed me live. Hard to be so angry and militant when you're a millionaire trotting out Queen Musicals. You see we all evolve!

I'm far more outrageous than Sir Ken, Les or Larry would dream of. I often wonder what Doddy would make of some of my more colourful Anglo-Saxon vocabulary. He was squeaky clean. Women particularly love foolishness and silliness and this element of campery and fantasy is so loved in British culture. You can't fail to warm to the charm of the team of imaginary characters you know but have never seen or met. It's fun. It's nonsense. It's old school. I LOVE IT! Doddy too loved this fantasy with his 'jam butty mines' and most famously the Diddy men and 'Dicky Mint' - his tearjerking imaginary son. Camp old malarkey = a cheap tattyfilarious comic device adding another level of mystery to your act. I too will have a 'Venting Belfield' for my second coming. A fisted puppet can't fail to melt the heart and say things I now can't get away with!

The second most powerful tool for any act is a good old catchphrase. BUT familiarity is the foundation of success - turning up on time is paramount. I don't know anyone who is at the top of their game who isn't 100% devoted to their craft and audience and takes it so seriously that it's their obsession. That fixation of commitment leads to perfection – or as near as you can get. 'Obsession' now has a negative connotation. But every great person I've ever met in sport, music, art or showbiz has devotion to get where they are. Doddy taught me this from day one. NEVER let your audience down. I pride myself on this. Truly that's why Voice of Reason became a hit. I was there every single day without doubt. Doesn't matter if the show was a doozy, I turned up and that bought respect. The jealous critics who want to be me never understand this level of commitment to the audience. If only trolls could put their energy in learning a skill maybe they could be more successful and less creepy, medicated and noncy.

No matter rain or shine, good day or bad, let alone happy or sad – you put on a happy face, stick on your shirt and do your job! To entertain! By 14 this was my mantra.

My first dalliance with showbiz didn't start on YouTube (it hadn't been invented yet!) nor at the North Pier Blackpool. I can remember as far back as eight years old whilst on holiday on the Isle of Wight. It didn't go very well but it wasn't my fault (your honour). Boy did I get a bollocking! If you hand me a microphone you take your chances! 4, 14, 24, 34 or 44 – I've never changed. The island was always special to me because my grandad was a long-distance lorry driver on the Isle of Wight.

Each year through my entire childhood my Mum and Dad would save and save to make sure we got a week on holiday by the seaside. As a little boy I can't describe the overwhelming excitement waking up for what seemed like an endless journey to Shanklin, via the ferry, to reach what felt like paradise to us, half an hour south of Southampton. My sister and I would sit in the back screaming 'are we there yet?' and we hadn't even reached Leicester Forest East on the M1 let alone the heady heights of Milton Keynes or Dunstable. Cowes was our Barbados! I remember one year Uncle Ken and Grandma coming with us. It was the coolest and most exciting thing ever! I desperately try to re-create 'that' feeling for the kids around me today. Memories are <u>everything</u> to a child. My parents are a magical team. Mum sorts stuff out and dad selflessly does anything to make his family happy without ever moaning. They love to love and couldn't be more devoted with old fashioned values - through thick and thin. The pay-off for their graft and toil were the most joyous times together. I can't thank them enough for this life affirming investment.

One memorable year dad was worried about the car. The days of getting a brand-new Hybrid HIV on Hire Purchase every two years was long from being invented. You were lucky to have an old banger so it had to last decades! Back then a car twenty years old was deemed 'almost new' let alone a classic. Our 1982 Vauxhall Vulva had seen better days years ago. I remember our bright red beast causing dad sleepless nights. He knew it was about as trustworthy as a Labour government. We made it over the water on the ferry but shortly after de-boating, waving goodbye to the seamen on HMS Ann Widdecombe, we reached a hill and BANG! It was game over. The Isle of Wight is a long way from Nottingham. Dad is a protector – he was beside himself. For us kids it was exciting……….especially when an RAC man turned up in a Merc to ship us home. Mum and dad worked so hard to save up for this. They were mortified. We got ice-creams at the service station, what better way to spend the entire week's budget! Remember, family is about making memories. This story outlives any fortnight in Marbella. We drowned in experiences, events, days out and love. Days out to Skeggy cost nothing but it is the memory bank deposit scheme that reaps rewards. What a lucky boy I was! Every bank holiday we'd go to a National Trust Park for a picnic. This was before all the woke LGBTQ+69s nonbinary flag flying ruined it. Bi's and Trans hadn't been invented in the 1990s and nonbinary wasn't even a twinkle in a sectioned weirdo's eye. I love the countryside, feeding ducks and clay badger shooting. We'd always go with Margaret and Ray, Mum and Dad's best friends and their kids Dawn and Sarah. Again, year after year this was so exciting with a cooler bag full of egg mayonnaise, tuna, ham and cheese sandwiches and a few scotch eggs and sausage rolls. Add in a few low-fat crinkles and cheesy puffs and this was the stuff dreams are made of. We'd walk, eat and play ball games. Incredible memories. Innocent and simpler times.

I don't know how, but they re-booked another holiday shortly after. I bet they wished they hadn't! This was an even bigger car crash. So back to my earliest memory on stage (stop distracting me), it was on the Isle of Wight. This was my introduction to the 'type' that is 'The Blue Coat' (although these might have been rainbow pink). Holiday camps created so many amazing acts like Shane Richie, Joe Pasquale and Bradley Walsh 30 years ago. These days it seems to be less about talent and more about pathological cheerfulness, screaming loudly and awkwardly over egging every omelette prior to becoming a drag queen in Brighton. Not my cup of tea. Each night the resident comedian would use the kids to make fun of, not funny. You'd never get away with it these days. This bright spark thought he'd ask two <u>child</u> guests to have a 'back and forth' battle with the naughtiest words they'd heard starting with 'silly' and 'stupid.' Unfortunately, I fell at the first hurdle, I'd watched a few too many Max Boyce videos. The problem for all wannabe comedians (turns) is that when you get attention your instinct is to keep getting laughs until you walk off the stage or are given the hook. This 'competition' crescendoed from 'daft as a brush' to me bringing the house down with 'you dopey cloth eared twat.' Remember, I'd got every 18 Certificate comedy video on Betamax (remember them?) from the car boots. Add that to my Roger Whittaker vinyl collection and I was hot to trot! Was this my first and last farewell to showbiz? I didn't need the fantasy channel on cable I wanted comedic filth and 5* whistling! Now as a grown up this story may seem mildly amusing but when an eight-year-old says it in front of hundreds of pissed up dads at a Pontins holiday camp you get a standing ovation, BUT my mum didn't see the funny side! This was a great lesson. I guess even back then I was my own worse enema!

Mum wasn't upset at what I'd said, but how I'd been set up to say it – history does repeat doesn't it! Thirty odd years later I could see that look in her glass eye again as she visited me in the hoosegow! I blamed a potty mouth uncle for saying it in front of me when he thought I wasn't listening. Rule One – I'M ALWAYS LISTENING! I couldn't admit I'd heard it on Mike Reid's smut packed genius collection. 'Turn it in' Mike! You got me in a right kerfuffle you pilchard!!! You could say he got me in a whole load of Cowes dung! Even now mum recoils from within at some of my content, that's her job, right? She ain't moaning when I pick up the bill at the Ivy though! Welcome to my world – I'm a modern-day Jim Reeves. This lesson was brutal - it has never left me! I've never fallen for this beartrap black eye since. Showbiz is a cesspit that doesn't have a safety net. For many reasons people will be encouraged to walk tight ropes over dangerous valleys and only you can save yourself from crashing into the cavernous abyss below. You HAVE to recognise the amber light! This was also the first time that my public life affected my family's private life – the worst by-product of being known. These are the 'life events' that never leave you. What a learning curve. I was like Sinatra walking around that place for the next week. Did I tell you my grandad was a Sinatra impersonator? There wasn't much demand for that in 1943. I just love family holidays – even to this day. My one and only time I went in a tent was with my Uncle Andrew and Aunty Jill when they took my sister and me camping. It was so much fun and so exciting. These bonds and memories are so precious. Their impact can't be underestimated. I hated the cold but loved the time with my family. It was a bit chiglios on the old chiglios!!! I'll stick to hotels from now on.

After the gobshiting 'incident' on the Isle of Wight my next pin focus would be four years away. In the meantime, I needed to turn my hobby into my job. I asked Mum and Dad for a karaoke machine. They probably thought it was to sing, but it wasn't. I'd shrewdly worked out that this 'all in one' unit with 3 x CD player and two tape decks were a mini radio studio and I could practise how to be a DJ. I never cared about the music, my obsession was how do I get in and out of the records and say something interesting in between. I would literally practise for hours in my bedroom going between TAPE 1 and TAPE 2 with the hope that one day I'd be as 'slinky linky' as the greats like the late Steve

Wright, Tony Blackburn and Ken Bruce. I still think they are the benchmark for consistency, professionalism and unwavering on-air positivity. Sadly, having a penis and being over 35 years old they don't tick a box so naturally the BBC have no interest in 'pale, stale and male' voices these days. They'd rather hire uphill skiers on coke that make you wanna choke!!! Wrighty was the big boned master in my book (incomparable and perfect as long as he didn't fall on you)! What a loss to broadcasting. Of course, the BBC humiliated him, sacked him off his incredible afternoon show breaking his heart leading to his untimely death in 2023. Sick, unnecessary and shameless. Naturally he's been replaced by a box ticker with a voice like Donald Duck and the creativity of a tax inspector. Snore. Bravo BBC!

My poor parents and sister would have to listen to my racket morning, noon and night for years. If I wasn't fingering my organ, I was pretending to broadcast to the world via a brick wall. It paid off right? Practise makes prison don't they say? My advice to any wannabe in <u>ANY</u> walk of life is that if you're blessed with a passion – practise! They reckon it takes at least 10,000 hours to qualify to do anything properly. Trust me Roman Kemp wasn't born that naturally gifted, hysterical and so natural at LIVE TV! He must really have worked to get where he is! #facetious. Anyway, that's not why you called! What a racket! That karaoke (studio) was my Xbox. What fun for <u>years</u>! It took me over ten years to actually be the 'real' me on-air. For years you're hung-up on neurotic notions of what people think and how you should sound 'professional.' You only master the stage and airwaves once you truly don't care and just slap it on the table and be yourself. The greats make it look <u>VERY</u> simple; Chris Evans was a master in the 1990s until he went to bed and woke up as Oprah with a soupçon of Meghan and Harry. Most disappointing. Bring back Wogan I say!

Throughout my life I've been so lucky interviewing so many legends, stars and hugely successful rich people. Guess What? That didn't happen by accident. I haven't met one who has stood the test of time by luck <u>alone</u>. It's a lot of hard work and determination to achieve longevity. Fame and success are fleeting. The media finds talent entirely disposable. It's down to you to survive amongst the savages who will eat you alive via jealousy. What makes stars tick is fascinating. These people are identical in their personality and mental strength. Driven doesn't cover it. There are very clear patterns in the behaviour and lifestyles of hugely successful people. Their childhood discipline is a given. Lazy people never achieve any discernible or long-standing success that's for sure…...well, other than on E4 or ITV2 reality shite.

The weird thing about my path is that <u>it</u> found me. I didn't have a show business mentor or inspiration in the family as a child, and I certainly was not born with any excess smarts, talent, 'a gift' or even a silver spoon in my gob! That's not modesty, all of my 'skills' are learned. I'm no prodigy or idiot cul intelligente (French for smart arse). Everything I've done and achieved has been found, learned and crafted. There was uniquely no nepotism whatsoever. It's as if it was my destiny. I never questioned 'it.' I've never done a proper job but instead sustained a life in the horrific, cut-throat world of entertainment and managed to survive the woeful jealousy and seething bitterness of those less successful (well up until the end of this book!). No one knows what to do with me and few can handle my brutal honesty. I just don't fit the mould, but that's what makes it interesting. Normal usually = boring! I've worked out that mostly in life people want you to be good – but not too good. Even as a boy I used to sit in class thinking 'you're talking complete shite' – the same feeling I get today watching Prime Ministers Questions. We've got a PM who can't define a woman or working person. It's bleeding hopeless. It's like a bullshit alarm going off in my head when I'm in the presence of a numbskull or absolute pringles! Do these people swallow the dickhead pill when they reach notoriety? When I see a plant pot talking cack, their head spins to me like a lighthouse during a storm. Most are blinded by their stupidity. They have so much smoke blown up their arse by hangers on they can't see the wood for the trees. I'm just busting to leave the room and head for zee hills! Covid proved how blind, gullible, stupid and weak people are. We are bred to be compliant. (Did you know gullible isn't in the Oxford dictionary?) We are trained not to ask 'why' but I love asking 'WHY, WHY, WHY' – in as silly and louder voice as possible. Could you follow and be brainwashed by a cult? Well, you did in 2020! Brainwashing and propaganda have never been more alive and kicking.

We moved house during Junior school and I moved to Stanhope School which was identical to the one before – a way to fill my days before getting home to the family – my only daily ambition. Here though was my first protector and encourager, Mrs Benson. Unlike so many other teachers who took the money and ran, Mrs Benson cared. She quickly spotted I had a longing for the public gaze. Mrs Benson allowed me on a Friday to do five minutes for my fellow students in assembly. It sounds so silly but I took this seriously. This taught me 'THE LINE' - an invisible boundary that would define my career. My whole act is about mounting 'the imaginary line' but not crossing it. Clearly the Clown Court aren't as convinced by my boundaries of taste. Not everyone can be a convicted stalker <u>WITHOUT</u> causing fear, alarm or distress – that's talent and discipline epitomised hey?! 'The Line' or 'amber light' are the most important single factor in performance. It's designed to trip you up and end your career. Whether you're performing in an assembly hall at school or in front of a thousand people in Blackpool – knowing where and when to stop is paramount. Mrs Benson was incredible, she used to love me to excite the other pupils with a song or bit of schtick, but then would gently raise her hand at the point I needed to stop. This was profound. I always listened and the next week she'd ask me back. I'm indebted to her. She conducted me to be great. Boundaries my friends – you see I can be produced and directed! Today of course 'the line' doesn't exist. Now it's just 'don't bother,' you'll be cancelled before you've finished the sentence regardless. It's not so much of a crossed line but more of a moving goalpost.

The confidence Mrs Benson gave me was immense. The faith and trust even were life changing. What a legend. If only she ran showbiz! Thank You Mrs Benson! Every kid should have one of those gems in their lives.

I'd now been having keyboard lessons with Steve for years. Learning the keys is not enjoyable. It's relentlessly, dull, repetitive and mind-numbing until you get it right. I got to about grade eight, nothing special for keyboard but it eventually went from a chore to a joy. I kept at it for about eight years and then one day I had an electrifying feeling in my fingers. I'm no Lang Lang but suddenly music was now 'in me.' No longer did I have to think about what I was doing. The keys became an extension of my fingers. A lightbulb came on and I knew this would be my life and my forever best friend. It became my career that paid the bills and was always my saviour when the shit hit the fan in radio. The insufferable hard work paid off. Having a sense of place and purpose and a clear ambition from being a kid was a huge blessing. I was now prepared for any opportunities. Maybe from birth – I always had 'it' in me. Now I needed to get it out….

<u>You Live and Learn</u>
My teenage years weren't about the old Columbian Marching Powder, it was more about finding my voice and discovering who I wanted to be and researching what I would believe and why I believed it. My heart and head were in conflict over my Labour and Union roots. I saw incredible hypocrisy that didn't sit well. I needed to educate myself. I always had a profound sense of right

and wrong born out of my love for people – many of whom in my community were ignored, illtreated and forgotten. I was very astute even as a kid and couldn't stand unfairness, lies, deception and injustice. My first ever (and only) proper job was delivering papers for Mr Singh on Wollaton Avenue next to the school. I thought it was marvellous and very grown up to be getting up at 6.30am woken by my dad who was already up and ready for his bike ride into work. This summer job at thirteen was ace. Looking back, it does seem very young to be popping up people's back passage to shove their Daily Mail and Nuts magazine through their cat flap. The little old ladies loved me on my rounds. We'd discuss the front pages. I did so much yacking I'd often be late for school. I'd often end up doing jobs for my silver tops and put their bins out if they'd got painful coccyx's. By the autumn my fair-weather sensibility kicked in and I packed it in quicker than trying to start a conversation with a Spice head in prison. Maybe this was where my love for current affairs and news began. It gave me my first insight into what real people cared about.

A new free paper had been launched called 'The Topper.' It was great as even back then people were reluctant to pay for two-day old news in the local rag. The Topper was given to everyone in every home whether they wanted it or not. My mate David had got the local contract but couldn't be arsed to deliver his five hundred newspapers and would regularly dispose of a few hundred in various wheelie bins. Along with PMT magazine it was a renowned monthly release. I was happy to be out of the house if it wasn't raining, so we'd get shot of them together in half the time and split the profit. You only got paid on what ads and leaflets were in the paper. For weeks on end, we'd earned a regular £10 each which was comparable to a week's daily papers before and after school.

As November flittered by, I noticed he became distant and seemed to be looking for a row. I was a teenager but even then, I could read the room quicker than anyone else. After the tenth time he'd deliberately tried to piss me off and I didn't react he said, 'we need a few weeks off. You're pissing me off Alex, let's try again in January.' I was gutted. My mate had dumped me from our walk around Gedling and I had no idea why. Moreover, it was about the only exercise I got. As December progressed, he came around and we were best mates again just before Christmas as if nothing had happened. Then I bumped into a mutual pal Adam down the road and he said, 'you know what that was all about don't you?' I said 'no.' He said 'the end of November and early December is the busiest time of the year for ads and leaflets. He facked you over so he could share the £50 a week with his brother.'

I was gobsmacked. Like a kick in the balls, I could not believe someone could be that manipulative. Guess what, people can! I asked him about it and he froze - he could not deny it. As a young lad I truly walked home crestfallen that someone, a mate, could be such a Judas over a few quid. It was my first realisation that a lot of people in life – in fact nearly all – are totally self-serving, utterly selfish and as I'd later learn – complete c@nts! I couldn't forgive him. To me it was such a betrayal. I didn't care about the money it was the lack of class. Weird right for a young lad, but I simply couldn't get over the calculated duplicity. Just tell me and I'd have understood. It's his round not mine, he's perfectly entitled to keep the big bucks. WOW! What a lesson. How many times in life does this happen with family and friends? You think you know a guy….! He would try to talk to me at school and even call at the house. It was in that single moment that I realised life isn't fair. But I had a HUGE awakening - I'll let people walk all over me – but not jump. He was out. It was a <u>GREAT</u> lesson so young! 'Business' is brutal……even if you're a kid on a paper round.

So, my first life lesson. People are mostly self-serving and look after themselves. Even at sixteen I realised 'management' believed they are a law unto themselves and will do and say anything to protect themselves. After several school stabbings and Dunblane all schools had newly erected gates and fences put up. The world had changed – it was no longer a cute or kind place. I was well known by the local papers as the local 'child star' and they asked how I felt. Ironically, I'd made the front page of the Topper on many occasions and The Post toilet roll. Well, naturally in true Belfield style, even back then, I milked the publicity. I did a fabulous 'prison' like picture for the front page of the Nottingham Evening Post with me poking my head through the bars like a paedo passing a local nursery. Oh, the irony that twenty-five years later I would truly be behind bars and about to stage another publicity shoot to promote my four prison HMP exposés. The headline was 'we feel like caged animals. They wouldn't treat chickens like this in a farm! Someone call the RSPCA.' In my usual tongue in cheek style, I ignored that they were attempting to stop murderers getting in, all I was bothered about was being prevented from going to Mr Singhs at breaktime for a couple of Mars Bars. You don't get fifteen stone at fifteen by eating couscous salad! The headmaster went nuts! "Who the hell do you think you are Belfield?" he screamed. I said, "I represent my fellow students who want our right to go to the chippy at lunchtime, we want our free scraps!" He said, "we're not stopping you going, if your parents say you can. Have you been authorised?" I pissed myself after. I never once went to 'Donna's Kebabs' – I had a lunch box of two fish paste sarnies, a penguin bar, a Happy Shopper bag of smoky bacon and no cash whatsoever! It was the mid-1990s – who did he think I was, Alan Sugar?!

This was the first of many media 'stunts' that pissed off authority. The paper naturally loved the drama! Was I bothered by the alarm and distress I caused the Head of Gedling Comprehensive School? I couldn't give two shiny shites. As long as people were talking about my cheeky 'he's a character' antics, I was over the Moon. In return for the story, they promoted my LIVE gigs and put my mum's landline telephone number at the bottom which was perfectly normal in 1995. How times have changed. There were no medicated trolls in those days. To this day, I don't know why people take me so seriously. It's nearly all nonsense mockery and teasing. You gotta have a gimmick. Sanctimonious and supercilious pricks tend not to get this. Hey Ho, no foreskin off my man sausage!

A step too far came when Mr Richards came into class and fell over pissed. He'd been drinking in the Tavern at lunchtime just minutes away from our now gated asylum. He went proper arse over tit. I, as quick as a tack said 'line 'em up barman.' He hit the roof. Of course he did – deflection. Instead of focusing on the pissed English teacher, the deputy head was now distracted with our argy-bargy which got me suspended for the afternoon and a letter sent home. I didn't give a baboon's red arsehole that he was drunk, I just thought it was hysterical to get a cheap laugh at his expense. This was my first lesson that people in power will do anything to cover up the stench of their own shite. Whether it's a jab that kills a radio DY, or daytime TV host, grooming young boys or an alcoholic teacher picking himself off the floor - if they can divert focus to you – they'll stop at nothing to throw you under the bus to pivot attention elsewhere. Even back then I had the hind of an elephant (and the trunk of a skin tag) to bat off this switcheroo. Deflection would define my life and career. You put a mirror up to authority and they'll kick back and double down like Mike Tyson backed into a corner.

My Mum and Dad backed me and spoke to the headmaster. "Alex why did you say it?" Mum enquired. "Because he fell over pissed." Fair doos right? I was asked to apologise, it would all be swept under the carpet. I did apologise, true to my word. I said "Dear Mr Richards, I'm sorry you were drunk and fell over. I should not have mocked and ridiculed you." We never heard another word! Don't ask about the time Mr Evans put an advert in the dating section of The Post. Oh my God we had a hoot. How that photocopy ended up on every girl's toilet door I'll never know. 'Teacher, 47, balding but fun seeks attractive and active lady 30+' I added underneath 'sense of humour ESSENTIAL' – OUCH!

## Teenage Bore

You'll probably conclude by the end of this book that I'm awfully dull. There's little scandal when you boil it down. Just words, that's all. I've never smoked a cigarette (smells worse than Piers Morgan's taint) no interest in sniff sniff (don't like any white stuff including snow or caster sugar) and unlike most in showbiz my annus erectus is an exit only! I'd have to be the postman not the post box, put it that way. I'm just saying I'd have to be the train not the tunnel if you know what I'm saying!!!! As my three corrupt and illegal police ransacking's prove, by those pilfering cuntstables, I'm up to the square root of bugger all. We all have boundaries - I don't do pain, that's why I can't watch The One Show. Anywho, that's not why you called…...

As I said at the beginning, this isn't a boohoo woe is me pity party publication. There was no funny business during my childhood, I was so ugly the creepy caretaker never even blinked an eyelid at my chubby ginger carcass. My Shrek-like qualities had few admirers outside of the Latter-day Care Home for the Bewildered. I was only ever a sex symbol for visually impaired seniors on their way to Dignitas looking for a final charity portion.

I wonder if in life you have to have one or the other? You can't be stunning, popular, cool AND creative whilst being disciplined and focused to master a craft? I don't think I've ever heard of a stunning genius. The Lord giveth and taketh right? I had no desire to be in the cool gang and frankly had an air of contempt even at nursery for halfwit knuckle draggers dribbling in the corner. School is identical to life – it's a pecking order based on confidence, wealth, looks, the way you carry yourself and personality. Bullies generally don't pick on quick and funny people as they can't take an insult bullet. They're weak and broken. Mockery, as I found out in 2020, is seemingly more devastating to sheep than any punch. The sting cuts deeper and lasts a lot longer as well! I wonder if now this pen will be mightier than the sword during this epistle?

I've always had the ability to find the Achilles heel instantly. I'm not sure if it's a gift or a curse. It's a magical innate ability to rock the foundations of the strangest of men (on the surface) and make them topple like the Berlin Wall in just a few words. A few touchy lefty women don't like being fingered (on-air) either…...ask Carol Vordernorks! #misogynist. Would I rather make hearts melt like a Cornetto in Phuket in the sunshine than snap back with a zinger? Of course, I would but that's not me. I don't do cute. I say it as it is and that leaves people girding their loins. We're only dealt the cards we're given by luck and I banked the Trump card. So, would I swap my acerbic wit for gorgeous looks? Look, I've met a ton of strippers, some have become close friends. Would I like to be hot, sexy and drop dead gorgeous – OF

COURSE I WOULD! Would I like a thirteen-inch love length……who doesn't (= Caitlin Jenner). But this is me. I'm born to bother the bullshitting backstabbers. It was never going to be a quiet ordinary life, mind you who wants that hey? Not me!!! I'll take my lot in life. I'm shameless about my actions all done in the best possible taste with the most honourable intentions. I'd spent a longtime learning, dedicating my entire formative years to words, communications and entertainment – so, could I now pull it off professionally and make a living out of my first love and passion???

## Chapter 3

## Puberty, Clearasil, Choir, Showbiz & The USA

Ermmmm People. Where do I start? 'Normal' people are fine, but it's like trudging through treacle trying to find them. The pitfalls are endless. The world is full of fakes, snowflakes and phoney baloneys and I have no time for bullshit. Some people have a sixth sense for ghosts and dead people - I have a sixth sense for twunts. I sort of have an inner radar for malarkey and zero patience to tolerate it. The friends of Dorothy have Gaydar – I have Prickdar! You see I naïvely believed people qualified at life and because they were old – or at least grown-up – they had to be respected. I stupidly believed they achieved position and greatness as they deserved and earned it! WRONG!!! You can never reason with stupid and presume a person in power has a clue what they're doing. You'll never comprehend the corrupt and you'll never work out closeted weirdos who will stop at nothing to keep you quiet. Sadly, life teaches you to turn the other cheek and block out human vomits and let them get on with it. I didn't know this in my teens. I believed in integrity, honour and doing the right thing. WRONG! I didn't have the tools or life skills and experience to navigate these treacherous waters. My formative years were as precarious as crossing the channel in a dinghy. I was up Dover Creek with a paddle…...or a whore (I think that's how you spell it). I suppose, even now, I judge people by my own standards. I guess sometimes you can be too perceptive for your own good. Often that 'inner voice' showing a red flag can lead to situations others would deliberately ignore! From being a small boy, I passionately believed honesty was the only policy. My Nana beat this into me daily. Right IS right. Looking back (and having read endless psychology) I realise all of these people from the playground to the boardroom who are triggered by my brazen honesty are trying to be 'King of the Jungle' or 'Willy Waggling' as I like to call it. People young and old are mostly insecure and are simply vying for position. Some will stop at nothing to be leader of the pack.

By the age of eighteen I'd learnt the biggest life lessons:

1. People don't change.
2. People don't listen.
3. People don't want to change.
4. People don't want to listen or change.

Arguing with an idiot is like watching Love Island for the intellectual insight. They're mostly as dumb as a box of rocks. Look at the tits and marvel at their bikini line and inability to say three words without a 'like' or 'errrr' in between. They're morons but hot ones. That's the ones who haven't killed themselves once the limelight fades. Bravo ITV!

By my mid-teens I'd found my calling was for radio, people, phone-ins and communication which grew stronger and stronger by the day. I don't know how, but I realised at this point that having an accent (well a strong Nottingham accent) wouldn't help my career - Duck! How did I know this? No one told me and I certainly didn't discuss it with my dearest. I just secretly worked on my diction and accent....to soften the blow. I love my home town. I've never spoken about this or admitted it before. I'm embarrassed to say it, but it's true, people make HUGE judgements on the way you speak. Back then I could hear and see that the harshness of the accent would hold me back. I didn't want to lose the vernacular but reduce the staccato or harshness of certain words. So, for months and months I trained myself to soften the tone without dropping my humour, sayings, character, charm, nuance of voice and colloquialisms. Some in my family didn't like it. They were confused by me saying 'barth' instead of 'baff'! It was taken as a slight by some who took it as 'he thinks he's better than he is.' I didn't, it couldn't have been further from the truth. I just wanted to make myself as 'commercially viable' to as many people as possible. How did I know this? It took over a year to 'transition' to a neutral accent. I wanted to work everywhere. Later I was proven to be 100% right when I hosted celebrity network specials for over a decade across the UK – even the BBC loved my 'generic' delivery. It sounds harsh but I knew I had to do it to be understood. Irish, Welsh and North East are probably the exception that work everywhere. Of course, these days you hear accents (mostly from Bolton) as broadcasters pretend to 'level up' the regions, but I know in my heart that the way I spoke would not help me become the broadcaster I wanted to be. Part of this training was to slow down, deepen my voice and talk more quietly……which (on mic) makes you sound a hundred times more butch!

One day I was listening to my local radio hero Dennis McCarthy on BBC Nottingham and he took a call from a lady at the Italian Mission in Nottingham. They needed a choir master for their St Bernadette's Church which was just five minutes from my home. Thirty Italians being taught to sing by a fourteen-year-old lad who couldn't speak a word of their language. What could go wrong? I called Josephine and told her my story. This angel gave me a chance and arguably changed my life forever. I got the job! Again, most lads still had a paper round – I had a choir. It felt perfectly normal. It was a brilliant learning curve and I fitted in with my Italian silver tops magnificently. The music was lovely, the people were fab and the food afterwards was Bellissimo!

I <u>loved</u> the Italian culture, spirit and sense of community. I belonged – all any of us really want. These people are loud! You very quickly learn if you don't keep up, you're left silent and quickly excluded. Their verbose and ebullient way of chatting was inspiring to me. If you snooze you lose! You have to keep up! My gorgeous gang of singers were mostly sixty plus and quite frankly well to do. They had bucket loads of class and culture. What an education. For over five years I played on Christmas Day and all the Easter Masses and became the peculiar ginger teen friend none of them could have predicted. Magical times. They'd bring me leftovers from their sensational dinners and invited me to their family dos and homes for parties. I was in heaven. One had fifty ice-cream vans, one had an Italian shop, others had restaurants and I was now part of the furniture. It was such an exciting time. How lucky was I? In the beginning of course I had to be picked up as I couldn't drive at fourteen....perfectly normal. My folks didn't blink an eye. Lovely Josephine, Concetta and Anna picked me up for years. Absolute pleasure. This was all perfectly normal. A fourteen-year-old choir master – hey ho!

We formed a group called 'Sing It Together' and we would play hospitals and old cockeries doing the classics and it worked a treat with me on piano. I had a hoot. The local press loved it; we'd often make a full page with a daft photo of me looking like a ginger Alan Carr with my three lovely ladies in their seventies in between me and my organ. These were great times to learn my art and most importantly stage craft, confidence and social skills. The most important thing about being an entertainer is how you walk in and out the room. The way you speak to your guests OFF stage is far more important than the act. I tried to master this. Turning up on time is critical. Far more important than being good. I believe it explains my twenty-five-year LIVE career without any issues or dramas whatsoever. Around this time, I felt I was ready for MY audience. With the help of endless adverts on BBC Radio Nottingham and features in the Nottingham Evening Post I'd become a local oddity that was reliable and got bookings out of pure curiosity. I remember after one interview on Radio Nottingham a lady (posh) called up from Mapperley Park and asked if I'd play Christmas Carols for her dinner guests on her grand piano while they ate. As usual, Mum and Dad didn't flinch. At 6.45pm they dropped me off and came back at 8.10pm to pick me up. £40 at that age is a lot of money. WOW! Piece of piss. Why would anyone pay me to have this much fun. I got a turkey butty afterwards plus a mince pie. I was as happy as a pig in shite.

At least once a month the press would find another angle to take a pic with the 'local lad done good' strap-line and they made me a local star. Ironic that the very same people revelled in my demise thirty years later for tawdry, cheap bullshit clickbait headlines. That's showbiz! By fifteen I was performing far and wide and my poor Mum and Dad would have to schlepp my organ from Blidworth Bottom to Likiend! Even the local council bought me a touring piano to up my game. For years I would play my keyboard in care homes, village halls, local WI's (Women's Institutes) and eventually the clubs. At this point in silence, not one word said - no ad-libs, singing, let alone jokes. It was nearly a decade before I went to the next level and plucked up the courage to talk to my punters – let alone sing. That was the moment I became alive. What a learning curve. I dealt with everything from falls, heart attacks to fights in those first five years. A club artiste's perfectly normal life. It's a magnificent apprenticeship.

Dennis got me my first big paid gig. I mean BIG! £75 to play the keyboard for an hour at Tibshelf Miners Welfare. You can't imagine how that felt. Dad helped me carry the new 'portable' (coffin sized) piano down the stairs, then my sound system the size of Sweden and off we went up the M1. Those punters sat so politely listening to my self-indulgent rehearsing of ABBA, the Baron Knights and Showaddywaddy classics. Poor buggers clapped and encouraged me and off I went. A snotty nosed fella came over and said, "you're not very experienced, are you?" I said, "I'm fifteen." He said, "keep at it, one day you might get better." A northern back handed compliment if ever I'd heard one. No chance of me getting an ego! I had a similar reaction at the Stanton Hall Iron Works Club. All the big manufacturers had a social room and they were the hub of the community. It takes balls to walk through a room where everyone knows everyone – other than you! Clicky doesn't cover it – I felt like I was sneaking in from ISIS. Ironically by the time you play theatres this stops.

Almost uniquely I've never been paid off in my career. Entertainers tell horror stories of bombing so badly, the plug is pulled, a brown envelope is thrust into their hands, and they're shown the door. Bizarrely I have never had this but trust me you know when you're flying – and you equally know when you're pulling teeth and they are bored stiff. I'm not saying every gig is a standing ovation, far from it, but I did manage to get to the end. Adding vocals, eventually, made a big difference. People are shy. Few will start singing alone. They will join in if you're singing…...even if it's badly! The days of fingering an unfeasibly big organ solo were over! I truly believe my current inner confidence along with a reassured sense of right and wrong was born out of every crappy club and pub I played for over two decades. You can't buy or be taught confidence and experience. It grows over decades not weeks. Knowing you are (mostly) only there to fill the gap in between the 'Top of the Bill' that is BINGO is truly humbling. It's a job. Very little (or no) glamour. BTW, dare go a minute over your time and you will be pulled within seconds as Bingo is ALWAYS on time. Seriously, you HAVE to know your place. No ego. Take the money and run. I had military timing to avoid all of that indignity. Never compete with a buffet, you won't win!

The other strange thing about my career that may surprise you is that I've never had an agent or manager EVER! I've busked and fought my whole life to survive and I just could never see the point of giving away half of my money to a fella sat in an office making a phone call when I can do it myself. Again – working class ethic. Remember they are still taking 20% for the rest of your career. At least Dick Turpin wore a mask!

As if my comedy (ridiculous) life couldn't get any more absurd, I became very popular with Father Maroni. Father was the senior High Catholic boss for the Italian community in the Midlands. As well as weddings and Sunday Mass, he also had to do funerals – which were seemingly endless in length and regularity. He asked me if I'd like to go on tour with him sending off stiffs from the dead centre of Minge Heath to Connie Lingus. I had never met anyone like Father. He was literally a law unto himself. Like so many in the Catholic church he ran a hugely lucrative business and seemingly had total diplomatic and legal impunity. I was basically a kid joy riding with a seventy-year-old priest. This man thought nothing of flying over islands without looking and couldn't give two flying facks about red lights. This man felt God's hand on his shoulder and had a total disregard for his brake pedal. It was truly like the wacky races. Hysterical and terrifying at the same time. I felt safe in the knowledge that Father was as close to the pearly gates as possible but was equally as mad as a box of frogs blinded by his own delusions of grandeur.

What staggered me about working funerals is that it wasn't remotely depressing. You just got on and did it. Another profitable department of SHOW business. At the end Father would have stacks of wooden plates stacked inches high with £10, £20 and £50 notes. That's on top of his show fee of course. I didn't work for charity. £80 for two songs at seventeen is quite a packet. A peculiar way to earn a living for a teenager, but St Peter would be proud! I wonder if his pile of notes were declared to the tax man? Asking for a friend. Regardless, I'd made it. I was professional. I earned a good living via my peripatetic organ.

## Belfield's Love of America

One of the most incredible awakenings for me was going to the USA. Land of the free and enormous bottoms! They appeared to droop 10 – 20 inches lower than in other civilised societies. I cannot thank mum and dad enough for making this dream come true. To me it was the land of opportunity (and true free speech) with every landscape available from the magnificent (and man-made) New York to the natural breathtaking epic enormity of the Grand Canyon. Mind blowing. Where did we land? DETROIT! Beggers can't be choosers! As a teenager I couldn't give two shites whether it was Detroit or Las Vegas. It was the USA and at $1.80 to the £1 – everyone was living like a king in the nineties.

Why Detroit? My Nana Lil's sister Alice married a Yank after the war and thus became the event of the decade in our family. When Aunty Alice and Uncle Bill arrived once a year it meant three things 1) A trip to Heathrow 2) Gifts 3) The American Optimism which I adored…a totally different way of thinking. I found the accent intoxicating and their stories better than Jackanory. It was like a mythical Holy Land. People are curious about the 'the American Dream' ideology but, to me it's utterly uplifting and inspirational……regardless of the 'have a nice day' fakery. Uncle Bill played the piano by ear and was a hugely classy and dignified man. Aunty Alice had gone from wanky Notts in the fifties to Yanky wonderment overnight. They were captivating to me. In recent years my entire trust in justice, journalism, politics and everything authoritarian has been rocked. Americans are trained from birth to be upbeat and believe anything is possible. I LOVE THIS mentality! This pure delusion of success, self-worth and confidence is nothing but fantastic to me. The British Donny Downer weighs heavy on my soul. Pep it up! Life is magnificent. Get lost with your anxiety and anti-depressants – get me to Key West for a full body massage for the love of God!

As I've previously mentioned, fitting in has never been easy for me. Who is he? What is he? Why did he……However, in America I've never had any of these problems. My amazing parents made me and my sister's dreams come true by booking four seats on a Fokker 100 (I believe) to DTW. This was our first foreign holiday. They'd saved for years. We were only able to do it as our board and lodgings were free. Detroit Metro Airport was where we were swiftly collected by my Aunty Alice and Uncle Bill, then quickly driven an hour north before we got shot. Detroit in the nineties was DANGEROUS! You did not hang around on the drive north out of the airport. It was the most exciting time of my life. I couldn't believe my eyes. A flight across the Atlantic was the most unbelievable thing that had ever happened to me AND to America AND to meet my new family – I was the luckiest kid alive! Can you imagine? All my Christmases came at once! Heathrow, a nine-hour flight and then arriving in The United States of America. Oy vey – that feeling still gives me a tingle downstairs even today. The smell of Cinnabon as you get off the plane, the scale of the buildings, the houses and their girth were unseen here in those days. Of course, super-sized fatties are ten a penny in the UK now, but not back then. I wonder if the 'fat jab' will work? Wouldn't a lock on their fridge be cheaper for the NHS! What a country. Roads without potholes and sixteen lanes on each side. Boy, I'm in a movie – living the dream! Everything was exciting from traffic lights to the bin liner sized bags of potato chips. Unfortunately, I was still too young yet for $10 titty bars! Then the most magical thing happened. I met the family and my life changed forever.

We stayed at my Uncle Jim and Aunty Rose's house and they had a daughter called Alice – single-handedly the most exciting, fun and amazing person I'd ever met! She was like a firework display going off. The loudest person I've ever encountered with the biggest heart and warmth. Her laugh could fill Wembley. WOW! I'd finally found my people. She was like my Nana on acid.

FEARLESS! Nothing went too far, nothing couldn't be said. Next came cousins Jimmy and Joe – the two biggest stud muffins on earth adored by the birds and the envy of their mates. God, if I could only be them. They were a few years older than me, in their prime as American football and basketball stars locally. I've never seen such adoration and guess what? Cousin Alex was cool too because he had a brilliant accent from 'overseas,' knew Princess Diana (because I was British) – I didn't by the way I was fifteen and from a pit estate! Suddenly, for the first time in my life I was in the cool gang. What a feeling!

It didn't stop there, cousins Mike and Joanne, Patrick and Brenda and Cathy and Joey were the kindest souls on earth and welcomed us into their homes and hearts like we'd known each other for our entire life as did Aunty Carol and Uncle Pat – they were all stunners! This gave me faith in humanity. The most fun I'd ever had in my life. As a boy I was a big boned lad. I truly never cared. I mean I wasn't morbidly obese like Piers Morgan or anything disgusting like that, but if you put a suitcase on my head I could pass for a fitted wardrobe. In America of course I was positively anorexic. No one cared. I had no self-awareness regarding appearance at all. I truly thought it was silly and a total waste of time and energy to worry about designer trainers or £50 haircuts. America was my spiritual home. Curiously and most surprisingly there's a dexterity to their use of language and passion for life that somehow doesn't exist (often) here in Great Britain. Obviously, I'm not talking about the morons on US reality TV who sound like a frog. You know the type who croak like

Kermit at the end of every line. Half of my Michigan family married Italians – this is another level of personality and culinary heaven. Cousins Connie and Maria are two of my favourite people on earth. Loud, hysterical, loving and generous beyond words – I've found my people. Oh, and they can cook better than Gordon, Jamie, Delia and Fanny put together. Italian stunners. Funny as hell. BINGO! Their mum, dad and brother – Josephine, Lorenzo and Joe and Nancy were such class. They all had style and elegance. I was blown away by their instant hospitality. Italians would play a big part in my life. Cousin Harry became a dear friend much later in life. I adore the bones of him and his twin brother Jack is a top man. They all had kids and collective would meet in groups of twenty or thirty. It was the BEST fun ever! I saw the babies, Josephine, Maria, Elizabeth, Maggie and Patrick all grow up to be stunning humans, now in their late teens and twenties.

You can probably see that there's a theme with everyone in my life that always ends around the dining table. This is the magic and the moment I adore. For years I would time my US trips to fall at the end of November to coincide with Thanksgiving - the biggest party ever in Detroit! Concetta's family are the best cooks ever. Stuffed artichoke, pasta fasul and the deserts – good Lord I was in heaven. I'm anyone's for a Cannoli. Lifelong passion was ignited in the 'D' – an amazing place riddled with US contradictions. You see Downtown Detroit is a shithole, well it was until they pumped billions into it to pretend it was no longer a dangerous ghetto. Drug and gun crime is out of control leading to unbelievable fear from those on the outskirts. 'White Flight' is a real thing. This is an unspoken reality born out of the evening news packed with daily (hourly) murders in gangland – mainly black on black. This has led to a very real fear that has created 'gated' communities (filled with white people and very rich people of colour) living completely separate lives who chose to buy security and leave society per se. I've never seen racism as it is in Detroit, born out of true fear. The media paint Detroit as 'reborn.' They sing the praises of Motown and the stars it created, but how many of them still live there? This reminds me of the legendary Liverpudlians who quickly moved to Surrey. My gang live in lovely areas like Birmingham and St Clare's shores – a world away from the endless murders less than an hour down the I9S.

Restaurants were ridiculously cheap back then, less so now. We used to go to a steak restaurant called Champs. It was a dollar an ounce for a steak. Preposterous with the exchange rate. I would eat out twice a day. Then I found the delights of Taco Bell, White Castles and Popeyes - small pleasures. Heaven for a teenage boy. No one goes to the US to diet although later, I believe, they're world leaders in the chop salad.

We're constantly reminded that life is fair and/or equal! IT IS NOT. There will always be the rich and poor and most importantly these issues will NEVER be resolved. It's not in the elite or establishments interests to sort it out. Don't get me wrong, America has its major flaws, but what they lack in political decorum they make up for in culinary diversity and hospitality born out of the cultural and immigrant heritage. A smile goes a long way, doesn't it? It does help you 'have a nice day.' Thank you, Detroit. You have no idea the happiness I have had flying into DTW a hundred times over the years. The best people on earth and some of the happiest times I've ever had. I feel free there. I can be me. No judgement. Just love and fun. No expectation. What a blessing to get a second family at fifteen!

On The Turn ….to becoming Professional
So, by fifteen I'd discovered America, dipped my toe in luvvie lake via my organ and got my own choir as MD musical director. I even had one of those conductor sticks. I wish I'd have had two and then I could have become a drummer as well. The best advice I've ever been given was by Doddy who drummed it into me that 'showbusiness is two words' SHOW BUSINESS. I've never forgotten this. From day one I realised the power of every pound I earned and there were no flies on me when it came to shafters and charlatans. You get a sixth sense. You can smell a scam. This game is riddled with scumbags and raving back and bottom stabbers! No point running a charity. Unpaid invoices didn't pay for my flights to Vegas! They were much simpler days. I kept everything and didn't earn enough to even pay tax after expenses. Now I have to pay 20% VAT, a further 20% to the venue plus another 20% if there's a booker, then 19% corporation tax – I'm left with £75 like I got in 1994 despite selling 1000 x £25 tickets on the end of the pier generating £20k at the box office. Doh! Work that out. Thanks .gov – genius!

One thing I've loved throughout my career and learnt early on, is that it's all about regular gigs. Every Christmas for twenty years I went to the Salvation Army for example and every Christmas Eve for years as a teen I'd play carols on my palatial organ, in front of the pub opposite the Co-op in Burton Joyce, for a local kid's charity. I would have paid them. It was my Home Alone moment with everyone dressed in tinsel and reindeer ears with buckets of festive joy clattering with donations. I loved it. For two decades at 2pm I'd go to my Aunty Dorothy's care home in Carlton for an hour for the very final gig. It was a tradition, not a job or work. The local press loved it as it gave them the obligatory yuletide picture for Christmas Eve's uplifting edition which got more bookings until Easter. I must have had twenty front pages over the years with various nincompoopery gimmicks. Radio Nottingham sent the radio car to join us throughout the morning one year. The local mayor and MP joined us to steal the limelight and pamper their egos; we had a hoot raising hundreds of pounds for kids who didn't have any of my luck and life blessings. Richard Bacon was the radio car reporter and reluctantly gave a bit of pathological cheerfulness to drag the public down to the arse end of Robin Hood County. He didn't seem to have the energy and pazazz he later had on Blue Peter. Mind you, he probably couldn't afford any sniff to pep him up in the mid-1990s. Like so many at the BBC, his 'Blue Peter' was the talk of the canteen. Anywho, it got a buzz and a bit of malarkey on Santa's Eve. These events became very normal at a very young age. I guess I've never known any difference. To me it was just my job, but to others I'd set my stall out as a total one-off and oddity with my strange way of earning a living. I just loved what I did and knew from day one this is all I wanted to do for the rest of my life.

The worst gig I did was at a pub. I was about seventeen. This boozer in Basford wasn't exactly the Monte Carlo of the Midlands. The rottweilers walk round in packs for safety. It makes Cleethorpes look like Dubai. I got there at 6pm for a 7pm start. I set up and literally no one was in. I presumed I'd be paid off but the landlord said, "give it twenty minutes and start." Rule one of showbiz – you have no pride! A job is a job when you're on a set fee and the 'bums on seats' is irrelevant. So many are led by their ego. Remember Show BUSINESS. On a set fee you take home the same for five or five hundred. Pay cheque before a warm hand! Anyway, I went to the toilet and there were lovely flowers in the gents. As I stood John Thomas in hand pushing fag ends around the urinal I thought 'it can't be that bad if there's flowers – surely?' – well it turns out a man had been killed in this very toilet the night before! The flowers weren't a distraction from the odour in trap two. They were in remembrance of a stabbed stiff in trap one. It could only happen to me. I did my two forty-five minutes set as the contract confirmed. Not so much a standing ovation, more a wake of hand wringers, pearl-clutchers and tear droppers in their G & T's. I got paid. I win. Onwards and upwards……That's Showbiz. Take the money and run (quick). May this unfortunate, departed soul rest in pieces.

I was on a roll! The bookings were pilling in via my mother's landline. Don't forget, this is the mid-1990s – no mobiles, let alone iPhones yet! A lot of old timers talk about work drying up and 'I can't get arrested' – by eighteen I was doing a world tour of the best care homes, dives, cesspits, pubs, clubs and car parks in the East Midlands! I did have same glamour though!!! I had a call from a lovely lady who booked me at the Marriott Hotel in a private room for her 80$^{th}$ Birthday in town. I did it for £100 – a huge amount of money for a teenager and my biggest gig by a mile yet! A proper stage and lighting. It was a huge conference room and my modest PA wasn't exactly designed to fill Wembley. The pressure was a double-edged sword but naturally and shamelessly I said yes! Firstly, I knew how hard my mum and dad worked. Dad left the house at 6.30am to earn HALF in an entire day, even now I never forget this! I still have massive guilt over this. My hobby and gimmick had become a real job – but how insulting to people who work their arses off for their entire lives for no round of applause and less money – life ain't fair, I've told you already! Don't get me started on nurses on £15 an hour and having to pay £30 to park their car. Bastards! The dress up box Twirlies in the West End hate me for saying that mincing about on a stage isn't a proper job. IT'S NOT! Talking is a gift we all have – it's not special. It's an honour to show off if people are willing to listen. OK, dancing is a talent and maybe magic but acting is identical to news reading – it's just saying words. Three-year-olds can do that! No, I can't accept we should revere or give awards to actors, journalists let alone TV 'celebs.' It's basically pissing about for a laugh. Look at Andi Peters!

Of course, the reality is that you rarely get 'amazing' gigs, let alone highly paid ones and you're forever hustling for the next hurrah! When cushy numbers come in, they're normally three hundred miles away. It's relentless. Anyway, the lady at the hotel must have had some kind of short-term memory loss. She was over the Moon as were her family with my performance. She wrote me a lovely card with a cheque for £1 in it – I was £99 short! I was so mortified and embarrassed. I was beside myself how to deal with it. I didn't want to ruin her day or offend. I didn't have the chutzpah or experience to say anything to her face. The second half was a blur as I tried to work out what to do about the missing money whilst pretending to joyfully do the act. I was still a kid in a big man's world which sums up my life to be honest. I knew it wasn't a stitch-up, but what to do? In the end I spoke to her son who was amazing and he sorted it out - £100 it is then! Always check your cheque people! He gave me 5 x £20 notes plus the cheque, so I made an extra £1 for the inconvenience – my first tip and bonus! The Lord works in mysterious ways! You'd be amazed by all the completely 'accidental' mistakes over the years in the little brown envelopes! Rarely do extra fivers slip into your pay packet…...incredible how easily they slip out! Whilst all of this was going on I was still at school doing A-levels and incredibly bored. I did it because that's what you <u>had</u> to do. Each year there would be a talent contest so at sixteen I thought the time was right to test my developing comedy act in front of two hundred teenagers and the headmaster. A VERY WRONG DECISION!

Crossing the Line

I've told you before about the imaginary line in showbiz. Bob Monkhouse called it his 'Amber Light.' Stop before it goes to red! At Gedling Comprehensive School, I had a fantastic venerable old music teacher called Mr Pilgrim. He had his own block and smoked a pipe in his office. Oh, the good old days. He saw a little something in me but to other kids he was a tyrant who wasted their time. Art and Music are not for everyone. I see no point forcing kids to do it – akin to me and sport. Hopeless. The buff lads dedicated their lives to winding him up and ruining it for everyone else. He had a hysterical drumstick that he thought he could conduct the class with, WRONG! Old school discipline had gone, this was the nineties and the kids had less respect than they did rhythm. The relentless 'attention bang' on the desk was just the stuff of ridicule. They couldn't wait for him to do his Phil Collins on the wooden table, battered to shit by him; a teacher in his late sixties from another age of compliance. Mr Pilgrim helped me in shows and even bought me a euphonium that I had to bring into school in a push chair! Have you seen the size of those bloody things? Could I be any more hysterical? As if my face didn't make me a big enough laughingstock. Now I'm carrying a bloody brass band case bigger than my bedroom halfway down Wollaton Avenue.

I had a very nice teacher and later fell in love with brass bands. 'Brassed Off' is my favourite film. Anyway, Pilgrim's days were numbered, and he was replaced. After he left, I swapped the euph' for a recorder to save the work out. I was orchestrated post puberty and had found my calling. I was still no genius but he did inspire me to move on to the third side of the triangle by the time he left. Top man! Being a pro muso can come at a price! I remember the embarrassment of 'Brass Player's Lip.' It must be like 'call girl fanny' in the early days. Nobody had told me to do three minutes max as the muscles in your face can't cope. I was mortified leaving my mother's back bedroom and taking the walk of shame to the living room to ask why I'd got the lips of Lesley Ash with a swollen face of Joan Rivers. This has been a metaphor for my career. Showbiz sucks so don't blow! Lips are a muscle. Years of training is required. This presumably explains how Kerry Katona made so much dosh on OnlyFans. Practise makes perfect!

By sixteen I was gigging and gagging and believe it or not I'd spent a decade learning my craft – seriously – I'm not working you from behind. My vocation became my life and job. What good fortune. Little did I know the endless pitfalls of this ridiculous occupation. Honestly, this is not for the faint of heart. Why couldn't I just change tyres in Kwik Fit or be the woman who hands you a glass of water in the dentist? You need relentless backbone to fend off the endless vultures who just want to bring you down. Even as a novice kid! I was about to learn a BIG lesson in front of the entire school. I thought I'd try five minutes of stand up at the end of year concert. Mr Pilgrim had long gone and now an enormous, big boned catastrophe called Mrs Shelley had taken over. We didn't gel as I was paranoid that she might eat me or worst still have a wardrobe malfunction and smack me in the gob with displaced back or roaming gunt flaps. I was given my spot and I did a mix of Doddy, Monkhouse and Tarbuck with the charm of Bruce Forsyth. I might as well have shat on the receptionist and had a dirty protest in the Thatcher like deputy head's office. Shelley was fuming!!! I honestly don't know what made her see her arse and caused such an argy-bargy but she was angrier than Judy Finnigan at last orders! This old cow was clearly riddled with cystitis and hadn't had a portion since Elsie Tanner was in the Rovers, but don't take it out on me! It was the audacity they didn't like. 'Who the hell does he think he is?' I was banned - even from the band. For some reason she took it as a personal affront that I'd slapped on the theatrical table my comic bent. Look it was cheeky, but it wasn't rude or inappropriate. I was exorcised from the music department quicker than a straight white male from the TV or radio schedules post BLM. Look, I didn't know better. What this fat pig should have done is said 'that wasn't the time or place' or 'why didn't you tell me?' Instead, as all crap managers do – she looked at me like she'd found a pube on her soup bowl and didn't talk to me EVER again. I've become <u>VERY</u> familiar with this look over the years. I couldn't care less. I might be an ostracised outcast and proud pariah but at least I didn't have a lazy eye, chaffing thighs and have a brain like a sieve and a brassiere to match!

Despite the 'fitting in' and boundary issues, I can promise you I had the best childhood on earth. Like now, I didn't care. The audience laughed (a bit), I learned – I moved on. That feeling of 'the naughty step' would happen a LOT! All I focused on through and after every shitstorm was my infinitely supportive, loving and amazing parents. Why should I care about naysayers. I had my Nana I couldn't adore or love any more, grandparents who were fab, uncles and aunties a plenty, cousins I loved being with like Emma, Alan and Tracey down the road and friends young and old who all had my back. I felt Teflon to the scorn of people who were worthless to me. This identical contempt continues today. It's not all bunches of flowers and blow jobs in luvvie land.

There was no social media or iPhone in the nineties so I didn't have any toxic trolling through my formative years. I was lucky. VERY LUCKY! I would not want to be born now. I pity kids today with their tippy-tappy clicking 24/7. You can know and see too much. I was in a sea of protection and comfort. We weren't rich. It wasn't glamorous. The smell of coal fires is still magical, but the world was changing. Radio was about to explode across the country with licences handed out like smarties and I needed to get on board! The novelty of a 'teen local star' wouldn't last long, so what's next? Time to grow up – the saddest part of all our lives. The 'real' world is not nice…...so, how could I continue in my blinkered bubble of fun and love?……How would I survive in the lefty brown nosing cesspit of luvvie land?

By the end of the nineties, I was at the tail end of clubland and local radio before it all sold and closed down. I managed to get the last couple of years to serve my apprenticeship before everything moved to Manchester or London – who on earth wants to live there what with the rain and foreigners respectively. That was lucky! By pure fluke I would be the last generation to get the opportunity to learn and practise my craft on-air and in real time.

I was about to meet royalty, politicians, stars, DJ's, creepy managers and BBC liars and cheats. What a bunch of characters……...

It's time to grow the fack up! Balls to the wind it was time to piss or get off the pot.

## Chapter 4

### Belfield at the Beeb – Radio Ga Ga

As my passion grew for talk radio and phone-ins I became consumed by politics and social affairs. The more I listened the more I learned about the struggles, inequalities, oppression, injustice and unfairness of life. Almost every article on shows like John Taynton on BBC Midlands was about <u>people</u>. He was quite brilliant and the first who taught me about being cruel to be kind. You don't always have to be nice. Edge is great! I listened to two other BBC Nottingham 'legends' called Tony and Julie who were popular…...until exposed as nonces in a court of law for sleeping with kids. Why are there so many lurking paedos at Auntie's nonce factory. What is it with so many perverts in the media? Broadcasting is the Pied Piper of paedos!!! Back to the script. Phone-ins are an amazing melting pot. I couldn't believe how many broken, ill, angry, hysterical, outrageous, dysfunctional and nuts people there were……who were willing to call a LIVE radio show. I equally couldn't believe how quickly politicians and PR people rallied to cover up, defend the indefensible and sweep over people's tragedies. Regardless, this was content and these interviews on a REAL human level were riveting and I wanted my career to be defined by holding arsehole public serpants to account.

'Sorry' is the hardest word. It's the go to word to get out of shit. People ruin other people's lives and think 'I'm sorry' which makes it OK. <u>NO</u>! "We'll learn our lessons" – no you won't! It does not wash with me Chunky! I'm the only honest guy in public life who will not be bullied into saying untruths to smooth the waters. 99.9% of people you watch or listen to are puppets and yes people puppeteered to pay the mortgage. I didn't have a mortgage for another twenty years. Fack it! I'd rather go to the pokey than be fake pretending to care with platitudes of fake 'sorry.' Balls to that! Arseholes to them. I'm not sorry! Now of course 'sorry' is replaced with 'mental health' excuses to dodge a bullet. It's the #1 excuse from spineless weasels.

I learned that through late night phone-ins you could connect with 'real' people like no other medium. Late night is intimate and so much more personal than you could be at any other time of day. I knew that I didn't want to be party political – everything is politics of course, but I wanted to stand back and look at both sides – then eventually pick one. Pick the right side. Hardly any of the fraud journalists I've had the indignity to work with are capable of this true impartiality. However, I was always on the side of every man…....not the rich and powerful man which most social climbers (nonbinary vegans) choose to suck off in the hope of a few quid or a promotion. So how do you 'know' your opinion and be sure you've picked the right side? Well, my moral compass would allow me to make the right choice. I always had that confidence of judgement. Astounding now I look back. You have to be steadfast in your integrity unbought by the many temptations. Most importantly, it ain't a popularity contest! This path has few powerful voices who will back you. Being stoic and consistent against all the odds (and dark forces) is the key. It's terrifyingly risky but bloody exciting!

My gran and parents instilled a passionate moral compass through their hard knocks working class values. However, that didn't mean I'd be far left, unionized and like everyone else on the pit estate. Even back then I knew I didn't like the 'sit on your arse and take benefits' culture. Equally I wouldn't just vote Labour because my grandparents did. BRAVE! But who would be stupid enough – or brave enough – to voice it?......especially around the Sunday buffet tea table! This now gets VERY tricky. #awks.

Believe it or not Sir Ken Dodd helped me find my voice. He was a passionate Tory and we spent thousands of hours discussing politics over two decades. He taught me a lot! Mum and dad weren't militant or even gobby about politics but were naturally Labour simply because their parents were. I didn't like what I saw. So, how could I exit the closet as a conservative kind of guy? It IS a 'coming out' moment. BIGTIME! When you're surrounded by lefties, they're a team. A sheeple of Stockholm syndrome seduced downtrodden suckers. I hadn't got any allies around my house that's for sure. Why do most showbiz tarts hate me – politics. They're blind far left box tickers and refuse to engage with anyone who differs. They're also scroungers who rely on the state when they're 'resting' 80% of the time. They're militant. In fact, they have to wipe out anyone who challenges their 'woe is me' narrative. I don't like free things – like the NHS and schools because people take the piss. The NHS wasn't set up for boob jobs and nose straightening because of 'mental elf.' Puke. No. No! It's there to save your life.

Our culture extreme/radical political division hasn't changed. Especially now with immigration globally. I still see people gasp when I have my Trump polo golf shirts on. They HATE him – but can never tell me why. My favourite thing with Tommy and Horse Face Hopkins haters is to ask them WHY. I'm yet to find one irate and furious ranting lefty who can quote what either has said. Post prison, I'm now in this cancelled club and 'disgraced' elite group of future predictors. I spent about a decade relentlessly listening to Talk Radio, LBC and phone-ins all over the UK to get all sides. I was like a sponge drinking in the art of opinion. I wanted my own view not theirs. I wanted facts not spin. I wanted to judge person by person – not simply red or blue. This made me the man I am today – loved by 100,000's but despised by a few narrow minded but VERY loud opposition who seemingly dedicate their entire lives to 'closing me down.' ONLY because of my politics at the core…….and success and 'influence' on-air.

My love for Radio has always outshone all other passions. Live entertainment is hard. You have to rehearse, get there, wait, dress up, wait, wait and wait and then drive home – all by yourself. It's isolating, lonely and triggering. If you're weak in the head you will <u>not</u> survive. You'll end up medicated to survive as so many of my dead peers prove. Showbiz preys on the weak. Attracts the vulnerable and spits out the least profitable without conscience or zero duty of care. It's all about £! Thank God, I saw it as a job and avoided all addiction. Seriously, I'm so lucky I'm not 'that type.' So many can't cope. This is a very tough game to endure and survive unscathed. Radio, I'll be honest, is easy for me. VoR via YouTube is just filmed radio. Identical technique. All of my 'skill' boils down to radio technique. You go in prepared and then have the time of your life for four hours talking shite off the top of your head. To me it is stressless and effortless – but sadly poorly paid in comparison to LIVE (for the effort and time involved). Nowadays Radio is a laughingstock. Any shit head with a crap voice can read a script and get a job. Have you heard of Capital or Heart? Amanda is to radio what James Corden is to Weight Watchers. This new 'celeb' generation don't even have to know anything about life let alone the medium on which they're broadcasting. As long as you've got more than 100,000 followers, you're on! Pitiful. Look at Radio 2! Wogan and Wright must be turning in their graves at the insults and imbeciles on-air that have replaced them.

Back in the nineties radio was creative, dangerous and exciting on commercial radio. Today it's automated, robotic and run by soulless accountants who know nothing about entertainment, variety, comedy, people, audiences let alone communication. I just wanted to keep learning. At sixteen I volunteered to answer the phones at BBC Radio Nottingham for Lisa Lynch. With boundless optimism I believed I'd made it just to be in a BBC building! I was in a radio station, watching a professional work LIVE and every twenty minutes the phone would ring and I'd have the honour of answering it. 'Hello. BBC Nottingham' WOW – Thrilling!!! Lisa was very generous. NO idea where she is now but she did weather on the telly for a bit. She was a pioneer. On-air for being good, not just because she had a vagina with a silly laugh as 99% of the on-air gobs on sticks prove post #metoo and diversity quotas. They'll stick a female cleaner on before a pro these days. Where I think I'm smarter than the rest is that I didn't miss a trick. LEARN. LISTEN. LEARN! I worked every shift for free to better myself for years. To me a radio studio was like a Cathedral. Beyond exciting. To me local radio was the best as you could directly talk to and get to know your audience that you lived with locally. This didn't happen in commercial radio like Trent FM as they had to play fifteen songs and twenty minutes of ads an hour - that was of absolutely no interest to me. I've never wanted to be a DJ – a disc jockey. I was all about the bits in between. Songs were an inconvenience to me. Over time I worked on other shows at BBC Radio Nottingham until eventually I became a BA – a 'Broadcast Assistant' on Breakfast from sixteen. Boy did I have my eyes opened!

That's when my heart was broken as I realised that showbiz is all smoke and mirrors. These people are dull, weird and creepy – I never wanted to become this. It's fake and disingenuous, pretending to care. I saw a room full of producer bores and a soulless set of presenters who read poorly crafted scripts. Zero originality who gave me the heebie-jeebies. My first paid job as a BBC BA actually put me off wanting a BBC contract for a decade. Seriously, these people were uncouth, classless, rude, riddled with bitterness and as funny as piles. I knew my niche was in cheekiness and being different but these were identical clones. Talk about a putrid dish of namby pamby, pinko liberal, Guardian reading, champagne sipping, oyster eating, Naga Manshushy types. A plague of locusts on all of their deeply dull private parts. Here's a word in your shell like, you wouldn't get me anywhere near their smegma ridden, muff diving, tyrannical unsavoury prawn ring. I don't wish to elucidate further but there's nothing like a spell in a BBC newsroom to leave you with erectile dysfunction. Their malarkey is enough to make you heave. Sadly, many of them look like Olive from 'On the Buses,' with glasses like re-entry shields. I was warned that one aging lass called Margaret who was in her forties and had been around the houses (and slept in most of them) was a hoot in the clubs, she'd flattened a lot of grass over the years and clearly, she'd got meat in her freezer older than me. The Breakfast show presenter said I'd need cahoonas the size of Judy Love to touch the sides but unfortunately before we got anywhere near hanky panky this woman who was reminiscent to Judith Chalmers caught one of the laser beams in the night club on her left lens and nearly gave me open heart surgery. I had to kick her into touch as I was far too young and naïve to wet my whistle with a woman who's only saving grace was a black belt in karaoke and when she took her IQ test it came back negative.

I'd dreamed all my life of working for the great 'BBC' but within a month it drained my soul and spirit of all hope, optimism and creativity. It was a machine. A factory churning out less than mediocre filler words called radio shows. No one cared. It was 'filling air time.' These people were so boring and dull, booming out shows instead of baked beans. Dreadful contempt. Their arrogance in BBC newsrooms was breathtaking. They HATED their audience. They were better than their audience and all appeared to have the arrogance of Jacob Rees-Mogg's posh uncle. They were <u>NOTHING</u> I EVER wanted to be! One was an alcoholic who often came in pissed, injured and was rumoured to be shagging a male 18-year-old intern despite being married. Two were renowned for cocaine parties and no one seemed to like anyone else. Utterly toxic! Two were facking school boys! We'll move on from that, I don't need another High Court writ – they know who they are……as do the rest of the despicable staff who kept schtum.

Radio is not exciting. It's like an old pair of slippers. To 99% of the dopes I've met, it's a job - I've never wanted a job. So, all these years of pushing up my knobs and slapping on my twelve inch in my mother's back bedroom – where now? Definitely not a staff job at the evil, creepy, repulsive, sycophantic and backstabbing BBC! The dizzy heights of 'Nottingham's Hospitals' Radio' seemed a promotion from BBC Radio Nobcheese - and it was! Yes, wireless for those on life support across the Queen's Medical Centre and City Hospital - this ain't a joke! It far outweighed the dirge of Auntie's London Road empire. Don't laugh! This is my life! A potential audience of thousands – all of which weren't listening. Yet, they still had more collective energy than the dullard news hounds at the BBC packed with naff over promoted traffic wardens.

Every Sunday from sixteen years old at 3pm my poor dad would schlepp all the way across town down Derby Road to the QMC. Even then I refused to catch a bus. I don't do public transport carrying headphones. Back then I was pretending to be important, talking to three women who'd just had a hysterical rectomy on the 6$^{th}$ floor. I was very popular with those who have dropped pelvic floors and loose lips on gyno N6. However, I was less in demand on the Resus and High Dependency Units for obvious reasons. To me, it might as well have been BBC Television Centre, I'd made it! My own Jingle and my first sacking – IT WASN'T MY FAULT - HONEST. You see I'm always thinking. I remember a most peculiar man called Dennis who ran the station. Just like at the BBC Local Radio, these places only attract people who weren't good enough to get a proper job or make a living out of the business independently. They'd do it for the delusion that they're still in the game and important. Dennis was actually quite nice to me, but he made a major mistake. He said, 'nobody ever rings in.' Every station I've ever been at have told me this. It's bollocks! If you're compelling enough, trust me, they'll ring in - even if it's to tell you you're crap!

I decided I'd go around the 'not dead yet' wards and offer my punters a free call on their brand-new phone and TV system installed at every bedside on a big bendy movable arm thing. I later found out it's 80p to make a call so of course they didn't ring! Hospital radio is like so many virtue signalling projects that waste money. It's just not thought through. Who would listen? If you're well up to listening you'd already be in a cab home for Christ's sake! Why would they listen? It's totally self-servicing. If you're in hospital you're going to have much bigger priorities (like not dying) than calling into request The Barron Knights on Belfield's 'Bed Bath Hour' – (I always had warm hands and a large spatula!). Anyway, I had a new idea, if they can't ring me, I'll ring them! Each Sunday I'd spend an hour before my show begging lonely silver tops and sedated smack heads to let ME call THEM for free! It worked!!! PERFECTLY legal and not remotely inappropriate. I'd get their number off their phone and call their bedside from the radio studio switchboard LIVE and chat for five or ten minutes to pass the time. They were bored; I was keeping the needles wagging whilst attempting professional showbiz entirely broadcast in the hope of getting a half decent clip for my demo. What more could they ask? Amazing right – WRONG! After three months when the telephone bill came in, it had gone up by £16,000+. They had a full investigation alas it was all my fault; 80p a minute over four hours (I always had someone hanging on in case one dropped out (or dies) – is A LOT of money! I told them I did what they asked, they begged to differ. I politely left quickly before being sued. They thought I was ringing 0898 mucky filth chat lines. Nope, just the equally expensive rip-off NHS private profit lines. Outrageous. At least Gladys got 'My Way' for three consecutive weeks before her end was near, and she faced her final curtain.

Of course, I couldn't give two facks. Like always I laughed my cap off and moved on to the next gig. It had served its purpose. I learned so much there over the year I played at radio. I also started interviewing at NHR. No one could believe it. From politicians to celebs, they all said yes! It was a learning curve the size of Mount Eiger. I was bold and fearless. I'd messaged local MPs like Kenneth Clarke, Vernon Coaker and even the odd vegan Lib Dem who all kindly obliged and popped in which taught me so much about on-air chit chat. I was so lucky to have this opportunity to learn my craft LIVE. With radio and the stage, you can <u>ONLY</u> learn and improve on the job! You just need a platform where no one is listening. Little did I know this would be my life and career for the next twenty-five plus years.

By seventeen I'd got LIVE work, Hospital Radio and things were going well at Radio Nottingham despite their insidious dullness and unnecessary obsession with cancer, death and dog shit on public footpaths. I just kept learning how <u>NOT</u> to do it. I always loved it when they were caught short and stuck on a dopey newsreader for three hours. Not so easy now hey clayballs. There was one odious poncy prick I had to produce one Sunday. They're not good at ad-libbing when calls mysteriously got cut off are they? LMFAO! These purvey News hounds aren't as clever as they think when it's not scripted! My big break came when I was given the opportunity to be a 'LIVE' reporter in the radio car. I bloody loved it. I got to go to summer fairs, council events and anywhere punters would gather in the hope we'd find some BBC Nottingham fans to chat to. That van was like a beacon. The aerial when aroused was thirty foot high. Finally, I'd found my niche away from news and with the audience. Such a fantastic learning curve. I could have happily done this for the rest of my career. Remember – If at first you don't succeed – scuba diving is not the sport for you!

I put on my first variety show 'An Audience with Alex Belfield and Friends' in 1997. A call came into BBC Radio Nottingham with a very nice couple trying to raise money for a very young girl with a terminal condition. They wanted to fly her to Florida for potentially life-saving treatment, unavailable in the UK. So, without any fear I staged the show with anyone who was willing to perform alongside me, including my Italian Choir. I wrote to every star in the country for raffle prizes and auction lots. So many replied, I couldn't believe it! As always, the Nottingham Post and local press got behind me and we took pictures with Meghan, a young beautiful girl in a wheelchair, and it sold out. WOW. A kid from Gedling made it happen! We raised £1000's. It was a huge success. Sadly, I later found out that the couple who raised the money (not her parents) also joined the girl in Florida and were pictured at Disney. Con artistes come in many shapes and sizes, not all work in the West End, on radio or reside in Parliament. Disappointing and hurtful – I felt cheated. I'd spent six months writing, planning, promoting and selling this show. Why the hell did I work my arse off to pay for those two fakers and con artistes to have a free holiday? This ignited something in me never to take <u>anything</u> on face value again. Blind faith does not work. How could these people sleep at night? Just disgusting.

Is this what they call 'school of hard knocks?' This may explain why I'm so interested in charity accounts today. My takeaway after twenty odd years is that there's no such thing as charity – it should only start at home!!! Have a poke around for Children in Need and Comic Relief costs. <u>Neither</u> are BBC charities by the way!

Two new influences came into my life in my late teens. Whilst falling in LOVE with America, I used to travel in the car to work with my cousin Alice. I went at least twice a year for decades and loved every second. Unwittingly I was also learning so much about humour and broadcasting. One day Alice switched on a guy she thought I'd like. I didn't like him – I LOVED him! Howard Stern is the #1 DJ (well talk presenter) in radio history. Howard is a rebel; he's the best interviewer I've EVER heard and the greatest technician of his craft in history. His radio show in the nineties was intoxicating. Unbelievably shocking at times but the funniest thing I've EVER heard on-air, unsurpassed today. He makes Ricky Gervais, Jimmy Carr and Roy Chubby Brown look positively reserved and saintly. He wouldn't last two minutes today. The namby-pamby pinko champagne sipping liberal Guardian reading lefties would have him cancelled before you could say piff paff pouf. He was the anti-Christ of MSM and truly their nemesis. He didn't miss a trick. So sharp.

He called out everyone. He was in no one's pocket. A law unto himself and the original BIGTIME influencer far outweighing that fat arsed Kardashian. He was the first person I'd ever heard who had no need for affirmation, praise or to be liked by the industry. He in fact revelled in being an outcast. They tried everything to bring him down until he was forced to leave FM and go on satellite radio in the early 2000's, where he was completely unregulated. The woke world couldn't handle his sheer sincerity and honesty. Breathtaking rawness on-air that left politicians and less than genuine celebs quaking in their gimp masks. He left FM radio for $500M over five years. Biggest contract ever. This was a sign of the times. Again, Howard was decades ahead of his time, but unpalatable to the hyper-sensitive millennials.

Stern is unique. A brain and vocal dexterity unmatched. He makes Chris Moyles and Piers Morgan look like Snow White. He was 100% fearless. Driven beyond anyone in the history of broadcasting and loved by his audience to an extent unparalleled. He truly was a cult. I'd found my hero. On 9/11 in New York where he was based, he stayed on-air whilst others headed for zee hills. Afterwards he begged Times Square hookers to offer sexual favours to emergency service workers in thanks for their hard work and bravery. Nothing was off limits. Years later I was invited into his Sirius Studios to see for myself the empire he had created. It was mind-blowing and utterly inspiring. His success came at a huge price, but what a legacy he would leave. Today, he, like so many of us, have been beaten by the lefties and sent 'underground.' His 'free speech' was of its day and <u>way</u> ahead of his time. Unparalleled success although even I cringe at some of it now, but you can't take offence at material beloved decades ago. He is the ultimate shock jock. A creative genius! Now he's too old to fight. He's taken his billions, moved to Florida and keeps his head down. I cannot underscore how outrageous he was, but how incredible his talent was. Sadly, now he's been bought. Despite thirty years of interview endorsing and encouraging Trump – he backed Cameltoe Harris. Most disappointing. Heartbreaking for me and millions of his devoted fans. That's showbiz – money talks!!!

Next came another comedy hero. I fell in love with David Letterman on CBS. Nightly at 11.35pm I wanted to hear Letterman's beautifully crafted opening monologue written by at least twenty script writers. You'll never know the profound influence this had on me. Stunning 'kerching' gags taking the pish out of the morons of the day. Brutal at times, but always with a glint in his eye. Ruthless to prissy self-aggrandizing attention seeking stars, celebs and politicians. I learned so much. Again, I was honoured to see him film LIVE several times. Now they would say he was cruel and detrimental to the mental 'elf of vulnerable multi-millionaire egotists! Oh, do piss off! I thought he was the greatest topical gag teller in history, <u>EVER</u>! These pros are in a league of their own. The Jonathan Ross's of the world don't even come close. The effort and crafting of every word is magical at US network level. Letterman and Stern both had a family of characters. I was learning there <u>is</u> a formula to success. People don't change, they cannot be forced to love you and there's nothing anyone can do about it. You have to create your own unique world. Invite people in and most importantly turn up. Both men worked five days a week for decades. They were happy to do so – even on $40 million plus a year.

Another life-long friend came into my life at this point. A lad called Stewart turned up one day at school to do A-levels and had a guitar. We became very good mates and he offered to drive me to gigs and we'd become a duo. Me on keys and Stew fingering his 'tar. We worked anywhere with a conscious audience who could stay awake for the hour. We made very good money doing it. I think it was £30 for one hour. That's £5 more than I got by myself on a good day. Finally, Dad didn't have to hump my organ everywhere. That poor old bugger had been schlepping me and my subwoofer to every shitty venue for years and waiting around listening to the same old crap over and over again. I bet he could do the act better than me. Enough was enough. What devotion hey? I'm forever indebted. It must have been torture for him akin to being a Taylor Swift roadie. Poor bastards! I'd use one of her wrist bands around my neck! I'd found a new accomplice to join me on stage! We had a hoot. So much more fun not being alone. Stewart is the complete opposite to me. He's a classy quiet and very clever man who is the nicest, kindest soul I've ever met. He's put up with my knob gags and malarkey for years and I'm proud to say he's still one of my dearest and closest friends today. I was honoured to be asked to be his Best Man at his wedding in the summer of 2022. His two sons bring me such joy. To share families and memories is the best thing about being a grown up. Mind you, calling me Uncle HMP is a bit harsh. That's a fiver out their birthday card.

I do attract all kinds of people in some less 'regular' partnerships throughout my life. Ladies of a 'certain age' often are mesmerised by me. It's only natural. When I ran the Italian Choir, I had a lady called Anne who drove me all over the country for gigs, shows, reviews and events. She loved it. We had a hoot. I've been so lucky to have been selflessly supported by people who 100% made me who I am today and given me the freedom to accept opportunities prior to passing my driving test. Two hysterical ladies called Pauline and Eileen were such fun I went all over the country with them. The laughs we had in Scotland, Cornwall and Cumbria were fantastic. I just adore great people who love a chuckle. Sir Ken falls into this category I guess as he was seventy plus. By now we'd known each other for several years and he trusted me. That's the word that underscores everything I'm about – TRUST. I would visit Ken as often as I could at theatres all over the country and he taught me everything I needed to know about showbiz etiquette. How to behave from the second you arrive until you leave. There's always someone watching.

Everyone wants a story and has an opinion! Bad news and 1* disasters travel quicker than 5* reviews bizarrely. Ken was flawless. No flies on him. A gentleman and the ultimate star! How lucky was I to get this education first hand from the greatest British theatre legend of all time! I do admit though, it is a bit strange a teenager surrounded by people three times his age but it was always so normal to me. I never saw age, colour or gender. Ahead of my time. I simply saw amazing peeps or arseholes – nothing in between. The wisdom and knowledge were infinite. I have no shame or embarrassment having these mentors and heroes in my life. I was blessed. Finally, though at seventeen I had to get on the road and open up my horizons. I took driving lessons and quickly failed my first test. I'd got a lot on my mind – I'm busy and distracted. FREEDOM, now nothing would be impossible. I couldn't believe my luck to finally be able to go anywhere, do anything, see anyone and I didn't need to beg or ask a soul for a lift. Now life could truly begin……

OK, it wasn't quite that simple. I failed my test seven times in total. It wasn't my fault, I was so busy chatting to the instructor and I didn't have time to observe red lights or passing pedestrians, let alone the lunatic police car who cut me up on fail 4. It won't be the last run in with Nottingham Police now, will it? Those cuntstables are a theme in my life story. I was so lucky that my Nana helped buy me my first car – a Fiat Punto. I loved it. Cheap to run, aircon, four wheels and it could go 25mph or more if two were peddling. I loved it in 'jet black'. Just enough room to fit my all-in-one Yamaha PA in the rear. I had three new Puntos in the end, every couple of years. They were cheaper than a tank of petrol in those days. Maybe it was in honour of my relatives in Michigan or my diamonds from the Italian 'St Anthony's choir.' It was small but did the job – fill your own punchline.

Doddy was the master of avoiding the showbiz shithouses. He wouldn't have any toxic box tickers around him and only _ever_ trusted his absolute closest friends who were allowed in his dressing room – respect built over many years. Stewart went off to Uni eventually so, now I could drive and keep all the money! Every cloud. Seriously I missed him. He was my mate and confidante as he is today twenty-five plus years later. I'm not a double act though – more a double chin act in those days. Now I had to make it by myself. Finally, my BIG BREAK came! A new radio station launched in Nottingham called Radio 106 – across the East Midlands (never mind local) – this was REGIONAL radio - so I applied. It changed my life forever!

I'm a Pro-fessional …..Megabucks and Mogadons

Up until now I'd been pissing about learning my craft quietly and getting away with meandering through life. I was a grafter no doubt, but now I needed to do it properly. My two years working weekends at BBC Nottingham and on Breakfast as a BA left me cold. It was a backstabbing, competitive, toxic building which has never changed since. They truly hated radio and their audience. Zero fun. No laughs. Just an office of boring, suit wearing, bitter and heartless lefty journalists devoid of any levity or perspective that they were on a dysfunctional and very average local FM. They made my teeth itch. Commercial radio (ILR) is the opposite. All fun. No journalism – everyone survives on success not because they've got a life sentence and pension paid for by the public. I remember once seeing a BBC Nottingham jock throw his entire stack of 'carts' (jingles) at the wall in a fit of rage. A producer ran in and picked them up. I couldn't help but think these twats are just petulant toddlers with a mic. Losers and deeply unhinged and unhappy people!!! BBC Newsrooms are truly the most depressing places on earth and as dynamic and exciting as Resus at the City Hospital!

My (relative) success came from hard work, practice and tenacity! Now I got the chance to learn from the big boys – and be paid good money for the privilege. Regional licences were given by Ofcom for virtually nothing and sold for £100M each. Radio 106 was the best learning curve EVER! By a very strange coincidence the man who gave the licence to its sister station in Manchester ended up running 106 and made a shitload of dosh in the process. Funny old game isn't it. Wheels within wheels……I saw with my own eyes that no matter the budget and experience – management are almost always clueless. Thankfully, once again I sat back and just drank it all in. I learned so much from this bunch, four 'big personalities' 6am – 6pm who were sacked so regularly they had to put a revolving door in reception! If this shower of shites put their heads together they'd have made a plank!

Launching a radio station, or any project on this scale is always exciting. Initial budgets are normally ridiculous, but usually the relaunch is booked before the paint is dry and the original cast and management have got their feet under the mixing desk table. You quickly learn that everyone is faking it – even at the very top! They're all clueless. Total guess work. Nearly everybody is there by chance (not even luck or judgement). It's there by the grace of God that they remember to buy microphones. Radio 106 was brand new and exciting but run by dinosaurs who didn't see the future; they looked to the past. MSM was dying, times had changed, the internet was reaching adolescence and the days of 'build it and they will come' was well over! Both bosses were former BBC local brainwashed old school and formal programmers. The world had moved on. The good news for me though was that where there's chaos, there's opportunity! The breakfast show was a disaster hosted by a less then charming BBC Local 'legend' who didn't understand this new format 'for grown-ups' needed irreverent content, not BBC Nursing Home 'Whatson' features and the greatest hits of Max Bygraves. It was dull and as poorly produced as Newsnight. It was patronising, boring and tried to attract an audience that were never going to switch from their BBC local as matron was too busy changing their catheters. I later found out that the station content had to be approved by the boss's wife who was a Godly type who couldn't stand any bad language, fun, smut or controversy. THANK GOD, she never met me! She liked 'local news' – a euphemism for mind numbing and piss poor! Tell a knob gag and stick on some ELO I say……Radio Heaven.

Next came Kevin Fernihough on mid-morning who is a massive talent with a long history in <u>personality</u> radio and he naturally became the star of the station. He should have been on Breakfast from day one. They were blind to natural talent. Pissing all over breakfast figures, he had warmth unlike breakfasts' arrogant and patronizing condescension. This was a good lesson. I learned a lot from Kev. He's had a dream career and survived the game for over thirty years. He and husband Clive are two of my favourite people and dearest friends that I've been lucky enough to meet through radio – RARE! The audience will always decide. They're no fools - you can't buy or manufacture this. Radio 106 gaffers spent £100,000's on PR and advertising. A leaflet posted to EVERY home. It achieved nothing. If breakfast isn't right, you can't win the market.

Through the afternoon Colin did the dull but professional slinky linky stuff which was of no professional interest to me whatsoever. Theres only so many times you can play Spandau Ballet without falling into a coma! In the evening was a very unique oddball presenter called Jake Yapp who, despite his comic niche, didn't click or resonate with the audience. Too wacky for Bolsover and Burton I'm afraid. He was too creative for the East Midlands. Like his mentor Martin Kelner he's best suited on sneery Radio 4 where they can talk down to us plebs, not directly with or at them. Then Mark Keen from 10pm. This is where I got my big break. I was paid to answer the phones behind the glass. Mark was a very nice guy who even drove me home at 1am for months. Mark was very different to any phone-in host I'd ever heard – let alone met. He was exceptionally laid back and didn't have topics. He just had a gang of callers who he grew to know inside out. This is not my preferred style of presenter as it's too familiar and cosy for me, but it worked for him big time. Keeny had been around for over twenty years and had nothing to prove. He had a lovely girlfriend and home in West Bridgford and went above and beyond to help support me. After the show we'd have a Kebab on Alfreton Road – that's the glamour of broadcasting.

I still can't get over the kindness people have shown. As time went on, we'd go into town drinking and I guess looking back he was thirty-five and that's the type of guy who I wanted to be as a teenager. Relaxed, not brainwashed by the biz, not precious and just on-air taking the piss. Until writing this I hadn't realised how lucky I was to work for him. So few in this biz make you want to stay friends and give you a hand up. I'd go up to see him in Preston, where he ended up living, we even took a trip to New York to see Letterman and now his son is at Nottingham University ironically. The circle of life. What a lucky start. It's all about timing. That was the first East Midlands licence. There won't be any more. Someone was looking down on me for sure. It was the last bite of the radio cherry. My first gig producing regional talk radio with a top man who genuinely helped and cared with no side or ulterior motive. Keeny once drove me to do a tiny gig at the QMC hospital to do a Christmas sing-along. He was humping my organ and it fell off the trolley smashing it to smithereens. This couldn't happen today as you'd never find a spare stretcher as they're cluttering every corridor with dying pensioners on them. Good times. I lost my £65 show fee and had to buy a new keyboard. That's showbiz!

Another life-long dear friend who came from Radio 106 is Giles McMullen who did the business news. He was fantastic! New to the game, like me, he was a one off! We had nothing in common. He was brought up 'proper' with an incredible education. But he was so unique, fun and funny. We clicked. We still speak almost every day. His wife and two kids have brought me massive joy over the last twenty years. I adore the bones of this very clever man. We're twins swapped at birth like in Blood Brothers. He's now ironically a huge YouTube star himself. It brings me great joy to see good people thrive! Another huge supporter of mine was the Sports Editor Tony Delahunty. I naturally had nothing to do with him as I was too busy pissing about in theatres, not at The City Ground or Elland Road. You'll read a lot more about this cunning genius later. Unfortunately, sport would play a big part in my learning curve. From day one I knew who I wanted to be around. The snarly mincers turned my stomach and pickled my piss - I'll pass. Moral to the story; pick your friends wisely and learn from the best! Equally ignore the dopes and the talentless. Write down all the fails of the losers. Knowledge is power. Ears wide open my friends!

I slowly saw the power of phone-ins and how the callers were way more interesting than the presenter. To me the punters were the king. Phone-ins should not be about the jock. The callers are the star! The skill and craft though, was to know when to cut them off! I was mesmerised by the format. No songs, just a switchboard. Terrifying to present but so exciting and exhilarating! Sadly Radio 106 didn't work. It was a mess and totally ill-judged in both content and totally bizarre, incongruous presenters with below average repetitive music you'd get in a lift or clap clinic. A commercial and ratings disaster. Then one day a hurricane blew through the station door and into my life which changed me forever! A man called John Myers bought the station and rebranded it Century 106. He was single-handedly the smartest, most creative and bravest man I've ever met. Leagues above all of the rest. Two facks he couldn't give. No bullshit. It's business. Seriously I rate most bosses three out of ten. This old school, veg avoiding Bigman was ten out of ten! Fifteen years later we'd become great pals. John became very poorly with cancer and during his treatment we'd talk after my gigs most nights. He never forgot that I did everything to make him laugh at his lowest ebb. He later told me he was so poorly he couldn't sleep and I was the only one up at 2am to keep him entertained and smiling. It was my true honour. We later had a beautiful breakfast together with his wife in Naples, Florida in 2019 just weeks before he died of a heart attack on the 18th hole of Gleneagles. I adored him. A fitting and spectacular end to this maverick and broadcasting genius's life taken way too soon.

Over twenty years he became the biggest radio influence in my life and many others too. So, why did John stick out? Well, he was the ultimate pro. Not a day under twenty-five stone, he was an enormous force on every level. What I loved about him is that he was the only boss who could do the job on-air better than anyone he trained and managed. A master, a Wogan standard class act. A voice as rich as his kid's inheritance. He knew 'nice' doesn't work. You have to force people to change the dial and give them a reason to tune in and that isn't via boring news or music – it's entirely the unique personality of the presenter. So, on day one he ditched the former BBC bores and then put in massive gobshites peppered throughout the day for what he called 'a penis on the page'…...in other words a spike for appointment listening. He empowered talent. He encouraged them to go too far and had a budget to pay the fines when they were given. A brave and brilliant radio God. It wasn't a popularity contest. He couldn't care less who he pissed off or screwed over. Ratings were king and the only motivation to keep anyone in the building.

The rebranding of the station was done in style with a TV crew following him, ironically the BBC for a show called 'Trouble at the Top.' It's still on YouTube. Do watch it! He only cared about audience reach. The most brutal sacking was Liz Jepson the Godly talker who had a ZERO rating. When John fired her, he said 'your figures are so bad – even God isn't listening!' OUCH! Even Judas covered his eyes with the Virgin Mary's Tena Lady! You can't argue with the figures. Bye Bye. Ruthless. He didn't care, it was all about the audience, not staff hurty feelings or favours for mates – the complete opposite to BBC mismanagement feathering their own nest. They'll keep any daft twat on-air for decades to spare their blushes. John was a tornado ripping through 106. Most hated him...because they were crap and he wanted rid. I had infinite respect and watched in total awe!

Sadly, the brilliant Kevin Fernihough was unceremoniously dumped as he wouldn't change his holidays for the relaunch. This is where radio is cruel and unnecessary. Total own goal by John, but it was all on his terms. He didn't care. His rules or use the door. He got this VERY wrong but it was a pissing contest and total impasse. Kevin was number one, I don't think anyone beat him in twenty years, but it was Myers way or the highway. This is the only decision the big man made that I disagreed with. This taught me a huge lesson. You're never safe. Kevin went on to have a magnificent life and career regardless. 106's loss. Myers later hired two men who blew my mind. Gordon Astley came to breakfast and Chris Ashley on late nights. He also hired the odd frog eyed gobshites who taught me exactly what not to do. I knew and loved both Ashley and Astley from BBC Midlands – the heyday of late-night network wireless. Old school gag men, rammed with personality, infinitely charming and beloved by the punters. Now I'd get to work with them. Wow. I was made up! The cream of BBC talent who did network late nights for years. They'd naturally been replaced by a now convicted paedo and his complicit wife if I recall correctly! Welcome to your £174.50 TV rape tax BBC! These two men taught me so much about personality and playing with the audience. They were the very last of their generation. Too risky now for the PC BBC. Too funny for commercial today. Their loss was defo Century 106's gain with its' 'BIG Personality' new tagline and relaunch. Now my education could truly begin.........

Gordon was a gag master who had TV success on Tizwas. Outdated now but a beautiful technician of cheese and topical gags. He's a talented magician and the epitome of an all-round entertainer. He used a daily joke service to keep it funny and I loved his style. He even had a reception bell for the punchline to queue a smile. So smooth and 'old school,' brilliant! Sadly, radio had moved on and like so many he was cast aside after decades of success. A travesty. He enjoyed a bevvy and was a hoot to be around. Chris Ashley was a tall, imposing and brilliant wordsmith with bucket loads of magnetic appeal. They asked me to produce Chris from 10pm. This rightly aligned my passions. The rebels of the wireless were my type of people. It was my job to pick the best calls, put them through and eventually write gags or comments on screen if I thought it could help. I was paid £50 per show and could not believe my luck. I remember one day some snotty nose young journalist minced over to me to recommend I go away for three years to get a 'journo degree.' I churlishly asked how much he earned a day, Mike said '£75 a shift.' I was already earning that in old cockeries for an hour singing Dusty, Elvis and Jim Reeves for two one hour shows and home by 5pm and didn't have £40k of student debt. What a pilchard! I smiled sweetly, said 'thank you' and shut my gob! His cards were marked. Have you ever heard of a millionaire news reader that you're envious and jealous of? Nope. Me neither. Ask Huw the paedo!

Myers brought in the shock jock phone-in guys and asked me to work with them too at lunchtime. John was fearless and believed if you didn't offend, the mostly interesting listeners wouldn't ring in. It worked but came at a huge price. All of these lads ended up sacked, unemployable and in many cases homeless or bankrupt. I loved it though, a masterclass in this brilliant art of windupery. The lunchtime phone-in at 1pm was off its head. He'd found a guy from Newcastle, 'The Mouth,' who outraged people. With his bull dog looks and sumo wrestler build, if only his career was as impressive as his press shot! Judging by his level of mass debate I'm presuming he trained at Dyno-rod FM. It worked until the day he went too far and was physically removed from the building. Years later this very strange little fella who was as wide as he was tall sued Myers unsuccessfully and lost everything and never worked again. Ouch. A valuable lesson learned at seventeen years old.

My eyes were wide open to this clearly unwell diddy man. One day he ranted about being raped as a child. Ofcom went nuts. He was suspended and ridiculed for this grave, ill-advised and ridiculous stunt. No one could work out if it was true or simply for ratings. Clearly no one wanted his private parts as an adult so it was unbelievable this would court attention as a disfigured gnome. Off his head but fascinating to watch the car crash unfold in front of my eyes. If only this frog-eyed closet spent as much time on his act, as he did dropping anchor in poo bay in Soho saunas, maybe, just maybe he wouldn't be sat at home on PIP today. I truly believe you learn more from watching other people's mistakes and unhinged egos dig their own grave. Some people are just hoist by their own retard! He lost everything and didn't even have the blessing of an online comeback. Spat out for NOT reading the room and taking the time to find the 'invisible' line that even I'd learned at twelve years of age at school. Such a shame. He wasn't the only one. The 'Shock Jock' era of talk had passed. Few survived. I distanced myself from this lunatic. You learn very quickly not to be taken down by association. I wisely haven't seen or heard from this loose cannon and deeply disturbed head the ball in over twenty years! What 'The Mouth' didn't have was likeability unlike Astley and Ashley especially who were so loved. With eyes bulging on stalks – this is not a way to endear your audience through looking like the uglier twin brother of Wayne Couzens. So creepy. I'm so proud that I reinvented the free form phone-in for 2020+ on YouTube during Covid. Very lucky my timing was perfect. I proved audiences haven't changed. They still LOVE to chat. You certainly couldn't do it on FM (Ofcom regulated). Look at Talk TV, an unmitigated ratings disaster. So, Gordon Astley was an education with funny radio, 'The Mouth' was the red flag to avoid in terms of being deranged, light on your feet megalomaniac, maniacal and a tyrant without knowing 'the invisible line.'

The gem for me, and the highlight of my production career was the loveliest man in radio Mr Warmth. Chris Ashley was a Nottingham legend from Trent FM in the seventies. He innovated radio and became a BIG star. This man had bucket loads of wit. He was instantly likeable and loveable no matter what he said. You can't buy that beautiful connection to an audience. I GOT IT! This is the KEY to being a radio great! He was a magnificent ray of light in my life on-air and off. He could tease and shock Oompa-Loompa the audience at the same time and they would love him more and more. Not always nice, he was 100% sincere and authentic. What a blessing to meet, know and end up being a life-long friend with Christoph Ashley an absolute LEGEND!

I also had the unfortunate opportunity to work on sport. I am to football what the queen was to double glazing, but I gave it a go. I worked with England and Nottingham Forrest legend Larry Lloyd and drove the desk for Darren Fletcher on the odd Saturday afternoon. Darren is probably the most talented sports broadcaster I've ever met. What a brain. His speed and reflexes were astonishing. So glad he's gone on to incredible national success. So well deserved. Throughout this whole year or so, I kept drinking in everything I could, learning from the best and working out who I wanted to be on-air. You gotta have a gimmick – they all did. Many to their fatal cost. How could I become 10% as good as them on-air? The only way is to do it and practice LIVE! You only learn from your mistakes. Boy I've made a few. Finally, the opportunity arose to 'help' with the 'Entertainment Update.' I eventually ended up presenting it. Ninety seconds of showbiz tat. I'd made it! You wouldn't believe how long less than two minutes could take a beginner to record! I now average ten hours on-air a week. Back then I struggled with ten minutes which took me all day.

Since the hospital radio days, I'VE LOVED interviewing. Let me be clear at 15-18 years old you are not going to be good, you're just unique. Stars had a curiosity to talk to me back then because I was different and I cared. I was well researched and unlike so many lazy bastards who couldn't care less, I made it my job to watch the show, read the book or listen to the CD. You'd be amazed how rare it is. I guarantee you that certain fakes on daytime ITV have no idea who their guest is until they're perched in front of them seconds before going LIVE. They simply read from an Autocue on the front of a camera verbatim having no knowledge whatsoever of their product or life. My mistakes were covered by pure enthusiasm. I got away with it for years. An angel in my life was lovely Lucy Thomas at the Nottingham Theatre Royal. For two decades she was the top press officer and stuck by me, delivering almost every star who came into town at our two biggest venues. I cannot thank her enough. That magical Matcham designed Theatre became my second home for over twenty years. The fun I've had in there. It was my playground in front of and behind the curtain. So, so grateful for the opportunity. One of my first big stars was Danny La Rue. He was a wise old owl who had had the best years of showbiz and was down on his uppers. He'd been bled dry by champagne sippers who leeched him to poverty and in fact he ended up living in his dresser's back bedroom after losing everything. Another red flag. After our first interview he looked at me and said "Young man, you're a very talented boy. You'll go far, but remember no matter how big you get, no matter how successful you become and no matter how rich and famous you end up being – just remember – THEY'RE ALL CANTS!" WOW. This couldn't be true surely, could it? Well, not quite – there's a few gems, but 99% people in this odious J-cloth sniffing biz are so consumed with jealousy, bitterness, issues and anger – they'd stab their own mother in the eye balls to get a break. Thanks Danny mate profound advice to a whippersnapper.

The Theatre Royal was of course home to Sir Ken. Every Christmas for years and years (from about fourteen) I loved welcoming Doddy to my home town on December 28$^{th}$/29$^{th}$ for two sell-out shows. I'd wait about 5pm at stage door (trying to avoid being knocked over by a tram) and wait to greet Doddy and help unpack the car. Every year Ken would point at the huge domed building with a clock on the top. "What's that slim?" I'd say "council house." He'd say "put me down for one of them!" Showbiz is a small world and as the years pass you naturally see the same people over and over again. Some you connect with. 'That' feeling <u>never</u> gets old! I later became good friends with so many stars and would interview them time after time on their tours. Welcoming them to 'my' Nottingham gave me great pride. I've probably been in Dressing Room One at TRCH more than anyone else in the country. Week after week from a teen until Covid when theatre virtually died, I was there with a microphone in hand. What an honour. Seriously! Every single chat taught me something. This was like my window cleaning round. I remember interviewing John Inman in the hope of getting news of Mrs Slocombe's pussy! He taught me as a novice chatterbox how to walk like Mr Humphries, vital advice in the cesspit of creepy shuffalos. BTW, Mr Humphries' Walk was only mastered by having an egg up his bottom and walking so that he didn't crack it! Oh, the fun we had in that glorious theatre. Can you believe I'd recorded twenty minutes of silence when I got back and replayed it at the studio. What a prized plant pot. This could NEVER happen again.

Theatre interviews are not easy. You're under great pressure, in one take, to get the warmth you'd generate over an hour if they came to your studio. You have to build rapport immediately. It's so distracting worrying about the tech on top of sounding like your totally relaxed and calm and you've been mates forever. It's quite a skill that takes years to develop. Once you can fake sincerity, you've made it! So many mates, legends and icons that I've interviewed over and over again throughout the years like Joe Pasquale, Lesley Joseph, Brian Conley, Christopher Biggins, Michael Ball, Daniel O'Donnell, Sir Cliff Richard and more recently Il Divo, Katherine Jenkins, The Osmonds and many many more went through that Concert Hall stage door annually - at least. I was a very lucky boy to have such unprecedented and <u>trusted</u> access. So, I would do ten minutes with these stars and put thirty seconds in the 'Entertainment Update' on Century and I kept my archive which quickly mounted up over the years. As far as I was concerned, I'd made it. No one ever said no. With a transmission area of two million plus people, I was first in the queue for everyone locally. What a blessing so young to learn from the very best at the top.

Writing this book is like therapy. So many things I'd forgotten. Write your own epistle if you get a chance. I never took my life for granted, but it did become very normal and months ran into years with this silly showbiz life. This was my world and had been since a boy. This has just reminded me of my first star encounter at twelve years old. A dear friend of my beloved Nana was an amazing lady called Pauline. She took my gran shopping weekly and was an amazing support and beloved friend. Many years earlier she was at the Co-op Arts Theatre in Nottingham in the 70's where a young, bonkers and fab lady called Su Pollard auditioned. They became friends for life. The story goes that Su worked at the theatre and one day left the entire week's takings on the back of a toilet having popped in trap two for a pee before sticking it in the safe. It was hundreds of pounds. We laugh now – but not then! Pauline did the kindest thing knowing I was a show-off. She was the warden at my Aunty Dorothy's independent living centre. This community was inspiring to me. I used to love their 'Get togethers' and Do's.' It was an education. From a tiny boy I loved listening to all those old ladies chatting. Flo, Gladys, Dotty, Clara, Mavis – you get my drift. My silver tops fascination was born! Salt of the earth legends. The pure sense of love and trust between them was inspiring. One day – probably when I was eight or nine years old during summer holidays Pauline allowed me to call the bingo! What an honour! This is still the biggest gig of my career! I got cocky after a while, and it all went very wrong. DON'T MESS WITH BINGO EVER! I'd come up with an idea; it would be funny to say '5 and 2 = 27' 'on its own 12' – '2 little ducks 33' – this did not go down well at all! A civil warning was issued. My first civil writ was served. Lesson learned. Bingo is like the United Nations – don't mess! I defo crossed that imaginary line!

Anyway, at twelve Pauline invited me to go with her to Blackpool to the North Pier to see Su in summer season with Les Dennis and Roy Walker from Catchphrase. Can you believe thirty years later I sold out the exact same venue? Wow – I just got a tear in my glass eye. Anyway, the following day she took me to lunch (without telling me) and who was sat there, lovely unique Su. I was utterly starstruck. At the end Su said, "you've got something, never give up." How kind. That was a magical memory. To think twenty-five years later I'd be taking Pollard to breakfast at the St Pancras and dinner in the West End as we've done for thirty years. I interviewed Roy at his home near Blackpool two decades later and Les and I have met a thousand times in his various productions. In fact, when I was at BBC Radio Nottingham, I went to Central TV to interview him LIVE at Family Fortunes. What opportunities I've had over the years. What a lucky lad. I 'sponged' all of their knowledge, insight, experience, wisdom and advice. I'm eternally grateful to them all.

So, it began. By eighteen I had everything I wanted. An amazing mum, dad and sister. I had more money than I could spend, earning £300 a week and had a job in showbiz plus a ton of heroes to learn from. Oh…... and I hadn't even left school! All of this whilst pretending to do bullshit A Levels that were totally superfluous. Then a job came along for me to be <u>the</u> '<u>Star</u>'……but sadly, it was in Africa! From the age of fourteen I had been paid to do the job I loved. Lucky right? There's no NVQ course in showing off, the only way you learn is by doing. There's, two types of people in life, those who bumble along and those who strive for the impossible dream and never give up until someone gives in and says 'do it if you'll shut the f@ck up and stop bothering me.' I cast no judgement as my lifestyle has cost me dear, but bloody hell what fun I've had in the process and I'm not even 20 (yet). I knew one day I'd get my big break, but why, oh why, did it have to be in another country? I was about to go global and officially become in-continent!

To this day Kev, Tony, Chris, John and Giles are still some of the most important and amazing people in my life. Thank You 106 – it's all your fault! You made me the man I am today. Blame them! To make lifelong friends from your first gig at seventeen is remarkable. For that I'll always be grateful and totally indebted.

## Chapter 5

## Hakuna Matata

I had been quietly learning my craft in my mother's back bedroom forever, studying my heroes and forming my own act from those I loved and respected since being knee high to a microphone. The problem though was that I didn't tick a box or even fit in. My radio 'act' was deemed edgy as it was topical, cutting and irreverent at a time the accountants started running the asylums. I was fearless – they were totally risk averse. I didn't just time check and play Kylie. BORING! The world was changing and people loved playing the victim. 'Sticks and stones' was a thing of the past. It was now costing folk their careers and £100,000's in the High Court to have an opinion and I was swimming against the tsunami of a new 'woke' – lefty media and universe. It was nowhere near the insanity of post Covid, but it had started. Diversity was becoming a real thing and we hadn't even started the new millennium. Curiously I didn't have ANY of these issues LIVE. Not one problem in clubs or with the public – only the med-yar. Pfft. Why? Bloody Uni brainwashed journalist types desperate to join a march or identify as a pillar box got right on my tits!

Jokes have a punchline…....that equated to 'victim' to virtue signalling losers and boohooers. I made cautious Top 40 trained bosses nervous. So, where could I go to practise professionally polishing my cack and churn out four hours of peak time waffle five days a week without too many people noticing? The Radio

Mag featured all the top jobs. Not online – that wasn't invented yet. A4 pages stapled together......oh the halcyon days! Life is confusing for a young boy like me – with a curious mind. 'Experience needed' is the go-to line from bosses who offer starter wages. How do you get experience if no one will take the risk and give you a gig? Showbiz is the stupidest game in the world where there's so much desperation around (and too many people available) that they literally bid each other <u>down</u> to get a gig. Not me though. MORONS. That's why the West End is packed with nonbinary vegans on £700 a week...even though their rent is £900. No class. No self-worth. No personal value for their well-trained talent. I just don't get it. You can earn £250 in a club for two forty-five-minute spots or earn £75 for four hours of local radio. This gave me a contempt from day one for radio. Honestly, truly, I promise you – I NEVER took it seriously as a job or profession………. because it is not other than for the odd few in London who probably have no background or interest in radio. I just loved wasting my time doing it. I suppose it was a hobby. Even regional radio was only about £150 a show. Hookers earn more than that per hour in Derby!

One job did catch my eye 'Capital FM Breakfast' – not from Leicester Square, London (it would be five years until I would walk through those doors). No this 'Capital' was located at Lonrho House, Nairobi, Kenya. I'm not shitting you, East Africa! Blimey, a job to be a Maasai of the media. I sent my demo tape to a lady called Linda Holt. She was an expat who was an Ab Fab Patsy type. She called the house phone. 'It's Linda, will you come and see me in London?' Expenses to travel to London and tea in a posh hotel. Will you go? Does Coleen Nolan sleep on her back? I told mum and dad but didn't mention the reality of the contract. Kenya is quite a long way away from a pit estate in Nottingham. Within days I was sat in front of this very posh woman, all fur coat and no knickers by all accounts. Linda thought I was cheeky and a phrase that has been said quite a lot through the years 'A breath of fresh air!!!' The deal on paper seemed incredible. Two return flights a year, a house maid, security, driver and £18,000 a year take home. There and then I pushed her up to £20,000 and this was tax free; my only costs were food, but it was Africa not Knightsbridge. How much could a pound of kangaroo or beaver meat cost? She'd take care of everything else, no bills. I accepted. On the train home it dawned on me that this was the birth of 'Belfield at Breakfast' but in return I'd given up my entire life – which was (for me) everything I'd ever wanted. Never ignore your inner voice. I knew this was preposterous, but what a story hey? What had I got to lose? Maybe one day it'd make three pages in my autobiography……..if only I had time to write it!

The curse of being a turn is that despite big audiences, most of your time you're lonely, constantly waiting, isolated and pushed to your own psychological limits. I didn't want to be like the rest – living for the mic. It's pitifully sad, pathetic and soulless on every level. That's why so many turns end up addicted and off their tits…...or tying a rent boy to a radiator for a laugh! These things can happen apparently in hotel rooms from the West End to Broadway. If you're not grounded, supported, calm and sane you'll end up 'self-medicating' by panto. Fortunately, I was always level-headed, boring and because I had such an amazing support system I didn't flinch. HOWEVER, at eighteen I learned a massive life lesson. It's not all about you! So many people love platitudes as an excuse to justify their own mistakes or behaviour. 'I'm living my best life' means 'I'm a selfish bastard so screw you!' 'It wasn't my fault' means 'I've dropped a bollock, but don't blame me,' and 'I don't love you anymore – it's me not you' means 'I'm shagging someone far hotter than you so sod off.' You catch my drift.

Contrary to popular belief I'm quite sensitive. Actually, I think all artists and especially musicians have to be. How could you play the piano (or any instrument) well if you are not? Music makes you very vulnerable as a human being to do it properly. You have to bring alive the pathos. Fortunately, this has paid off for me in my private life but has been very costly in the biz. Professionally I'm as hard as nails as any criticism is water off a duck's back and should never be believed. Privately I thrive off the love of my friends and family who I adore. Could I cope without them? I paid a big price for Kenya. As I told you I adored my Nana, she was actually my best mate if I'm being honest. I loved her so much and we had the biggest laughs and best time together. Equally mum and dad are my rock. Now I had to break the news (and their hearts) that I was leaving forever. It all felt very terminal. You can imagine the fake smiles and pretend joy. In reality this went down like The Titanic.

My mum is a strong lady but was visibly shaken. My dad is as soft as grease and couldn't take it in. He's a northern chap who says nothing and lives for his family - I knew I'd broken his heart. Next came Nana. She was devastated and showed it. None of this 'live your dream,' it was 100% obvious I'd ruined everything in her entire life and she made it clear. What a weight to bare and a conscience to carry. I swear to God I must be catholic with all of this guilt. To me this was the opportunity of a lifetime, my own breakfast show. To them talking shite on the wireless was irrelevant. I was leaving Nottingham forever for a dopey radio show in 'Bongo Bongo Land.' To my face they were 100% supportive but Nana especially was almost grieving and couldn't hack it. Remember, there wasn't Skype, Zoom, iMessage or video calls pre-2000. It was those blue Royal Mail A4 (folded three times) letters that took three weeks at least to arrive. Basically – in her mind I was dead - dramatic, but true. I might as well be in prison, right? The reality of this opportunity didn't dawn on me for a good month. Nana was heading for the nearest car park with a short piece of rope. Ahhh - guilt! If it hadn't been for the two-hour queue behind all the dark web trolls, cyclists and eco warriors – she might have tossed herself off. Thankfully Corrie was on at 7.30pm so she had to get back to see what Jack and Vera were up to in the Rovers. Dad started wearing a turban and singing songs from Sunset Boulevard. My training in the Italian Choir at St Augustine's was finally kicking in. I must self-flagellate immediately! Surely a few Hail Marys would solve this.

A few weeks later the contract was signed and my seat was booked on Kenya Airways. I'd had my jabs and this was now very real. You have to be careful in Kenya. There're so many things that could kill you like lions or a salad. I had no idea where I was going and everything was done on trust. Why on earth didn't my mum put her foot down and say I couldn't go? One very sad morning I said my goodbyes to Nana – heart wrenching – and my folks drove me to Heathrow. "I'll be back" I said. "When" they asked – "I don't know" – awkward! They checked me in and walked me to security. Why was I worried? I loved planes, loved travel and had flown alone to Michigan loads of times by myself. But Michigan had family and people. It suddenly dawned on me I was <u>alone</u>. 'Alone' – the kryptonite of Belfield. I mean Lion King alone! Even Simba had a warthog and a hairy beaver to guide him through the savanna. All I'd got was my gag book and a few nicked jingles to keep me company in the bath.

My cousin Ross came to take the edge off it in the car. It's a great tactic I've learned over the years. At any hyper-emotional situation bring someone who is level-headed and not emotionally involved and it does dilute the pain and rawness – simply by pure distraction. Stiff upper lip stuff. We hugged and kissed goodbye and off I went. My head was spinning like a Lazy Susan. A big boy, a man, a know it all……..and now a Radio Star! In reality, I was simply a daft lad who already missed his mum and dad and I hadn't passed Duty Free. It then dawned on me that I wouldn't even see my sister who was working in childcare in Skegness. In all of the fuss I hadn't even had a chance to say a sincere goodbye. It was just another job. I was through security. It was too late to pull out. I went to the lounge for a drink. I love a lounge. Free bar and half decent food. But I wasn't a big drinker……until that day. Five voddy and diet cokes later I was steaming. Eventually I sat on board and immediately it was weird, I don't mean there was a rhino and zebra serving the warm nuts, no, they sprayed the cabin for deadly diseases. What the actual fack? OK, wine please matron! Before we took off, I was as sick as a dog. The snotty air stewardess thought I was a drunk. I suppose I was, but truly I was just stunned and heartbroken……self-medicating if you will! I felt as limp as a vicar's handshake. I needed the skimmed milk of human kindness not the sneer of some trumped up trolley dolly who couldn't get a proper job in Wetherspoons!

Flights are like prison, right? It feels like it lasts forever but the second you get out you instantly forget the torture. I landed in Nairobi and there was no going back. I got my bag and hoped someone would be there to greet me. What if this was one of those shitty Noel's 'Gotcha's' – well, at least I'd get to go home! They were there waiting with huge smiles. Linda and her significantly younger boyfriend collected me and took me straight to The Stanley 5* hotel. What did this twenty-five-year-old stud see in this sixty-plus multi-millionaire I thought to myself? What must they look like naked was my next thought? Nothing gets past me. I'm always thinking! Anywho, I'd made it! Tomorrow, they'd take me to dinner and explain <u>everything.</u>

I was taken to my suite in the best, most iconic hotel in the city and I was warned not to leave it 'because of security reasons.' WTF. This wasn't a joke! The radio studios are a two-minute walk from the hotel but every day for three weeks I was given a driver with security into and out of the building! Excuse me? As always it was all perfectly normal. So, I waited in my room all expenses paid. This is the life! I'd made it! The dream, right? I unpacked my bag, had a shower using three towels (because I could) and five minutes later looked at my reflection in the mirror. I literally asked myself 'NOW WHAT?' It wasn't even 10am and I had nothing to do. This feeling would define the rest of my professional career on the road and be the one emotion I despised and would try to avoid at all costs.

You spend your whole life believing you want to work, travel and stay in hotels and then once you make it, all you want is your own toilet, kettle and sleep on your own mattress. All I really wanted was to be in the bosom of my amazing family and friends at HOME. The gut-wrenching reality of being paid to perform in foreign parts is an evil twist of fate. It takes YEARS to normalise this emotion and I had an elephant/hippo/Alison Hammond sized baptism of fire. I hadn't even considered I'd given up my family for a dopey radio show. What about my friends? I'd stupidly given up everything for a couple of grand a month. What a prized twat! The problem is I'm too boring for sniff and I've never had the wrist strength for self-touching endlessly on Tug TV. I quickly developed tactics to stay busy and combat this devastating abandonment. I sat in my room and very quickly became ill for three days. That'll be the malaria tablets, right? More evil and sickening than the BBC licence fee! The food, water and shock got the better of me. I literally lay there with the room spinning like a whirling dervish and couldn't even speak. I took more pills than Holland and Barrett to sober up. I eventually called my mummy, but I couldn't hide my despair. I was in floods of tears – ill, exhausted and devastated. She was powerless. Her little big mouthed boy had flown the nest. If you're big enough to sign the contract and cash the cheque…. Home sickness for a kid is catastrophic but now I had to begin a new life and a new launch show and my new best friend was rolling Sly News on TV 24/7. Please <u>God</u> take me now!

I've learned a lot about time throughout my life. 'Time flies when you're having fun' is so true. Equally a minute can feel like an hour when you're as miserable as Katie Price's agent and accountant. Within a few days the 'Kenya Tummy' had passed and I felt human again. Being ill and emotional is the worst. I totally get what it's like to be pregnant or a Question Time viewer. I was so ill my arse went down for a drink! More painful than root canal surgery or reading the Guardian. Malaria pills are enough to make you get the next plane home. Now I had to do something much more terrifying than moving to Africa, I had to enter a radio station and replace a 'legend.' Deadlier than any croc in a river! BTW, Hippos kill more people in water than any other. Might look the size of a labour backbencher but they can move like a fat lass at a Chinese buffet - but that's not why you called! Yes, taking over a breakfast show leaves you hated before you even start – a feeling that I would become <u>VERY</u> familiar with throughout my career.

I was driven <u>literally</u> across the road from the hotel to the radio station and I asked why I couldn't walk. The very nice gentleman of colour said "Err, look in the mirror. This is East Africa. You're ginger, British, about to be a star and have money – you're not walking anywhere alone on my watch." This was very Whitney in the Bodyguard! Point taken. Who am I to argue? He was right I never did. I don't remember this bit on the job advert! I had a car everywhere and security to escort me no matter where I went in town. Suddenly this didn't feel so fun. I feel Prince Harry's pain. I was now 'a target' not only by terrorists in Nairobi but much deadlier media colleagues who almost certainly felt they'd do a much better job taking over breakfast than I. They probably could, but get over it – you weren't picked – that's showbiz! Why on earth would <u>ANYONE,</u> do this for a living? This is a real thing by the way. The delusions fuelled by lots of ADHD and autistic conditions create the most hysterical awkward moments with big heads that are convinced they can do your job better than you. That's where imposter syndrome comes from. Absolute nobodies with even less personality convince themselves they're not just excellent, but in fact rival Wogan, Bruce and Wright put together. They're blind to the reality that they have zero experience, talent or discipline of a fair ground dodgem! You've heard of Aspergers syndrome…...the media morons have Assbuggers disease. It's a terrifying hallucination of grandeur.

I went up in the elevator and on the 19th floor, was Capital FM. The biggest radio station in East Africa and I was taking over morning drive. I replaced a man called Phil Matthews who had been there decades. Old school pair of hands and now me, the gobby maverick. I couldn't believe he was in the office when I walked up. It's excruciating. The fakery that proceeds is even more buttock clenching than those election defeats where the loser has to pretend to be happy for the winner. I'm talking Lorraine Kelly interview levels of pathological insincerity. The MD Linda greeted me in her usual flamboyant way and all the team were great. I politely said 'Alo' to everyone and then trotted into the studio. This is the only place I've ever felt safe in any radio station. The nest of viper's newsroom is my Gaza. I'll Pass! I've seen so many careers ended with office banter and shenanigans off air, even back then I knew to keep my trappiness for on-air. These days I'd have to wear a muzzle. I'm notorious for turning up on time but not early and leaving quickly. I try to avoid as much risk of unnecessary interaction as possible. Even twenty years ago I knew there was no yield in idle tete-a-tete. I went into Studio 2 and worked out all of the knobs. Radio studios look like the cockpit of Concorde, but you only press about three buttons. It's all show. Phil popped into say alo, classy move. He was polite and clearly had done his time at Capital. A radio gig isn't an entitlement. A refresh was much needed. The following Monday I was on-air after five days of publicity. Posters went up all over town and they spent a lot of money launching 'Belfield at Breakfast.' Capital owned all the billboards so it was a city-wide campaign. But what would I say at 6am? That was never a problem – finally, for four hours I could feel at home.

Capital FM was trying to be a cool US sounding top forty station. With an American voice over, very sexy 'JAM' jingles identical to those used in New York and LA, it felt and sounded BIG! I was impressed. I'd heard a lot of Rick Dee's in America and now he was syndicated from LA to Kenya. He was the epitome of cool. What a voice and talent. I realised the instant power of success. Let's face it, I'm somewhat unique looking. Thanks to YouTube, I now can't go anywhere without some delicious soul saying Alo, but imagine me in Africa? I looked like a sausage roll in a bag of Twiglets. Trying to fit in would be like trying to disguise Mount Etna by putting a bobble hat on it. So, I needed a catchphrase. 'Amuka' is good morning in Swahili, so I camped it up and 'Amuka to you lovey' started to take off amongst the giraffes, emus and gazelle in the Mara. You gotta have a gimmick….

The morning came to launch the show and the car was waiting outside the hotel at 5.20am for a 6am start. I slept very well, it's only radio for the love of God, hardly brain surgery or anything important…...to anyone other than me. Perspective is so important. Blowing stuff up out of proportion will cause havoc with your nerves. Deadly for success. I guess the biggest talent in showbiz is keeping your head when those around you are losing theirs. Swan time – BIGTIME! This did feel big though! I'm hardly Jay-Z or Ludacris…...although my nob gags and unique campery (to the impalas of Kampala) did make me a preposterously popular overnight sensation. Curiosity was my gimmick here. I was basically a freak show. The circus was in town, and I wanted to be the ringmaster – not a big shoed, red nosed clown! Everything went great! I did it. Four hours of pretty cool radio. The 'EQ' (audio processing) on my voice made me sound delicious. I'd never sounded mellifluous, butch and as ballsy as a 70's porn star. I fancied myself. I made Barry White sound like Julian Clary! Trust me voice/mic technique and processing is 95% of a top jock…....that's why all the TV totty on-air these days sound like mini mouse after puberty blockers. Clueless.

The music wasn't my cup of tea, but we had a lot of R&B like Destiny's Child, Boyz II Men, Backside Boys cack Mary Shackles springs to mind and for some reason the Thong song. Proper nineties guff. I grew to tolerate it. To me it was music for drug dealers. I wanted some Dusty, Bacharach or Tom Jones' Delilah…....sadly there's no demand in the Nairobi slums for Cilla's 'You're my World' or Roger Whittaker and his whistling even though he's from this neck of the woods and savanna. I didn't care I just filled the gaps. The show could have been broadcast in the UK. No local content at all. They wanted a US/UK sound as escapism, and it worked. Why the hell couldn't I just do it voice tracked or down the ISDN from my mother's back bedroom. At 8am we had a full switchboard. 'You're a breath of fresh air' – that line again. Then 10am came. Now what do I do for the next twenty hours? I did the walk of shame through the office. Trust me, this is when you know whether the team are a bunch of bitter vultures or whether they're behind you and you stand a chance. Remember this is proper radio. Commercial radio has to be <u>sold</u>. It's not public funded 'keep the needles wagging' horseshit. Fifteen years later at BBC Radio Leeds I walked out of 1A to stoney silence and Radio 4 being pumped out across the office in a show of 'you're so shit we'd rather fall asleep to The Farming Hour.' I was glad they hadn't heard me slagging them off, mocking how crap their figures and DJs were. Touché. Weird though how those creeps would go home and make notes from listening again. Cuckoo! Hideous breed, but thank God, the Capital FM gang were over the Moon. Actively coming to me to congratulate and pass on their excitement. You have to understand Radio is a <u>business</u>. If sales and marketing aren't behind you, you're finished. You can't ever sell a product unless you sell the person behind it. I minced over to the boss's office where they all sat crushing stones with their bare hands and gurning into spreadsheets. Was I on the naughty step or did I survive my first day?

Thank God it was good news. "You're brilliant, we've never heard anything like it" said Linda's boss's boss. I replied, "you need to get out more." You quickly learn in this game it's run by group think. These people are robots. They don't even know their own mind. The BBC is the worst – they agree their personal opinion by committee. You're hired by one woman in London but sacked by a team of snitches in the provinces of Botswana – most of which have never heard of you and have a vested interest to replace you, with someone who has slipped them a fiver or shares dark web 'images' with. (Nothing to see here).

By 10.15am I was in the car and back to the hotel. Feeling better after the three-day 'Monkey Pox' hangover when I arrived, I then realised I'd have to fill my day one way or another to get to tomorrow. I now love hotels, well the really nice ones. I have a theory that you should never stay in a hotel less nice than your own bedroom. I'm like Stephen Fry (other than the fact I don't appear to have married my great grandson) I could live in a hotel like The Savoy! Who wouldn't if you could afford it? Why would anyone choose to make their own bed? I do hope I'm like Thatcher and snuff it in the Ritz. Marvellous. So, I'd go to the gym and use the pool, by day. The buffet breakfast was open until 10.30am so I never missed that. I'd get room service at 5am prior to the show – full spread……….half of which I'd still be eating twelve hours later for my tea. That Northern ethic never leaves you. Then after the show I'd have my second breakfast of croissants in continental breakfast and a bit of bacon and then pop back to the office for meetings mid-afternoon if I got bored. I'm not daft. I had a double room so slowly I'd make friends and ask them to join me at Capital's expense for breakfast. Nothing gets past me dear! Very nice perk of the job. However, luxury and decadence quickly run thin. How many triple breakfasts can one man ingest?

A couple of weeks later they gave me my own house with a maid called Flora. I hated that. This didn't sit well. Firstly, I loved doing my own chores as it passed the time. She wouldn't let me wash a cup let alone do some low dusting. It's good for the soul and something to do of course. I truly believe a tidy home is a happy home. A clean fridge is a clean mind. However, I draw the line at cleaning the oven and washing the car. Best to get a man in. Life's too short to be on your hands and knees at eleven o'clock in the morning having a squirt and a wipe. Not for me. But having a modern day 'slave' was classless and abhorrent……..however, welcome to white life in Africa. That poor cow had my upright in her hand morning, noon and night.

My biggest reservation about Flora and the driver/security was their boundless devotion to their job for a laughable wage. About $25 a month. I couldn't fathom how these three people were literally saving my life on a daily basis yet only being paid collectively (a week) less than one of my show fees. This was shocking to me and still haunts me. $25 will feed an entire family of twenty people in Nairobi. There were about a million living in the slums with absolutely nothing and my 'team' were the envy of their entire community. Everything in life is relative. Until the day I left I could never fully comprehend the levels of poverty, corruption and desperation I encountered in Nairobi. I equally never felt comfortable with the unspoken racism and inequality between black and white. A bit like Detroit I guess – never the twain will meet. Those who serve and those who are so entitled they believed they should be served. Hideous. The colonies have a lot to answer for, however, for now I was outrageously complicit.

Nairobi is one big contradiction. There I was, not even twenty, a loose cannon flown in as the 'new big star' and put up in a 5* hotel whilst 90% of my audience couldn't even afford a roof over their head. This third world town was so disturbing. Massive wealth and luxury – seconds away from slums. A total mind fack and unconscionably indefensible. Was I helping or part of the problem? As I drove home the streets were littered with my face and AMUKA to 'Belfield at Breakfast' on lamp posts and billboards. We would pass hundreds of kids – under ten years old – crying and devastated by their drug addiction. It was terrifying and heartbreaking. Time went on but it wasn't easy. The longing for my loved ones was desperate. I think I'm probably just too sensitive as a human being to be in proper showbiz. To me fame and success by myself was utterly pointless. It served no purpose. This lifestyle was for sharing. It's a bit like being the sexiest, most beautiful and well-groomed stripper during a power cut. They all taste the same right? Snort. Total waste of time, right?

I was allowed one free phone call a week. No internet and very expensive international calls. It was gut wrenching. I did make friends quickly and John and Liz became my besties. John was a consultant from the UK who had done the business for years and had been the programme controller of Capital prior to the launch of KISS FM – our biggest competitor. I don't do competitions. No one could compete with me. You either loved me……or you switched off. As you know, I have little time for consultants as most put the c@nt in sultant! John was good though. He knew the game having worked for GWR in the UK who ran he biggest ILR stations like Chiltern, Ram, Wyvern, Capital and Trent. He totally understood my schtick. I truly wish he was my boss. The problem with being 'pop' (popular) is that eventually someone cooler comes along and you're redundant. Thank God I've never competed in that cesspit. You have to be pragmatic. Being 'popular' has never been my schtick. I'm about as cool as Jacob Rees-Mogg's cravat whilst sat in his baronial hall on GB News.

John's Mrs, Liz, was not only a stunner but a really smart and a lovely girl. Collectively we became very close and would go food shopping together and one by one visit all the best restaurants. My biggest passion in life. What's incongruous about places like Nairobi is that you might imagine it's all spear chuckers and Maasai wooden figurines, but in places it's very modern and has beautiful, decadent and elegant country clubs, bars and malls. Only for the very rich and successful of course. I never understood how the obscene poverty could literally be within seconds of 5* luxury. Bonkers. My favourite restaurant was The Carnivore. Wow. A now famous eatery with meats carved Brazilian style on to your plate and you had a flag to wave when you gave in and had had enough. Now when I say meats, I'm talking everything from steak and lamb to buffalo, warthog, snake and crocodile. It was basically a bush tucker trial. BUT it was great fun and delicious. I loved it. It couldn't open in Britain it would be deemed racist by vegans and accused of cultural misappropriation!

Within weeks I was recognised everywhere – a feeling that never sits well, even now, but it's part of the job that I've learned to appreciate and enjoy - especially since VoR. There's no getting away from it. You know when someone 'knows.' It's the weirdest feeling. However, it does have its 'bonus' for upgrades and better tables in fully booked restaurants. In my entire UK career, I only got recognised from Capital FM and VoR. The rest no one gave two facks. Fifteen years at the BBC achieved nothing other than 5.5 years Pleasuring His Majesty. It's as if inside the nonce factory you're deliberately anonymous and incognito. That's what I love most about radio – total privacy. Meghan Markle would hate it! Fame comes at a price. Awfully embarrassing when checking into less than salubrious massage parlours. It's never a happy ending to your session if they spend the hour discussing your opinions on the latest cast of The Lion King or the inefficiency of the IMF. Whilst splashing out on a bit of pampering, that's well awkward….so I'm told.

Another angel who came into my life was the most beautiful woman I've EVER met. Pinky Ghelani was the mid-morning presenter who followed me at 10am. My God, she was cut from diamonds. I've always (believe it or not) been shy around beautiful women as I have such absolute awe. Look, I have gifts – many – but beauty ain't one of them. Pinky was the first Miss India Kenya. Another level. Unlike the dreadful slappers on TOWIE and Love Island today who have lips (upstairs and down) the size of a puffer fish on speed, she was born perfection. This to me is the greatest blessing of all in life. If only I could turn heads…...they all end up spinning once I've finished ranting and raving. Added to her staggering loveliness was her fab personality and talent. We became top mates. If I was beautiful, I'd never leave the house! Pinky is now married with two gorgeous kids and living her best life as a Kenyan social media mega star. To think she could have married a convicted talker with a micro penis! Her loss! Years later she came to visit me in Nottingham. One of the things she taught me was that stunners often have insecurities far greater than a chubby ginger gobshite. I have no pressure to look anything. No one cares. I roll out of bed and on-air in fifteen minutes. She has to be 'camera ready' 24/7. I'll pass. It's totally liberating that all I have to do is turn up. Puts me in mind of the male strippers I've interviewed. They have to set their alarm at 2am and 6am to eat six boiled eggs. Balls to that, imagine the windy pops!!! When you're at her level, everyone is judging every part of you forensically. I did once propose to Pinky. She declined, but she said we'd be perfect for panto one day……Beauty and the Beast. Ouch.

Home sickness, longing or just plain sadness has to be managed. The key, in my experience is distraction. The busier you are, the less you think and indulge in your own self-pity or negativity. I've been widely critical over the years for the sickening trend that doctors offer anti-depressants to any Tom, Dick or Harry simply for Dick's feeling low……..which is a perfectly natural human disposition. It's now known as 'Anxiety.' Grow Up! This is not clinical depression. I read there's over seven million people now medicated to get out of bed in the morning. How do you know when it's passed if you're off your tits on uppers or downers? Of course, those clinically diagnosed as mentally ill should be helped, but you don't need pills when your Aunty Fanny pegs it! It's 'normal' to be sad. Grieving is natural and frankly loving, losing and missing people makes you blessed with empathy and compassion – not on the road to insanity. It means you're alive! Grow a pair and stop moaning. Seven million – my hairy white arse.

Over weeks and months, the show kept growing. My predecessor was forgotten. A dear radio mate of mine gave me the best advice ever – 'they've forgotten your name before you've left the car park.' There is massive truth in that brutal ego wounding line. I promised myself I wouldn't waste the opportunity to enjoy Kenya, but I knew it couldn't last. There's a pitiful darkness to Kenya but also a 'Simba and Mufasa' magnificence that you can only find in Africa. Nairobi has a fence – literally, that borders the Maasai Mara. The first time I went I couldn't believe my eyes. No joke, it is just like the Lion King. Nairobi ends and the savanna with Nala and Rafiki begins. The pride stuck together and the giraffes peak tall above all the rest. 'Tame' is a bit strong, but they're certainly not scared. They're smart. It's as if they know tourists keep them alive, protected with plentiful amounts of food! Arguably tourism finances their protection. You drive amongst the animals and they don't blink an eye, ruffle their mane let alone wag a tail of concern. It's life changing and magical. Animals have always been my heartbeat. I'd much rather walk a dog and clean up its poo than talk to a lefty. Similar to the Grand Canyon, Africa puts EVERYTHING into perspective. I loved it! Mum and dad visited Kenya years after I left to retrace my steps. They felt the same – utterly amazed. Africa will touch your heart and soul. It's a truly enchanting and enlightening place to see. Wonderful and kind hospitality from people who will never have our riches. One of my favourite things to do at the weekend was to literally hand feed the giraffes via a man-made podium. They are totally wild with legs to escape for hundreds of miles should they choose. Instead, they love and want to be there, they appear to adore human interaction, a tickle and thrive off the eternal adoration humans have for these majestic and gracious animals. So powerful. The definition of wonderous to me. I wouldn't mind a tickle myself come to think of it! It's been a while!

Sadly, there's a dark side to Nairobi, Kenya and Africa wide. The obscene poverty will never be resolved. Politicians have guaranteed that. The gap between rich and poor is utterly mind blowing. I cried many times when driven past the slums. All this bollocks at G7 and 'Crock of Shite 69' (COP) about climate change, and we still ignore people starving to death. Pitiful. What comes with poverty is risk. Obviously, I was a major target for criminals and terrorists. Imagine the value of a Brit DJ captured for PR – nothing to do with me personally. I should never have gone there in the first place, but boy I'm glad I did. Life affirming and humbling. A year or so before I arrived there were hideous floods and thousands died. The IMF granted $100's millions and the then President used it to build an impenetrable wall around the outside of his palace and pump the water over the fence to drown Nairobi. The rest of the money seemingly disappeared.

How do you combat this level of political vomit? I laugh when I hear the evil MSM discussing 'blackouts' in the UK. In Nairobi it's daily and for hours on end, however, not for the President. He has a direct line to the power station. Amazingly all houses in the straight line in between get power too, 24/7 – guess who live in those houses/mansions? Yep – rich white people. You couldn't make it up!

As my driver drove me into work, I'd regularly see dead bodies on the roadside as families simply could not afford to bury them. This is just another reality of the third world daily disgrace. Haves and have nots. This may well explain my disgust at boohooing millennials who cry poverty and use food banks whilst still smoking, using their iPhone 26 and watching Sky. Of course, the real heartbreak was the supermarkets. I used to go weekly with John and Liz. The doors were surrounded by lines of babies, toddlers and kiddies 'desperate' for help. Many had their noses running like taps. "Why is that" I asked? "They're addicted to glue" I was told. Again, how do you possibly help? Utterly desperate. There is no safety. No one cares.

Back on-air I did my charity work by trying to get laughs. We all have our purpose. This is all I'm good at. Suddenly the audience went from whippersnappers to more mature women forcing their fellas to sit through my cack. I've always known the women wear the trousers. Get them and the men will follow. My act (show) is entirely a business decision. If a lass says 'I'm not listening to that shite' – you're finished. My cheeky topical and political brand of humour seemed to hit although I still had to approach the boundaries cautiously to find out where they were. I still did topical humour. Twenty top stories a day, I would repeat them in rotation throughout the show. One day on-air President Mugabe was top story. At the end of the news bulletin, I said to the news bird "have you heard that old poem? Old MacDonald had a farm until Mugabe took it off him?" – Silence. I hit the jingle and played Shakira. Her hips don't lie……but my sister Vera's hips, lips and thighs definitely do – and chafe together! After the show I was beckoned into the boss's office. I was told in no uncertain terms NEVER to do African political jokes whatsoever! UK and US gags, no problem but shushy on Africa. I later asked John why they had 'overreacted,' he replied "This is Africa. If that gets flagged, they'll come in, take the transmitter, cancel the radio station and lock you up." Jesus - imprisoned! You wouldn't get a British gobby DJ in Britain locked up for jokes and free speech now, would you? Barbarians those Kenyans!!!!

Aside from the reality of Nairobi it is a hop, skip and a jump away from the Indian Ocean. It's stunning. We used to go to Mombasa for weekend get aways. It's the Skegness for Uganda! Again, how can this decadent 5* luxury be so close to such despair? I'm talking Barbados opulent! Its stunning beaches are breathtaking. Of course, after I left, the terrorists destroyed its reputation with an horrific attack. Unimaginable. Honestly, would I go back to Kenya or Mombasa now? I just couldn't risk it. A travesty really. I'm nervous enough playing Blackpool! Finally, my happiest memory by a mile was the incredible Sheldrick elephant sanctuary. The baby big trunks are still the cutest thing <u>I've EVER seen</u>. OMG. They make Doddy (my cockapoo) look like Shrek. Their mums had been poached so human mums (with guns 24/7) guard them, protect them and feed them seven days a week. For one hour in the morning, you can pay to go and watch them play football. It's the most beautiful thing ON EARTH. So inspiring. I was in floods. Hadn't been that moist since the Girls Aloud reunion!

But after nearly six months the letter came that I was dreading. Nana was in hospital and couldn't talk. This was a shot to the heart. Bullseye! I just couldn't take it anymore. Despite my bravery to carry on it was just pointless. I was putting my sanity and devotion to my beloveds second to radio……..

Why, Why, Why? What idiot would do that? It wasn't 'life.' I had no intention of staying there forever. I'd relaunched the BIGGEST FM licence in Kenya, and it was time to go. How on earth could I broach this with Linda? Well, she knew. Honestly, not for the first time in my life, I think she hired me to take the hit of the shitstorm when the 'legend' left and do my Razzle Dazzle to distract until people had forgotten. No one really noticed. It's only radio. She knew that after me she could put in a local DJ who could carry on forever at half the price and a third of the risk. Six months is nothing in real life, but when you're living it every day it is testing – why continue the skullduggery? For what purpose? I'd done it and succeeded – it was time to go! I'd caused a Belfield Storm and had increased the audience listening figures

(Emus up 20% and Hyenas were through the roof 'over the fence' in the Mara) – but enough was enough. It was time to book my Christmas tour in little old lady land. Linda was gracious and booked me a flight home. I'd whipped up a storm and I'd served my purpose. I was paid on time and spent virtually nothing. For the first time (and last time) during a departure it wasn't acrimonious – it was inevitable. Everyone had won, I guess. Africa wasn't for me long term, but I'd grown up, learned a lot and got £10k in my pocket. Those lizard things running up and down your walls all night (INSIDE your bedroom) was a step too far - 'I'm a DJ – GET ME OUT OF HERE.'

You cannot imagine what Kenya did to me. It made me a man. I had no idea at the time. On the surface it made me a 'star' – huge billboards and double page spreads in the newspapers everywhere I went. But that's all horseshit. Nairobi taught me about perspective. When I hear about Gen Z describing the poverty of mummy and one of their daddy's telling them they can only have one £300 Taylor Swift ticket, not two, I laugh. The horrific, deprived and indefensible poverty I saw every day was humbling and life changing. The despicable corruption that leaves these millions of humans with no hope is undeniable. Why do governments turn blind eyes and not say a word? So, when you hear me rabbiting on about some BBC turd's expenses or dinghy divers staying in 4* hotels at £7million a day – it comes from a genuine and real place of experience and despair. My heart was touched forever by East Africa.

Physically I focused on getting fit and eating well. There was no McDonalds or Starbucks with 1500 calorie Frappuccinos. Meat and veg was the backbone of every meal. I lost almost three stone exercising and eating well. This changed my life forever and I never went back. Thank You Africa. Thank you, Linda at Capital FM.

Nana's illness was the straw that broke the camel toe's back. A bit like the slammer, when you go away – no matter where or for how long – family pay a far bigger price than you do. Life is cruel creating a human you adore…...and then they leave you. I agree 'what doesn't kill you makes you stronger,' but I do ask myself why bother putting yourself in a situation like that in the first place? Life's learning curve. I don't regret a second. What an opportunity so young. The first time I'd even lived alone. Africa made me a man, showed me the reality of this evil and stunning world and gave me more compassion and empathy than I'll ever use in my lifetime. What a blessing. My days of watching Sly News for fourteen hours consecutively was over. It was time to board the flight.

Mum and dad met me at Terminal 3 Heathrow immigration. All I remember thinking was 'Jesus, is this the queue to audition for the Jeremy Kyle show?' No, No. All I remember thinking was, I did it! Invaluable experience and something to put on my CV (not that I've ever needed a CV, nor has anyone ever asked for it. Another 'careers' misnomer at school). It felt like a blink of an eye. Isn't the mind incredible. But what now?……

Nana was the excuse I needed to get back to Blighty, but I was truly sick with worry. This woman was my bezzy. I loved the bones of the old cock. I could say <u>ANYTHING</u> to her. Boy I wish she was around today. She'd say 'arseholes to PC and wokery' – music to my ears. That generation were miraculous. So strong and built on fortitude. British bulldog spirit oozing through their veins. Proud to be born in this septic isle set in a silver sea! I hadn't yet lost anyone in my life, but I knew deep down that I was the cause of Nana's apparent coma. She'd given up. My whole life I'd spent every Saturday night in her house and the family Sunday tea. I loved her and her 100% uplifting, inspiring and optimistic personality. She was a human firework to me. Even in my teens I'd go out to the pub and still sleep at hers, a compromise she was happy to make. I'd have two (4 slices) bacon sandwiches waiting for me wrapped in cling film after an hour in the Cavendish, Tavern or Windsor boozers – oh the glamour! All three pubs have since been demolished just like my faith in anything government related.

I went straight to the hospital and there she was, a shell of her former self. I held her hand and said a prayer. I talked to her and told her all about my trip. She was as vacant as Angela Rayner at Prime Minister's Questions. I left even more heartbroken and deflated than when I'd come in. This was far worse than they'd let on. As the Bigman is my witness, the following day that manipulative genius was talking, back on her feet and home within 48 hours as right as rain! Nobody could believe it. I could. Her boy was back and so was she! My old gran was reborn. Back bigger and better than ever. Phew, just in time. So cunning and almost hysterical. Not daft those silver tops. At my Nana's council house, I had my own bedroom with a double bed (very posh) and my own office with a gorgeous handmade desk. Since being about ten years old I'd sit there practising my schtick and writing down every great line and gag I could remember. In the garden she had two pear trees, a ton of rhubarb to prune and an outside lav that froze Nov – March. I remember as a tiny big boned kid doing pretend plays and shows at the top of her stairs and using the banister to lower bed sheets on string as my makeshift scenery. I had a relentless imagination. I loved to create. I took it awfully seriously. I guess this life was always my destiny from being in nappies. Sir Ken used to say politicians are like nappies – they need to be changed regularly…...and for EXACTLY the same reason! GENIUS hey?! Not dissimilar to Bob Monkhouse I still have hundreds of pages of one-liners all saved in categories and all in alphabetical topics 'just in case.' I believe Joan Rivers did the same in huge filing cabinets. It was a Godsend for a good ten years of my career. I had a gag for every occasion!

How did I know to do this from so young? That still fascinates me. No mentor, no role model just a born passion to connect words to make people laugh or think in a different way. I would spend hours writing in that office. Lately my style has changed and I haven't even looked at my scribblings for the last ten years. Now they're all stored in the Rolodex in my head. So many, many happy weekends and school holidays sat at that desk whilst Nana watched 15 to 1, Countdown and Going for Gold. As soon as I'd finished for the day there'd be a home cooked meal waiting for me. A truly peculiar, unique and blessed childhood. More love than anyone could dream of.

# Chapter 6

## A New Century Dawns!

After the dust settled, I picked up the phone and rang Ian at Century who was now station manager. He'd started as a production guy and worked his way up the veined management pole. We'd both started as lowly dogsbodies from the launch almost two years ago. He'd done very well for himself. We got on great even though he loved his silly 70's Smashy and Nicey style, as if he was constantly eating a banana or cucumber whilst I loved winding people up and taking the pish. He so graciously offered both lunchtime and late-night phone-ins back with the chance to cover overnights on-air. WOW! It worked. Now my career could begin in Ernest. Who was Ernest BTW? As the old adage goes, sometimes you have to walk away to grow up, man up and come back. I did. 'Tea Boy' syndrome is a killer in the media. You also never learn and grow if you don't work in different stations and formats. Nobody became a genius reading the same book in the library – same in the bedroom BTW – I'll leave it with you. Practice and variety make perfect. My unintentional timing was divine.

By now 'The Mouth' (lunatic lunchtime phone-in gobshite) had been sent back to obscurity after a couple of Ofcom complaints put the final nail in his three-foot wide and two-foot-tall coffin. I'm told he apparently gave the fashion industry the idea for shape zero. Century brought in a much safer, sane and boring pair of hands before cancelling the 1pm phone-in altogether.

Sadly phone-ins were seemingly dead in the water everywhere. The era of risk had gone. The innovator Myers had gone off to run Guardian Media Group so the days of him protecting provocateurs on-air had long gone. Radio didn't have room for ego-driven, deranged, closeted loose cannons. They were costly, time consuming and frankly embarrassing. I'm genuinely grateful to this warthog faced sloth for a 5* education in what not to do. It was invaluable! But now it got exciting, I was given two final bites of the cherry with legendary radio rebels, Chris Ashley, and next Scottie McClue. God did I learn! Chris was incredible working three shows a day in Shropshire @ 10am, Luton @ 4pm then Notts @ 10pm with me. His professionalism and stamina were astounding. 'When it's there, take it' he told me. I love him to this day and he and his wife Margaret are two of the nicest, kindest most supportive people I've ever met. From day one Chris had nothing to prove, saw a glimmer of talent in me and pushed for me to get on air, learn, grow and shine. We still speak regularly after twenty years and I've visited him in Spain where he's still booming out the woofers daily at eighty years young. If only all showbiz types could be like him. Thank-you Chris, I adore you and the current (and final) Mrs Ashley!

When Chris was unceremoniously disposed of, he had in his briefcase an open resignation letter ready. The boss called him in the office and said "Chris, bad news" to which Ashley in a gnat's fart replied "yes, it is, I resign" and proceeded to flop out his resignation printed off 'To Whom this may concern' Ta ra! "It's not working, is it?" the limp wristed boss continued on in his silly mock Tony Blackburn voice. Chris replied, "I think you'll find it is, but I'm leaving anyway." I love that man. 5* genius. A pro, scholar and gentleman. What balls, such talent and so smart. I sat opposite him night after night listening to his immense craft and vocal gymnastics. So fluent and instantly likeable. That's your X-factor. A raucous laugh and superb timing. I so envied his speed. Eventually all good things end. A teaboy from thirty years ago was now his boss. It didn't end well. These departures proved to me that no matter how big you think you are – no one is safe. No matter the skill, talent, years of experience or ratings – when they want you gone, you're facked! It's almost never about you. Times were changing as quickly as the management and content relaunches. Radio was suddenly less fun and a lot less risky. Accountants in suits now outweighed programme controllers. Networking is cheaper. It's not personal……but they always blame YOU!

This new boss ran a very 'selective' mafia at Century 106. No, I'm not being discriminatory. However, undeniably he was clearly only looking for a certain demographic to fit his nightly drinks parties and soirées at his city centre apartment. I understand there were lots of nibbles like low fat crinkles and cheesy puffs. I clearly didn't tick any boxes. I don't think gingers went down well in 'The Two Cocky Sailors' wine bar on Maid Marion Way. I'm more Friar Tuck he's more try-a-f@ck! There are many advantages to being wolf ugly with B cup man tits. The Lord works in mysterious ways, doesn't he? It was quite obvious the 'new' style of management was a club – an inner circle which I had no interest to penetrate. A lot of young lads appeared to be far too willing to compromise their morals and gentleman parts for a promotion or gig. They went down far better than me at the 'board' I'm sure. I guess that's a 'head board!' I wasn't even twenty, but I could see the blatant perils of wanting to 'fit in' in the media. I'll pass thank you. And people wonder why I don't socialise with creepy luvvies and media types. I much prefer my Nan's back bedroom to the boss's cottage! Apparently, team building days involved walking to the pub which is nice. I believe they had a lot of fun at poolside gatherings and BBQs. I overheard that one prepubescent and over promoted right hand man (boy) said that he 'fitted in' a lot better once he sniffed the party poppers and tried a chipolata. Most peculiar hey?

It's all seedy, creepy and sadly still common place today. Just disguised more cleverly I suppose. All of this is a euphemism for 'if your face fits....' – ask Phillip Schofield's work experience lad! I would have no part of this cult. A sickening brigade of unprofessional back and bottom slappers. If I hadn't spent £400,000 on lawyers (so far) for defamation (and nothing but the truth) I could do a whole book on 'creepy perverts in media!' who prey on lads wanting a helping hand and promotion. They use money and power to 'buy' horizontal influence and refreshment. Pfft. Theatre is even worse it really sucks doesn't it – not in my book it doesn't. I'll happily remain an outsider, pariah and unemployable thank you. Anyone who denies this went on is a liar! Sue me. #Metoo? More like #Fyou!

None of this affected me. I refused all 'drinks' parties. I never went to <u>one</u> and that's what pissed the 'club' off throughout my career. I was available, reliable, popular, enthusiastic, my breath didn't stink and I didn't fall over the furniture – what more could qualify me? Makes my inner thighs chafe in disgust what goes on at these places. Phew. The cover-up in newspapers, TV, radio and theatre will never change. It preys on the vulnerable and desperate. The only option left is to bankrupt, ostracize or imprison those who open pandora's box. It's a whole casting couch of wrong!

One day a true genius came into my life. The greatest and most talented of all the phone-in presenters I've EVER worked with for 'my' type of tomfoolery. Scottie McClue is a comic creation from hock-eye the nicky noo land by Colin Lamont. He's a master communicator and probably the most naturally funny and witty man I've EVER heard on British radio. Warmth personified…...with a porta loo gob. Of course, he hasn't worked professionally in the last decade as he's too risky and edgy for feeble, frail, weak and miserable mainstream media - which is a travesty. There's a pattern here isn't there? Who survives, succeeds and who doesn't. Anyway, Scottie was networked across Manchester and Nottingham and I would produce the East Midlands link. It was the best job on earth. I was basically paid to listen to this icon and every twenty minutes play in the adverts. The honour for me was chatting to and recording twenty minutes with Scottie before the show. No joke, we would laugh until we couldn't breathe. I've been around the houses, but I can tell you Scottie has the most natural charm of any talk DJ in history. His Scottish lilt and canny catchphrase 'Dinky Doo' is pure radio gold. It's so sad that like almost every other big personality and talk jock of his era, he was doomed. There really is only James Whale left and he's hardly Ricky Gervais slumming it on Talk Radio. James disappoints me on so many levels. It's all so schticky and lazy now. 1990's Whale was authentic and cutting. I guess eventually you earn too much, have too much success and lose the fight – a bit like Stern in America. Scottie is trying to break through on YouTube but sadly the success I was blessed with was one in a million, I only wish he could enjoy the same profile. Frankly he deserves it. Maybe time hasn't been kind to his style, it's a bit 'cute,' but what an awesome talent and quick and brilliant mind. A good lesson about talent – it ain't all looks or luck.

Finally, after just a couple of months of being back desperation got the better of the bosses and they needed overnight cover. I didn't care if it was 6am, to me it was a gig! I had made it on-air, got my own Century jingle and a captive audience. I toned it down a bit from Capital Breakfast, but I was encouraged to be me. The tagline of the station was still 'Big Personalities.' I don't believe in luck, but my timing was impeccable…...and I was ready to do myself proud.

Nowadays most stations only have two daytime presenters max and they'll be gone soon. There is literally nowhere to learn. I took it very seriously and could screw up in private whilst the world was snoozing. I practised and planned and treated it like my own (very) early breakfast show. Overnights would be crap on a 'normal' station, but this was regional. The entire East Midlands had a potential audience of 1.99 million. The fact 99% were sleeping didn't bother me! I was huge in the factories and 24-hour petrol stations! The night owl crowd were great fun. It was a tremendous secret community. They used to listen on headphones in the noisy factories - 'on the muff'- you could say! I'd made it! All you need is preparation to meet opportunity. I was ready. I was now an FM regional presenter by twenty!

I also carried on doing my celebrity interviews and reviewing the big shows that came to the region. I was very polite in those days and never said 'mean' things – or 'the truth' as I now call it. Back then I was just glad for a night out. When I became a pro-critic, I ended up sitting through so much shite I couldn't wait to sneak home at the interval. This sent precocious luvvies apoplectic. I met so many stars. Some starting off like me. I regularly interviewed new comics in the pubs. I met one man who I thought was magnificent and had him on overnight as much as I could - before anyone cared, let alone would pay to see him. Whatever happened to Peter Kay? 'Discovering' new talent is so thrilling. Seeing them thrive is wonderful. He's far too big to chat now. I know exactly how Dave Spikey feels! I hear he's been poorly recently. I hope he's OK. There's no doubt Kay will be forever regarded a legend and master of stand up.

Every day I would talk to or meet someone so talented and interesting. So exhilarating, exciting and inspiring. Nottingham

Arena replaced the ice rink where Torvil and Dean started so that offered bigger national bands and stars. Other celebs I did 'down the line' on ISDN. I had more showbiz types on the show than I could shake a stick at – all for twenty seconds on the entertainment update and then repeated at 3am. A free plug at this level was worth everyone's effort. I worked hard to develop my interviewing skills. I'm most proud of my interviews. It's VERY hard to make it look so easy and feel so relaxed. When you only have five minutes it's a lot of pressure. Technology was in its infancy and the paranoia that you hadn't recorded it would keep me awake at night. I was in the right place at the right time to fulfil my biggest passions. I'm indebted to Century 106 for the experience, platform and opportunity. Today entertainment reporters don't exist locally and overnights are automated; I was the very last generation to be given my LIVE on-air apprenticeship. Times had changed. Personality Radio was on life support. Phone-ins were a gonna and overnights were doomed. I was offered a new gig to keep me quiet.

It's during this period I first fell in love (and hate) with musical theatre. Musicals are so silly - but can be incredible. Musicals are where a fella gets shot and instead of bleeding to death they sing a dopey ballad. One night a terrible thing happened when Jason Manford was in 'shaving Ryan's Privates the Musical' and unfortunately, they didn't use his understudy. Worst still his microphone was working. It was a devastating press night for me. I got to see EVERYTHING for twenty plus years and Lord have I endured some shit. In the beginning, I'd walk-in full of eastern promise and sit through everything regardless out of sheer politeness. By 2020 I was as limp as a filleted haddock at the thought of another show tune in a cheap jukebox musical starring Jake Quickenden, Beverley Knight or some other twat from a soap. I quickly learned life is too short and left the very second that I wanted to eat my own testicles without an anaesthetic. Within ten years I was the most honest/deadly critic online at Celebrity Radio – my new own website. The twirlies <u>HATE</u> me as I burst their bullshit bubble and put a mirror up to their lunacy. My 1* reviews became more popular than my 5* praise. Very revealing about the public and their warped sense of curiosity. Twirlies ignored my good reviews and made me their punching bag for the car crashes I didn't enjoy. It was all my fault for not liking their cheap tat at £65 a ticket during a full priced dress rehearsal. The venom towards me was (and still is) extraordinary! It turns out theatre schools (and the new generation of cross-dressing delusionists) teach a fantasy world of cutesy Disney wonderment that does <u>not</u> exist. They believe because they're paid £10k for a certificate to say they're marvellous and can read words, I'm required by law to agree. WRONG! Honesty would be my forte. I wasn't detested for being wrong, I was a pariah for hurting precious snowflake twirlies' fragile feelings. It made me a star for being 'real'……and also landed me in jail for pricking the pomposity of this closed mafia, mostly self-serving and vile community, with false smiles and jizz hands a plenty. The truth hurts.

Look I gave thousands of 5* reviews. I RAVED about incredible talent before they'd even been 'discovered' twenty years ago like Hannah Waddingham, Mazz Murray, Sharon D. Clarke, Lee Mead, Dean Chisnall and Jenna Lee-James and many more who are supremely stunning and incredible on every level. Yet, when I slagged off a shithead from Eastenders their heads exploded!

Century 106 was my radio baptism of fire. I drank in the good and the bad and was surrounded by some of the weirdest, creepiest, most talented and plain peculiar talent in the biz. What an education. As months went on, I worked with Ian Skye on Breakfast which would be my final gig. I was his on-air producer paid £140 a shift - £20 more than overnight. I didn't care for him. I just couldn't see any talent. He didn't have a funny bone. Too cool for school. I saw no passion. Zero pazazz! But each to their own. We never had a row I was just indifferent. In Ian's defence I'm not a co-host. Too much to say. I had no interest in his laid back 'ad-libbed' content and he cared even less about my sarcastic and facetious replies. To put no finer point on it, it was a match made in desperation not heaven. Century was now utterly toxic and pointless. For the first time I didn't get a tingle on-air and I struggled to get out of bed. I was ready to retire at twenty years of age. I worked with Ian for six months or so. I learned another good lesson. Be very careful who you agree to work with. The 'Ant and Dec' chemistry is very rare. You're thrown together but no matter how hard I tried I just couldn't be bothered to make it work. What a woeful admission. My heart wasn't in it. I was done. Pathological cheerfulness is hideous. I'll leave that to travel birds with Botox and big knockers. I didn't want to be part of this mediocre broadcast.

The Breakfast show is always regarded as the dream gig. It is not, trust me! You're up at 4-5am, done by 10am, bored all day, eat six meals in between as you're permanently jetlagged, exhausted and end up morbidly obese like Piers and forced to go to bed when everyone else is going out having fun. So, after three years on and off I was given my marching orders from Century and my work was done. It was a self-fulfilling prophecy. I should have walked sooner but regional money was incomparable to anything else at the arse end of 1999. Even Prince would have taken the money and run! It paid for my USA trips which became my obsession. Century <u>never</u> found its feet. It rebranded twenty times and is now a national Olly Mursfest. Snore. At the time it was tough to leave as this was my proverbial 'first love,' but what an opportunity to rise through the ranks, learn my craft, practise on air, host my own shows and begin my lifelong curiosity of life story interviews. I'm also grateful for the lesson on the pitfalls of nepotism and why you should compromise yourself for success.

Back then I didn't have the introspection, experience, confidence or dexterity to admit it was over and walk away. I should have gone to the bosses and asked to go back to overnights…….but they'd been axed, to (a DJ free) jukebox. I now recognise I'm not a producer for one simple reason - if I don't respect the talent, my contempt is palpable, I just can't hide it or fake it. It's not in my make up or personality to make do sadly. The show also did things I morally didn't agree with. We gave away cars putting the public at great risk. 'Hands off my Punto' was a cockamamie idea to get ten listeners to hold on to a car until they were so exhausted they collapsed or dropped dead! Fab publicity hey?! This resulted in one being taken to hospital and two seriously unwell. I didn't get the concept. It's radio – where is the content? It was pre-YouTube and social media so there was no video content at all. This was about as moronic as the radio station who got listeners to sit on blocks of ice. It basically froze their private parts causing infertility issues and landing a massive lawsuit. You see 'they' don't care. No conscience, it's just money. Heartless. Anything for publicity. This was my biggest takeaway from life and career so far. This was my first insight into the unconscionable stupidity of management. All of the competitions back then were fixed regardless. If a winner came in on day one to a £100,000 giveaway, I guarantee they would 'never' be picked for weeks. Competitions are only designed to generate income and revenue for the execs – far outweighing the prize money tenfold. Sadly these £2 call comps are mostly entered by poor, desperate and vulnerable people who can't afford it but buy into the hype. Shameful!

After I left Century Jeremy Kyle took over from Scottie McClue. There's not been a broadcasting travesty this breathtaking since Scott Mills pissed on Steve Wright's radio grave on Radio 2. Back in 1999 whilst Jeremy Kyle was a presenter at BRMB they did a controversial competition called 'Two Strangers and a Wedding' and famously 'gave away' a bride to a lucky winner having never met the groom. The winner's marriage lasted less than 4 months and, in a twist of fate, the bride subsequently ended up marrying Jeremy in 2003. They had three children together and the marriage lasted until 2015 with the bride citing unreasonable behaviour as the reason for wanting a divorce. Jeremy then ended up marrying the family nanny. Even Jeremy Kyle's first wife claimed that he had taken money from her bank account without her permission to fund his gambling habit and addiction, and had faked a life-threatening heart condition and run up debts at the bookies and on betting phone lines. She said: "The man I married wouldn't have been out of place as a guest on his own show. The programme is crass and embarrassing and for Jeremy to act like some kind of agony uncle is sheer hypocrisy." Kyle opened up about his long battle to beat his gambling addiction in his 2009 book. That story should have been on his own TV show! Kyle sums up the disgusting hypocrisy of media monopolies. Despite his own moral compass clearly being lower than a snake's tit on his hideous BONKERS baiting TV show – he continues to broadcast and no one blinks an eye. After his controversial talk show was axed following the apparent suicide of one of his guests, he was paid off a million quid by ITV to slither away laughing all the way to the bank and Murdoch's laughable atrocity Talk Radio. You couldn't make it up! In 2005 I worked with Jezza at Capital Gold. I'll tell you about that later! Not my cup of tea.

Seriously, radio is shameless like the rest of the entertainment. Years later I covered at Chiltern FM for GCap (now Global – they own everything). They gave away £100,000 on the NETWORK (all

40+ stations) but had me record a fake call with the winner as did the other DJs on all their other forty stations to make it sound like it was a local winner. Shocking contempt. Disgusting. The caller's answers were edited in. Totally unethical and undeniably misleading to audiences. Balls to Showbiz – A wake-up call of prolific proportions at twenty.

This period had a lot of life lessons. Dad had been knocked off his bike shortly after leaving work in the rain and fog. I told you bicycles are death traps. This was the first time I understood the true feeling of helplessness. A lady type driver had pulled out of a side road and despite his lights and reflective gear she was too busy doing her hair, makeup and putting on her panty girdle sending him over her bonnet. It was bad. Pushbikes are for six-year-old boys, not grown men. Cyclists need to be protected from themselves. Dad was ahead of the game saving the planet – which nearly cost him his life. File under 'own goal.' I've never forgiven him for being so stupid. Drive a diesel like a proper adult. Sadly, he didn't have a Go-pro strapped to his private parts to put it all over social media. Twatter hadn't been invented yet or he could have had her sent straight to prison. The ambulance took him to the Queen's Medical Centre and mum was sent from work to be by his side. My sister insisted I went to work saying 'there's nothing you can do, mum's there.' By the time Dad's twin brother Ken arrived mum was on the hospital bed next to him. He was in such a state she fainted on the spot. Now we've got two soft sods flat on their back.

Unbelievably, to my amazement, when I got home to mums at 1.20am he was in bed. 'It's just a scratch' mentality - the bravery of that generation is astounding. I could have bawled my eyes out. To see your hero, mentor and rock crushed was terrifying. I had to help him out of bed like a frail old man. This six-foot working-class hero was battered and bruised but there was no way he was going to stay in hospital – men from pit estates don't do bed baths! That's for sissies. It's another level of tenacity and strength. God, I love that man. To see mum devastated was even worse than seeing Dad look like he'd had ten rounds with John Prescott. All any son wants to do is be his Mum's hero. I was useless – we all were. This is when family comes into its own. Within weeks dad was fighting fit and back to work. What a hero! He dumped the stupid bike for a less supercilious, sanctimonious and anally probing form of transport.

Now it gets Exciting

It's now late-1999 and I had been talking to a unique diminutive character called Tony Delahunty. He was the launch sports boss at Radio 106 and a one-off. He left with the original bosses and had been in sport broadcasting since Marconi invented it. At two foot tall but twenty foot in confidence and bon ami, this original Diddy man made up for his lack of length with a gob the girth of a giant. I loved the cut of his jib. He had launched a tiny little station called Mansfield 103.2 just up the road a few months earlier. This was one of the new 'ILR' independent local stations intended to 'bring communities together!' They only exist on good will by local, desperate and out of work DJ's who are willing to work for nothing. Often these types are most peculiar, special, talentless – but available, reliable and compliant. What they lack in talent they make up for in willingness to work any hours for petrol money! Mum was now working at BT in Mansfield so I thought it would be perfect to cadge a lift if needed.

Tony is still one of my dearest friends and I adore him but he's tricky to work for. He's basically a turn, a show off and plays to his staff for laughs and drama. He's a nightmare boss but bloody fun and will give you as much rope as you need to hang yourself to his infinite enjoyment! He's a brilliant MD who managed to make Mansfield FM profitable – no mean feat! In fact, twenty-five plus years on, his tight ship is still on the air unlike hundreds of other stations who went bust in minutes. A canny and shrewd operator is Tony. HUGE respect! After almost three decades he's still reading the news simply to save £25 a shift on a cheap AI journo robot script reader. He saw something in me but knew I was risky and nothing like anyone he'd hired before. He encouraged me. Fatal Error. This man loves trouble.

Tony loved sport and had exclusive rights for Mansfield Town commentary, but he wanted rid of it. For a start he couldn't afford to continue the contract so needed an exit distraction strategy. This bloody genius decided to use me on a Saturday afternoon not to cover the football, mock their defeats and take the piss out of the fans in the hope the club would cancel the contract to save him money! How was I not lynched? I naturally obliged as it sounded like a hoot. Like so many gigs in my bizarre career I went in knowing it couldn't last. In fact, I've felt the same for <u>every</u> gig ever since. By week two there was mutiny at the radio station and the football club was seething, no raging – demanding my head on the block! I was being 'cancelled' before it had even been invented by the mental lefties. A pattern that has plagued my career is that I'm too good at 'the act.' So often my critics had no sense of humour and couldn't suss that I was 'acting' and playing the part that I was given. I'm amazed I haven't won a BAFTA. It never dawned on them that it was a gag for cheap ratings. People believed I cared and fell for my schtick. I was just literally sat there mocking the afflicted and having the time of my life at fart heads expense with no knowledge <u>whatsoever</u> of what I was angry about. The non-football punters loved it. Total piss-take. Pure nincompoopery. So many people fell for my bollox. Humourless lefties and the fourteen Mansfield Town fans just didn't get it. 'Shocked and appalled from Sutton in Ashfield' and 'incandescent with rage from Hucknall' made radio gold. I drank in the circus.

The less I cared, the angrier they got. The more dismissive and flippant I sounded the more outraged the reaction. The rest of the audience thought it was hysterical (including me). Some thickos cannot understand I'm a tease, a wind-up merchant and an entertainer. DELIBERATELY! This ain't an accident. It's still disappointing to me that jealous wannabees in the biz choose to miss the gag. I knew nothing about football and cared even less. I didn't have a single opinion about Mansfield Town and still don't. It was a game to get a reaction. IT WORKED. It <u>WAS NOT</u>

PERSONAL. I didn't know any of the Mansfield Town players or bosses. Delahunty had worked out there were so few football fans that he couldn't lose. Using me for moron baiting and pillock fishing was a much bigger winner than costly commentating! I would quickly become the biggest fish in the very tiny Mansfield, Ashfield and Bolsover Pond. In other words, more people would tune into me mocking Mansfield Town than supporters listening to get the score. Tone was clever – a VERY simple business strategy. The 'talk-ability' (as marketing geniuses call it) was massive. Boy was he right! It was a pantomime from day one and everyone in town couldn't wait to watch the fallout from the sidelines. It's the biggest broadcasting car crash and laughingstock since Gemma Collins diet pills on QVC.

Tony cleverly picked Matt Genever as my reporter and producer. Matt was Mansfield through and through. He loved the club and his hometown but didn't know what to make of me in the beginning. On show one I crossed over to him at 5pm for the Live report with my infamous killer question "Matt, today your beloved team lost 2-0. Why are they so crap?" SILENCE. My radio team stared at me through the glass in shock, disbelief and amazement. They'd never heard such vulgar audacity. They looked at me with that now familiar 'who does he think he is?' Look, silence is still WAY more powerful than anything you can ever say. It's my job! That's what I was paid to do. I left the dead air hanging. Excruciatingly delicious. A full switchboard lit up for the next hour. "Who do you think you are?" they asked – "I'm the big man sent here to educate you" I'd reply – pure parody and piss take. I channelled my inner cyclist to have such pomposity and insolence. I loved it as did anyone with a sense of humour that wasn't medicated, mental or longing for an identical opportunity. Did I care about Mansfield Town? Did I bollocks! Did I love causing a storm and triggering the hard of thinking? Yes, I bloody did!

Delahunty loved it. Classic radio, BUT, then the tsunami of boohooers, as always, began their campaign to get me sacked many of whom worked in the building. Come to think of it I might have invented cancel culture in 2000 – ahead of the curve again. Doh! Tony held his nerve, but a thunderous Matt Genever needed calming down. He was rightly furious. He saw it that I'd humiliated him LIVE on air for a cheap laugh – which I had! Sadly, this is a by-product of this type of entertainment. Like all jokes, you have to have a punchline and fall guy. I knew it was a ratings winner. On Monday morning both Tony and I sat Matt down and explained the act, the show and he got it immediately. A lightbulb moment! Straight away Matt was the smartest man in the room always far exceeding my state comprehensive smarts. From then on, he set me up to create more intentionally awkward moments to keep the buzz of this radio maniac brewing – me! All planned. Fans felt sorry for the 'timid' and 'bullied' Matt Genever. He was far from it! So creative and encouraged me to go further. My lot loved the banter and bollocks. All choreographed schtick. Matt and I literally became best friends over the next ten years in real life until tragedy struck. To this day Matt was the kindest, most generous and switched-on producer I've ever worked with. I will be eternally grateful for Tony bringing us together.

As the weeks went on the momentum of the show grew and grew to preposterous levels. The smaller the TSA (transmission area) the quicker you rise. Word of mouth has always been my best friend and it's much easier to shine in a small community where the jungle drums beat. People started turning up at the radio station whilst I was on air, some to bring flowers and others to give me a kicking. Then one day it happened – radio gold and my first media shit storm. Some people accuse me of being childish. Well, they started it…...

<u>Crossing the Line (again)</u>……
Where is 'the line?' It doesn't exist! I've already told you! In politics it's called 'toeing the line' – historic maritime rules where you can't cross it, but it's a real line drawn on the floor for your eyes to see clearly. On air and in showbiz everyone's line is different. Many intentionally blur lines as they do in court for their own edification and agenda. One bloke's fun is another woke's offence. One kid's mentor is another noncy groomer's next victim. You get the idea. Delahunty was without question brave. He did the smartest thing I've ever seen when a furious Mansfield Town advertiser had heard Chinese whispers but hadn't heard the programme. Witch- hunts were harder to ignite pre-social media, but they did still exist over the phone. Post convids, Twitter is the home for the crackers' mentalists in their mother's back bedroom who fight other people's battles and 'close down' anyone they

politically disagree with. This was a much more innocent time. Research proves 99.8% of these box ticking, kneecap knobbler imbeciles do it dressed in their mother's knickers and granny's britches after dark. Bless their gimp socks. Back then 'trolls' had firstly to hear it in REAL TIME. No clips on YouTube or playback to the whoop-de-doo bandwagon streaming services. They'd have to ring up thereby removing the anonymous cowards who are Lycra wearing mincing girls' blouses. A phone call came into reception on a <u>LANDLINE</u>! Remember those kids, we gammon's lived by them if the fax machine was busy. The caller was spitting feathers. 'I'm cancelling Belfield' he is slagging off my team and therefore me and my company' – what a pilchard. I've encountered a lot of these Mr Angry's' over the years. You kill them with kindness. Tony heard it coming, picked up the phone and said "John if you're ringing to add more adverts on Alex's show, because it's become rated number one, you'll have to join the queue. You're the third today, I'm out of slots." GENIUS. After a brief silence John said "OK, can you let me know. I'll add another three months if you can fit me in." Doesn't this sum up people's faux outrage and fickle flights of fart head fancies? It's all a game as I know too well. This was my first outing handling a pile-on by a bandwagoner of bovine intelligence. Over the years these 'events' became very normal and blow over very quickly. You walk into the storm and milk the shit out of it. You see people want a drama and fuss but rarely are as offended as they claim. They see it as a game and love to teach you a lesson to make themselves feel important. These days it's an Olympic sport. Never more so than now do these delusional morons believe that bringing you down will raise them up. <u>WRONG</u>. It never happens. In fact, quite the opposite. Karma.

Can you believe that right this second there will be a mob of shitheads reading this book who believe they hate me. They've literally paid 99p in the pound shop (bargain) to be outraged by my life. They can't walk away. It's an addiction. I guarantee you half of my sales of this epistle will come from the BBC liars, trolls, petrified nonces, corrupt police and HMP public serpants and the odd Clown Court Judge simply to satisfy their insatiable need to find out gossip about me in the dark belief they'll 'catch me out.' What a creepy, unfathomable and weird bunch hey? It's the definition of mental illness born out of some subliminal jealousy. What a compliment – all be it back handed! These dopes have made me the man I am today. I think of them every time I sell out a venue or turn left on a British Airways Fokker 100. Delahunty recognised the game and power of public chit chat. He'd been in the game a long time. You have to provoke to grow and switch the dial to see what the fuss is about to find new audiences. 'Nice' is boring and makes you invisible. I think we can agree VOR proved that! He backed me 100% but the endless Judas' in the building didn't help with constant sabotage from provincial no talents who'd be lucky to get a job at a taxi rank call centre let alone a proper radio station. I totally get it. No one wants to be the Bridesmaid or pale into insignificance next to me. It's all tactical moves. Another pattern I would see a lot throughout my career. Again, Tony fended them off with the knowledge that 'bums on seats' equals profit and kept them paid and the station open, on-air and alive – his ultimate MD defence. Sales were cock-a-hoop and Mansfield 103.2 was the talk of the town for the first time! My reputation went before me. The Mansfield Town players were pissed off! I didn't have blind reverence. I couldn't care less naturally.

The phone rang one Saturday after a match was postponed. I'd said on air that it was because the players where so bone idle and that they'd rather be in the pub than get cold and moist at Field Mill explaining the cancellation. It was of course due to the weather. I'm not limp under the cap. My tease was for entertainment purposes only. Matt answered the call and it was a football player called Darrell Clarke. He was a big star at Mansfield Town and incandescent with rage that I'd insinuated players are pissed up slackers. HE CALLED ME FROM THE PUB!!! His first mistake. He was FUMING. He'd fallen for the Belfield trap so I shouted, "get him on-air!" Off I went, ten minutes of on-air wind up until he slammed the phone down. Hook, line and stinker! Bait and BOOM – Bingo! Radio GOLD! Magical content. I still have the clip of the call and cringe at how raw it was but marvel at the gag. A gag he didn't get nor did his three sheets to the wind colleagues sat along the bar nibbling on Nobby's Nuts……as he was thrown under the radio bus.

This would define my career. The punters LOVED it, but why did he not get it? He'd clearly had a couple of Babychams and stupidly had called up from the 'Minging Muff' pub somewhere near the ground. He wanted to 'teach me a lesson,' 'bring him down a peg or two' and of course that classic line used throughout my Clown Court case from people I'd never met or spoke to – 'I just HAD to say something.' <u>Oh no you didn't</u>. You take your chances! A schoolboy rookie error. My advice to <u>ANYONE</u> who is ever triggered by a gobshite like me - SWITCH OFF. It's not for you. Do <u>not</u> engage! The last thing you EVER do is think you can win by ringing in. You can't win!!!! I have the microphone and the fader! You don't stand a cat in hell's chance. This is the motherload I've rehearsed and prepared for and waited a career to broadcast. I revelled in the lunacy. God, that was fun! Again, the precious souls in the station clutched their pearls and tickled their tits but Tony and Matt knew it was both radio and comedy gold. Our friendship was cemented for life. Childish, naughty schoolboys. Never to be taken seriously! That might be the best call of my life. 'You don't get it because you're as daft as a brush and not the full shilling Darrell.' How the feck did he <u>not</u> know I was working him from behind? 'Get it in your thick head, I'm brilliant! You're a footballer dear boy. You kick something for a living. Anyone can do that Darrell. I've done it with my balls since I was a toddler.' For the love of God. What was he thinking? This was the first of many 'set up' bits that blew the minds of my enemies. I mean enemas.

Within weeks, my work was done. The 5pm Saturday 'football' phone-in had a full switchboard. Ten lines all flashing for sixty solid minutes. Peacocking frosty knickers lads went bonkers thinking I was an infidel from Nottingham Forest. So silly. These were the very best days of radio where hurty words didn't matter, victims didn't exist and boohooers were told to stick a cactus up their anus horribilis and blow their nose until the pressure equalised. Get a life and get out of mine. Take a chill pill....and an anti-depressant whilst you're at it. What fun times ruined by lefty Guardian readers and champagne sippers. Tony loved the chatter and reaction around town. It was joyous. It'd take him half an hour to get out of the Post Office. 50% angry, 50% pissing themselves and 100% listening. For good or bad, people were talking about his station for the first time, so he extended the phone-in to weekdays 1-2pm and 'The Mega Phone-In' was born! Matt produced it and I had made it! <u>£25 a show</u>!!!! Three times the minimum wage. I'd have paid Tone the £25 to be honest. This was entirely a vanity project. I didn't need the money. You couldn't write it – well I am, I guess. I couldn't believe my luck. Most days Matt and I would go to lunch and spend my show fee before I'd even been paid. Couldn't care less, I'd still got my profitable LIVE gigs. Radio was just a laugh and chicken feed. I'd have to top up our budget if we had a pint. It was simply a hoot to see how long I'd be able to get away with it. The best fun on air that I've <u>EVER</u> had. Why? THE PEOPLE! My punters. My public. Diamonds! This patch was sensational. Every caller was a character. I was on fire and at my most real, outrageous and honest. The lunchtime phone-in was pushing it by radio standards but not for the metropolis of Mansfield listeners. Know your audiences – the recipe for success. This ain't Knightsbridge. Amazing salt of the earth people who can smell bullshit from a hundred paces. My people with whom I'd spend a lifetime living and loving. My show has never had airs and graces. Also, my act hasn't changed from 1999 to now. I promise you. NOT one degree difference in style and content. It blew the mind of snobby and patronising BBC twerps - that also makes me happy. Very happy. Why should I have 'all fur coat and no knickers' and be a complete fraud and fake it to 'fit in.' I don't want to fit in.

Language is my tool. The word 'slapper' for example outrages some people. I think it's hysterical for a start because it paints a picture yet means <u>nothing</u>. A local area called Kirkby-in-Ashfield had the highest teenage pregnancy rate in the UK. The scum sucking pondlife at the BBC would dress that up in mink and mules. I simply asked, 'why do we have more slappers in Kirkby than anywhere else in the UK?' To me that is crafted and <u>MOST</u> importantly funny. Switchboard full with every slapper in the county – plus their mum, dad, aunty, sister and grandma who felt compelled to defend their little Chanice or Tamika over her mucky 'one, two, buckle my shoe' habits. Once you've triggered the sensitive, it's pure gold dust! 'Lovey, did you drop your drawers?' How could anyone take that seriously? Some do. Oh yes, they love to be outraged! 'It wasn't their fault' they'd say. 'Well did the stork bring it?' It's a joust. My audience is made up of 10% triggered dopes who miss the gag and 90% pissing themselves who would NEVER ring in. EVERY single show was similar to this....An identical format of silliness: 'Should women be banned from the third lane of the motorway?', 'Should thickos be given an IQ test before getting up the duff?' and 'Why don't we pop the dinghy divers balloon boats as they leave France?' 'Can't we use the wind turbines in the channel to blow back the immigrants?'

Who would take this foolishness seriously? Righteous, do-gooding, born again eco-cyclist types will never get this. They're too spectrumed to see the sheer sarcasm. What fun winding them up. It still makes me smile even writing this now. It's ENTERTAINMENT. These days I do this exact tactic with lawyers, BBC managers and probation officers. It blows their tiny, prejudiced lefty minds.

Matt Genever was the first and only producer I met who got my rhythm and encouraged my malarkey. It's so exciting to get on air. We'd built trust. Boy did he get it! A couple of years later Matt did a year around the world trip and had the time of his life. I arranged to meet him on the way back in Las Vegas which became my favourite place EVER! I wish I could relive that first trip again. It was mind-blowingly amazing! I'd found my Mecca and Lourdes. An awakening. My second home of entertainers, great food, showgirls and strippers! It's truly the most stimulating, exciting, sexy, indulgent, decadent and fun place on earth. Well, it was then. Not now – it's a rip-off. Neither of us had been before. We couldn't believe our eyes!

During this period my love for America was getting bigger and bigger. I'd been going to Michigan a fair few times a year with a stop off in New York on the way. I was truly in love. Vegas though has another level of bedazzlement! For a guy who adores showbiz, this was truly the entertainment capital of the world. Vegas was ever so slightly better than Blackpool! I landed in Sin City, and we stayed Downtown, that's all we could afford. Back then 4* rooms were $20-$30 and buffets were $20 with drinks! They just wanted you to go and be there. Since the accountants stepped in it's now $200 a night plus $80 'service/resort' fee and $50 for a decent buffet which kills the buzz and fun immediately. Back then you felt like a king. Now you feel like Prince Andrew. Vegas is ruined by soulless accountants and greed – identical to radio, TV and LIVE theatre. Who can afford a West End ticket. It was an entertainment and gambling town, then a food town, then a day club town, then a nightclub city and now it's all about sports. I'm out. I was so excited that Matt and I could explore this Disneyland for grown-ups. It didn't disappoint. The lights, the noise and the smell of the casinos where intoxicating! Tits and knockers on every corner and in almost every showroom (other than the Chippendales - why people want to look at furniture in Vegas is beyond me). Every one of the properties were different. The early 2000's was the heyday of excess and obscene indulgence and decadence. I'd missed variety and the good old days of TV and Radio in the UK, but I was bang on for BOOMING Nevada!

We had a blast exploring every corner of this disgustingly OTT, opulent and audacious town. We got to see David Copperfield, who I loved as a kid. I adore magic which plays to my childlike joy of suspending disbelief. I'm a big kid at heart. David was the master back then. Years later I would interview Copperfield several times before a big showbiz bust up. I wonder if my assassins asked him to help make me disappear? After days of 'All you can eat' buffets we hired a car and drove to the Grand

Canyon. It was life changing. Balls to Vegas, 'God' pissed on the chips of any man-made monoliths that deteriorate over time (like the BBC). The Canyon is beyond comprehension. A scale indescribable. It's bigger than Sarah Millican's lady garden. It's equivalent to Jason Manford's ego. Every time I go, and now more than ever, I can't help but think <u>NOTHING MATTERS</u>, we're all so insignificant. 100% perspective. That's been there for millions of years. We come and go. Our little impact on the world is rarely remembered but the Grand Canyon is the epitome of colossal enormity and will stand the test of all time. We both silently stared into the abyss agog. Utterly magical! Now more than ever, perspective is my BEST friend. Look, nothing really matters, does it? Everything is just a story for down the pub. Virtually none of us make a difference. It's just our little life. We had a blast. I couldn't wait for him to come home in a couple of months. For now, he was having a hoot going from the West Coast back to New York City and then to fly home.

My best radio mate and I had made it from Mansfield to Sin City in a flash. However, on Matt's return he struggled with headaches, no one thought anything of it. Something wasn't right though. He'd call me in agony. He powered on and even worked in the BBC Press Office at one point – he hated it! Wasn't he suffering enough. Desks full of snakes taking home bucket loads of cash for counting paper clips and pushing pens all day. Enough to make you heave. It's a wonder that didn't put him in the Priory! He had a lot of tests in London and was diagnosed with a brain tumour. He wasn't even thirty. Devastating. I hadn't dealt with serious illness yet let alone a tragedy like this of a dear friend. It knocked us all for six. I was helpless. What could I do? What could anyone do? Well, be there for my buddy, I guess that's all. We've all had that feeling of 'life goes on' as someone is suffering terribly. Platitudes of 'it'll be OK' and 'say a prayer' are utterly inappropriate. The little religious faith I've had over the years is always rocked at times like this. WHY? For months all I could do was visit. I remember going to a London specialist hospital one day to see him. Heartbreakingly he'd gone from a sixteen stone strong sportsman to frail, thin and weak man. I cried. The silly old soft sod that I am couldn't help the situation one iota. It left me so angry 'why God' didn't help? The cruelty of cancer so young gutted me. He was very confused. Kept ringing me over and over. Life can be so cruel and shitty. I was powerless. I saw genuine fear in his eyes. I said the right things, but it didn't work. Shortly after Matt met a beautiful girl who was a doctor and became his confidante, protector and ultimately his carer. This was especially tough for Matt's mum and dad who have the kindest hearts on earth. He was literally their baby – at twenty-nine. Aren't we all? You know what they say, 'he's only your son until he has a wife and is then gone for the rest of his life.' It's tough but true. I did get incredibly close to Matt's family which was lovely and comforting. Heartbreaking for his adorable sister Siobhan who I adore. Matt did get engaged which brought joy momentarily. My inner voice underscored that time was our enemy, no matter the occasion or celebration.

Matt got increasingly tired. No amount of money or meds could help. Towards the end I took him to the cinema to see Batman Returns and he loved it. But he paid the price for days – gutting. Matt passed away aged thirty. It was devastating and a kick in the guts personally. I adore his mum and dad, Pat and Ted – two angels who do not deserve the pain of this tragedy. We've always kept in touch. If nothing else, I try to keep the stories and his remarkable legacy alive. I even took his fiancée to New York on his behalf after he passed. Nothing helps but it does distract. 'Life's not fair' hey?! Even in the darkest times there's levity and humour. I made the unforgivable mistake of taking her to see a mate of mine star in Les Misérables on Broadway. BAD MOVE! Oy vey. At the end of that Samaritan's sponsored wrist-slitter the entire cast are dead – they're the lucky ones! I saw Matt Lucas in it once – it was a bad night…...his microphone was working and the lights were on. The unforgiveable technical hitch that the trap door broke during his 11 o'clock number is galling and a travesty of the West End.

I don't think grief ever goes away with an untimely, incomprehensible and unthinkable tragedy like this. I think about this remarkable man a lot. Matt gave me the faith and confidence to be _me_ on-air - 99.9% of the industry tried to destroy me, undermine me for their own profit or run a mile, some even wanted me in prison. Miss you Matt. He and his family are always in my heart.

So, I'd lasted a few months at Mansfield 103.2. I knew I'd be sacked sooner or later. It was inevitable. One thing that my type of gobshite recognises is that it's only a matter of time. You always sleep with one eye open. You can't keep up that level of energy and outrage to generate the calls and not ultimately 'go too far.' NEVER in my life have I felt safe or that I was doing well. Every gig (including The Voice of Reason) is tinged with 'when will this end.' It's not paranoia, it's the reality of 'walking the tight rope,' 'head above the parapet' and the complete inevitability of our 2020+ woke broken world I'm at total peace with. That's why I have such contempt for the business. Delahunty and I had a few argy-bargies. Most famously he sacked me LIVE on air when I needed a day off. All planned. An old stunt that always works a treat to rally the troops and gets you in the papers! That clip still lives on to both our amusement. Making a 'the people's hero' a martyr is the best way to cement credibility and kudos. Ask Tommy Robinson or Jesus.

The biggest problem with my show is that the punters don't understand the legal boundaries or rules - that's my job. I didn't have a delay or a 'Dump Button' to delete the odd Anglo-Saxon or defamation. In fact, I've NEVER had a delay. That's a button where you can edit out seven seconds of the programme LIVE. This is normally crucial with my style of broadcast as pranksters quite rightly just want to scream the C word for fun to get you sacked. People think I can say <u>ANYTHING</u>. Far from it. The DJ is always the head of blame even when it's not you. Arse covering is a big part of radio and life – especially in this risk-averse dull climate of committee brown nosing.

Eventually the show had got out of control. Amazing radio but with Ofcom breathing down Tony's neck he quite rightly had to 'mayday.' I truly forget exactly what happened, but I remember 'THAT FEELING.' Being sacked is normally humiliating, costly and annoying. Not here though, this was a hobby for beer money and a fun lunch out with my best mate. I've spent my life 'being me' and entertaining audiences at the cost of constant upheaval, heartache, drama and initially bewilderment. Eventually you don't ever flinch whilst those around you are losing their heads and their knees, legs and torsos are jerking. Look, it's a job but it's also personal. These people lure you to push the boundaries – an invisible boundary. They make the rules. They decide the finishing line. At this point though it didn't matter at all. The money made no difference as it was half the hourly rate of an old cockery sing-along, I was still living at home with the folks and all I really wanted to do was bugger off back to Benidorm.

I was twenty-five before I 'got' the game. You have to go in with the realisation knowing you'll leave. You have to set yourself up so that you enter with an exit strategy that protects you from cost and any personal stress. I mastered this in the end, but it took a good decade to sort out the showbiz sham and work out the contract SWIZZ. Basically, anything in writing is worthless. Not worth the paper it was written on……which is why Delahunty (an ex-lawyer) never bothered! I've dropped an awful lot of bollocks over the years! Learning curve, they say. My safety net has <u>ALWAYS</u> been working LIVE. The second radio 'does one,' I go back on the road with no rehearsal. Tony has always stuck by me despite the choreographed dramas. He's now eighty and still the diddy-Bigman of broadcasting. I adore his diminutive spirit. What he lacks in height he makes up for in audacity and torment.

## Chapter 7

## Millennium Madness

As the twenty first century took hold my time in the metropolis of Mansfield drew to an end. Before 'I left' I did spend 31$^{st}$ December 1999 into 1$^{st}$ January 2000 LIVE on air at 103.2FM. I certainly didn't regret or miss any New Year's Eve parties. Far too much pressure for me to have fun. I'll pass. All I need is a bag of camp classics and a switchboard full of punters and I was away with the fairies and as happy as a pig in shite for the final countdown to the millennium. My LIVE work was still the backbone of my business. Imagine EVENTUALLY going from £25 a show to £25,000 a night in Blackpool? I prayed this millennium would be kind. <u>Never</u> lose faith. This business works in mysterious ways. What a difference two decades can make! Finally, having passed my test and now driving a Punto, I could perform anywhere in the country and didn't have a boss. By twenty-one, it was blatantly obvious that I viewed the world so differently to most people that I encountered especially those around where I lived. Just like school I would never fit in with any of my colleagues who were delirious with cheap ASDA sushi and woke ideology about climate change. It never stopped pissing down or got above 15 degrees in Mansfield we fantasise about global warming! By some curious twist of fate my unique slant and cynical bent seemed to give me an edge and advantage and finally it paid off! I'd found ME!!!!

All that mattered to me was family and friends. Showbiz could only ever be treated with the utter contempt it deserves as Mansfield FM proved. It's frivolous malarkey to pass the time and fun for the ego and creative juices – but – it's not real. Rammed and riddled with creepy perverts – top and bottom – I wanted no part of the circus. Radio is not reliable, but it didn't matter, thanks to mum and dad slaving away to pay for piano lessons I'd always work regardless. After six or seven years of only playing the piano and testing gags, I now had a new confidence LIVE to talk to, play with and tease the audience. A MASSIVE step forward. Inspired by my success on air I started adding in singing to the act knowing full well I was no Andrea Bocelli, BUT frankly the bar was so low in Nottingham, I couldn't fail. My voice is nothing special, but I can hold a tune. I had a few lessons on how to bring my voice out - some people suggest that it should be pushed back in! I could eventually reach three octaves – I had my legs stretched. With jiggery pokery of my decent sound system and echo, I could actually sound less horrific. I don't mean autotune – I'm not Britney or Cher – I just used to swim in reverb. Then one day I did something that changed my life. I realised the piano was my comfort blanket. It was a lazy prop. I hid behind my organ which is a disaster for rapport. Doddy told me at fifteen that 'you have to build a bridge between you and your audience – it's an imaginary piece of thread.' The piano was a physical and literal barrier preventing that connection happening. No wonder I wasn't feeling it and hadn't found my rhythm. So, every fifteen minutes I would stand up for two songs on 'track.'

Again, I was canny. I used to get my backing tracks from an incredible Aladdin's cave on Broadway called 'Colony Records.' It had the most authentic Backing Vocals I'd ever heard. They were $35 per track, but they were class! This changed my act, success and ultimately my life forever. I could now go to the next level opening up hundreds of new places to schlepp my schtick to. Once you stand forward centre stage a miracle happens. You connect with the audience in a second. It was like a lightbulb came on and I finally became a performer. I felt like a 'proper' turn - not a keyboard filler spec act. I'd wasted six years hiding behind a coffin with keys. What a tit! God works in mysterious ways. It gave me a chance to build my confidence (and the act) quietly. Identical to overnights on Century talking to insomniacs on diazepam, all those years of doing the shittiest gigs had given me the apprenticeship to handle <u>anything</u>. I'd seen it all from fights to silver tops shitting themselves. They fell over like ten pin bowls – some days they'd go down like dominoes during my wartime medley. Now I could 'own' the room and have the confidence to deal with all 'situations.' Drunks fighting and let's just say 'the odd spillage down-stairs' from those unable to clench with excitement – I wouldn't even flinch! It was time to shine….

Within six months I'd totally ditched the piano and almost never played it ever again until the big variety shows years later. To think years later at forty-one, I'd play the Baby Grand piano at the Joe Longthorne Theatre in Blackpool. A sold-out show, 1,400 plus 'bums on seats' gig. This was a dream come true, a gig of a lifetime. What goes around comes around hey? Magical! Despite our theatrical divorce, the piano is still my best friend in the whole world. But know your audience. Play to the crowd, not my own comfort zone or ego. Times had moved on and the punters needed more than one man and his organ. I'm no Liberace. Thank God I'm not even Bobby Crush! My tracks were exceptional and put me ahead of the pack. It's critical to be better than everyone else with the audio and also the suit. I invested £1,000's to be re-booked for things they didn't ever notice. It's all subliminal but REALLY matters.

Another bonus of dropping the piano from the act was that I didn't need to carry it. I downsized my sound system to a brilliant 'all in one' Yamaha set of gear. I could now set up a show in less than ten minutes – seriously! I'd take down in five and carry it in one go back to and from the car cutting my prep time by thirty minutes. Marvellous. When I see old turns taking two hours humping speaker after sub-woofer into tiny venues I laugh. The punters don't care. Tech is so good now it's totally unnecessary. Currently I play pro theatres with worse sound than my touring handheld PA. Less is more – a moral for life and definitely in my bedroom. Everything now fitted in my Fiat Punto boot instead of laying my huge organ across the passenger seat like a body bag with a huge set of Rob Beckett sized white gnashers. RIP to fingering my organ in public! All good things come to a sticky end! It was a health and safety bloody nightmare down my mother's stairs and up my gran's back passage.

The next revelation was about to hit me like a ton of bricks. Now I was stood 'public facing' my appearance became even more important and for the first time did matter.

Let's be honest, no one is booking me for my looks. I'm no Cheryl Cole. Punters notice far more than most credit them for. Only in recent years have I worked out the key to my success. The way you walk in and out is more important than the show. If you go in all toffee nosed and all fur coat and no knickers – you're finished. Game over! I didn't know I did it (back then) but it turned out bookers loved the fact I communicated with their guest before I'd even set up. I was just being me. This was a huge USP. Apparently, this is rare, but I'm a chatter box and love to gossip to find out what's going on. I'd often add this flannel in the show which punters love. I also realised I hated being on a bill – a show with more than me appearing. This wasn't anything to do with pride. Firstly, I don't like waiting - EVER! I like to come, go, get on and get off as I'm busy. Secondly, some of the shitheads I had to share a dressing room with made my teeth itch and inner thighs chafe. Live acts are not as creepy as DJ types admittedly, but not far off. I'd much rather rock up on time (but not early) cause a scene and bugger off home as quickly as possible. Unlike so many who hang around like a bad dose of syphilis, this isn't my style, it's my passion and job not life. Never outstay your welcome – another great bit of advice. Always leave them wanting more and don't peak too soon, I say!

The next revelation is the lack of 'class' by male turns. Most are to fashion what the Megan Markle is to everyman and sincerity. Lady acts go to great lengths to look fabulous. My mate Jane McDonald built her act on it. She looked a hundred times better than anyone else and had the best lighting and tracks. It made her stick out and ultimately a star. The women loved the tunes and the fellas loved her jelly wobblers and ball gowns. Smartest theatre star I've met. Show-<u>business</u> remember. I had to up my game. There'll be no jeans on my show! Fellas wear stinky old black top and slip on (and off) bottoms. Mistake!!! I quickly learned that women (99% of my LIVE audience) take shoes and shirts <u>very</u> seriously. The old advice was right, they'll never remember your name, but they'll remember how you look and how you made them feel. 'Can we have the ginger fella back with the fantastic jazzy shirts and shiny shoes' – my number one gimmick! Seriously, I'm not working you from behind – it got me re-booked time and time again. You have no idea how important polished 'tuxedo' shoes have been in my career. You can get them for £20 on Amazon, yet most dopes wear scuffed old school shoes or trainers from Jonathan James. My shirts and jackets weren't cheap. I've spent a fortune on them over the years. In the beginning I bought the flamboyant jackets from the 'gospel' (gentlemen of colour) stores on $32^{nd}$ Street, near the Empire State in New York. Now I get my 'Graham Roberts' shirts from Naples in Florida. I truly believe the way you look, the effort you make and the time you give in and out is 100% the reason I've been re-booked for twenty plus years. They're all tax deductible, so why not? Basically, I'd found my Mojo, a rhythm that worked and for the next fifteen years, as I continued to polish my act to within an inch of its life. Who knew if this dedication would ever pay off? I'm no nostrum anus! I believed in my heart it was worth a shot. Regardless, I loved it.

For some sadistic reason I still had a secret desire to work for the BBC in the belief that it was the Holy Land of broadcasting and impartial journalism. Little did I know it was a nonce factory, home to the likes of Huw Edwards prowling the corridors. A job came up at BBC Radio Leicester so off I went to that dump of a building in the hideous centre of town. This was my first full time job at the BBC after years of pissing about at Radio Nottingham as a BA (broadcasting assistant) and in the radio car. This hideously toxic building, rammed with lifers more institutionalised than my colleagues here at HMP, was identical to ALL the rest. Soulless, clueless, hapless, hopeless and classless. I was so lucky to work all over the country for the BBC, but their Leicester hub was more of a care home than usual. This sleepy station had a line-up of dinosaurs led by a Pterodactyl! He was later swept under the BBC carpet after shagging a young female journalist. What these woke, lefty Guardian readers will do for a pay rise hey? They were very nice to me to be honest but fack me – it was just like Betty Ford Clinic In-House Radio!!! Snore fest!!! Top stories - shit on the pavement followed by cancer, potholes and then the same article in a language that 99% of the audience didn't understand in order to pacify the box tickers and diversity quotas thrust upon us by the virtue signallers in London. Urggg. Hideous. Ten years later at BBC Radio Leeds <u>NOTHING</u> had changed. It's a cabal of self-protecting, lazy, contemptuous, publicly financed drains sucking the life out of the few remaining delusionists who feel compelled to pay their licence fee.

BBC Leicester was a monolith and even I had to go softly softly. They hired me to help with the re-launch of the station. Louisa James who's now doing brilliantly on GMB and Manish Bhasin who is a top man and doing gang busters on BBC sport started at the same time as me. So thrilled they're deservedly shining bright. I did my best to polish the rest of the outputs turd but sometimes I'd listen for four hours and couldn't find a single clip to use in the promo. It was soul destroying. So f'in boring! It was just a job to those HMP Leicestershire Lifers who took the money and ran. No malice or vitriol like Radio Nottingham. Their apathy outweighed any aspiration or ego. I'd already learned my lesson not to re-locate and drove every day from Nottingham. It was the first time I knew I'd become 'one of them' if I hung around too long. I was putting my name to some appalling content for £25,000 a year – a staggering wage at 21 for literally clocking in on time and not falling off the chair. I went to see the horny boss and after four months he offered me a pay rise to stay. I'd had enough. It was £8,000! WOW! Now £33,000 a year!!! But how???

This was when I knew the BBC was one big cockamamie scheme and shameful swizz. He added on the £8,000 by pressing one button saying that 'I could be asked to work different shifts.' This top up payment was called the UPA – 'Unpredictability Payment Allowance.' Thousands were on this at the BBC even though they

NEVER worked shifts. For the record I never worked a different shift either. Even at twenty-one I knew this was outrageous, unethical and totally immoral. A total abuse of public money which hundreds <u>still</u> benefit from now despite it being banned after several of my Sun exclusives a decade later. Aunty's 'scams' left me cold and furious. I went up 35% of my salary without a single raised eyebrow, just to stop me jumping ship. It worked…...I was 21 - but it didn't last long. Welcome to public money radio! More like FU to the licence fee payer. It was around this time that a legendary BBC Nottingham presenter invited my gullible mate for dinner. This married BBC mincer plied him with booze before sexually assaulting him. Apparently, this shameful fifty plus disc jerker guaranteed this 25-year-old apprentice on-air gigs for a blow job. My mate fisted him for the offer – and gave him a black eye. The following day this pervert claimed he'd fallen down the stairs. Two months later he was paid off and never seen again. Another staff lifer paid £50k for twenty plus years. This shameful abuse of power happened all the time at the Beeb and all over showbiz. Double life living creeps would 'audition' desperate and easily influenced young lads with the threat that if they didn't oblige, they'd never work again. Toxic.

You see in the early 2000's there was still plenty of work around. I could resign at midday and have another gig by 3pm. Within seconds I'd get replies from radio bosses and I never struggled for a gig. With such unrelenting ambition and tenacity, I felt untouchable and never took these gigs seriously – even with such preposterous pay rises. It was a job. No emotional investment.

It's talking. It's not a proper job. Getting or leaving a job never felt a big deal. I suppose working the clubs are like it. Get in and out and off to the next gig. As long as you're paid, who cares? NEXT! Move on.

My world changed forever in late 2001 and it was a wake-up call. Nana had become increasingly frail and age had got the better of her. After I returned from Africa my old gran got a new lease of life but by eighty-five, she'd had a couple of falls and we made the hideous decision to move her to a warden-aided flat down the road. To see your hero deteriorate and be unable to climb up the stairs is heartbreaking. We've all been there when you put the keys in the door praying that everything would be alright on the other side. You know it's time to do something. Nana never lost her speech, but she did lose her spirit. She still made me laugh out loud though. As often happens at a certain age your lady part muscles have seen better days and when she'd roar with laugher, she'd, well, wet herself Niagara Falls styly. So, we got her some Tena Lady fanny absorbers. One day I went upstairs, and one was on the radiator. I hit the roof! 'What the fack are you doing?' We speak as we find in the North. 'Waste not want not Alex, they're expensive' she said. I said, 'You taking the piss Nana?' She laughed so hard……...she pissed herself again. Ironic hey. She was ahead of her time with recycling. She literally wanted to reuse them to save a few quid. Eventually we got her guttering around the bed. If we ever had to share when the rellies were over, I'd always ask to sleep in the shallow end!

Her council house still didn't have central heating and that bothered me in the winter, especially overnight upstairs. To whippersnappers this is unimaginable – cost of living crisis wouldn't have made any difference back then. She had ice on the inside of the widows in the winter. The council found her a lovely flat five minutes from all our houses and she had a chord for Matron if she was in danger or in Nana's case fancied a chat. What broke her heart more than anything was that the flat was too small for me or anyone to stay. I loved the bones of the woman. Her obvious decline was heart wrenching. In fact, it was cruel. Nana managed months in the flat but eventually she had the humiliation of a care home after going arse over tit once or twice rehearsing for her comeback in Amsterdam working those windows. It was tragic. Bit by bit she faded away. I did a couple of gigs for her in the old-cockery. Bittersweet doesn't cover it. She'd lost her fight and acid tongue. She knew eventually she'd lose her marbles, which was a step too far.

Eventually her time had come to shuffle off this mortal coil so the family gathered at the Queen's Medical Centre and my sister was called home as an emergency from Skegness where she was working. Nana hung on until she arrived. A heart-warming miracle. As she passed, I felt 50% relief and 50% devastation. I finally understood true grief. My dad was so brave but like me he's a big softy and ultra-sensitive and despite his working man's stiff upper lip his heart was broken. I could barely speak. I walked the three or four miles home to clear my head up Derby Road. The poor old bag had to listen to me rehearse for years and years and never once screamed 'SHUT THE F UP!' Not once. As bad as I was in the beginning, she would always say I was fab. Her pride was inspiring. She taught me sarcasm, wit, speed of comeback, the power of love and the importance of family. This has to be the biggest gift in life.

I arrived home knackered and waiting for me was my best mate - the piano. It never let me down. Over just a few minutes the dagger in my heart worked its way out like months of therapy at the end of my fingers. Very quickly I forced myself to delete those last images in the mind's eye and forget those remaining final moments. As I played, I began to remember the feisty incomparable angel of the 1990s who I adored more than words can ever explain. Time does heal but what I'd do for a hug from Nana today…...not to mention a mouthful of yakety yak about this inept and hideous government and state of our country's affairs. THANK YOU, NANA! What a legend!

A couple of weeks passed and the funeral was packed. Close family to bingo mates all had stories of 'our Lil.' I was asked to sing at the funeral – now there's a gig I'd never do again. The distraction and chaos of setting up the gear was bad enough but singing and playing 'Bring Her Home' from Les Mis (gender fluids version!) was a monumental challenge. You have to literally zone out. Another good lesson. Turn off the emotion by telling yourself 'It's a show' is the ONLY way to get through it. You have to remove yourself from the event, occasion and of course sentiment to stop the kettle boiling over. I got through it. The wake was too much for me, I left. Too many words and platitudes were heartbreaking. I've never been one for hand wringing and pearl clutching. No one knew her better than me in later years. It was a bitter pill to swallow losing her. I couldn't accept it was real. I went back to her grave in Carlton and stood silently by myself and told her what she meant to me. As God is my witness and on Doddy's four-legged life, a piece of paper blew across the cemetery onto her newly covered grave and it had written on it 'I'm OK.' I swear this is true. How? Why? Sometimes life has miracles.

I walked away with a smile. She'd still got it. The headstone on the grave next to her was dodgy and had a wire holding it in place. I said, 'Don't worry love, I'm going to get you a landline put in like your neighbour.' Life is precious. I went home to play the piano for twenty minutes and then returned to the Wake. Weddings and funerals are the same in our house, just one less drunk. It was a great party. We had loads of things on sticks…...pensioners! Thankfully I didn't catch the bouquet at the end. My poor Aunty Fanny did. She fell into a paper shredder five days later. May our Fanny rest in pieces!!!

So, it was a new era and a new beginning. The circle of life is unbearable – but unavoidable. As Nana's pure love left this earth, other angels presented themselves. I became closer and closer to Nana's sister Mary, now in her eighties and Aunty Marje too was a formidable battle axe who I adored along with her husband Uncle Tom. Grandma and Grandad (mum's parents) now had new meaning. I haven't talked about these angels, give me a chance! I've only got one flaming pair of hands! As time went on, they all became heroes and five-star silver tops who I adored. I guess it's their innocence from less complicated times. They love you for you. It's impossible to find that anywhere else these days. The loss of Nana underscored my love for family. Now I had the car I could take them places like the seaside or even just Tesco's. It didn't matter. Half an hour of my time meant an awful lot to them. I was very busy but I made time. I am proud of that looking back. Life goes on. I only wish these people could have seen my incredible success thanks to the Voice of Reason.

Whilst at BBC Leicester my 'LIVE' skills caught the attention of the council entertainment team. Oh, I forgot to tell you this was all during the Greg Dyke era as Director General trying to modernise the BBC with his 'cut the crap' campaign. Sacking about 15,000 would have done it! The General came to our rat-infested shithole and asked us how we could improve BBC Leicester, I replied 'try a terrorist attack' – he laughed. The staff didn't. I always knew it would take a Dyke to turn around the BBC. Anyway Chunky, the phone rang and it was Leicester City Council. It was the Queen's Jubilee baton relay for the 2002 Commonwealth Games and she was coming to Leicester on her tour. They wondered if I would like to host the event? WHAT? Would I? Does Dolly Parton sleep on her back? YES!!!!

What an amazing day that was, 40,000 people packed into the city centre for two hours. I kept them entertained for an hour and then finally her car pulled up and in front of my very own eyes Her Majesty and the Duke of Edinburgh got out. They walked for a good thirty minutes as I followed them, microphone in hand. What an honour. They could have chosen anyone. They asked me. One of the many unbelievable moments of my life. A pinch me moment that they can never take away. As Her Majesty stood next to her Limo I roused the crowd into three cheers and thanked her. I couldn't have felt more proud. She nodded and waved. Not bad for a lad from a pit estate who thinks her ginger grandson is a prick. My time was up at BBC Leicester. You can lead a horse to water, but you can't make it swim on its back. It could never modernise. It was as dull as ditchwater and moving the deck chairs around the Titanic won't help. Despite my indefensible pay rise…. I was off to pastures new!

Over the next few years, I never stopped working, but the backbone of my business was the LIVE gigs, travelling further and further afield across the country. In between some radio gigs came and went for fun, but my heart wasn't in it. I knew deep down my days were numbered as nearly all of my mentors had now been sacked and were 'resting' – showbiz speak for unemployed and completely redundant. The decline of 'personality' presenters happened over-night, they were just too risky. You're more likely to see Prince Andrew open a primary school than hear a gag master getting a gig on FM. Fortunately, despite the Mansfield debacle I was not grouped into this category. I was still a total enigma and anonymous and it was pre-Google, so I carried on regardless. At BBC Leicester I had started offering sixty-minute specials to the BBC Local Network and it was not only lucrative but a huge boost to my ego and confidence. Mostly I <u>loved</u> it! This had never been done before at the BBC (or since) and these celebrity interviews, packaged as hour specials for each individual station, were truly my dream gig and played to all of my strengths and passions. They had ZERO controversy. Can you believe I ended up doing this for ten plus years and appeared on over eighty stations around the world, including over twenty-five across the BBC Locals in the UK? Using the BBC's brand and resources it was easy to get guests. The reach made my pitch a slam dunk for PRs and managers. From the very beginning I punched high and did annual specials with my hand selected favourite people. Sir Ken Doddy and I did fifteen one-hour specials in total from 1999 to 2012. I knew the BBC Local audience and which stars were good talkers. I loved producing and presenting these shows. Back then bosses appreciated this, now they'd rather play Dua Lipa or Sugababes and get the travel presenter to fill in between. I was the last generation of creative DJs to thrive. It was so exciting but a lot of work to produce. Again, you only get out what you put in.

One of my first hour specials was Il Divo who I was lucky enough to follow through their entire global success. They invited me to New York to launch their Christmas album at Sacks on 5$^{th}$ Ave which was a total thrill. God, I love NYC! The first time I went I could only afford to stay on about 112$^{th}$ Street – miles north of Broadway but it was brilliant. Invigorating and the most exciting place I'd ever been. I couldn't believe my eyes. It was like a movie. All of my favourite things packed into one tiny place. Everything was electrifying from the taxis (yellow of course), the shows (a league above the often-lazy West End), the smells, the steam from the drains and of course the food. I still can't believe my luck whenever I land at JFK. That skyline – WOW! I've probably been fifty times over the years, if not more. I recorded 'Belfield on Broadway' for over ten years, talking to the stars of the 'Great White Way.' That refers to the white light bulbs on all of the theatres illuminating the billboards. Whoopi Goldberg recently suggested that it's a racist name. I despair. Try putting black light bulbs on billboards dear and see how many tickets you sell. Dope!

Anyway…...I had a great time walking miles, then we stumbled across a man asking if we wanted to see a TV show filming? "What is it" I asked. "The David Letterman show, have you heard of him?" Had I heard of him? By now, I was obsessed. I've watched Letterman's every single episode from the late 1990s trying to learn why he was the master at chatting to famous people. There's a very simple answer – they liked him - and eventually loved him. He wasn't starstruck. In fact, he was the biggest star and highest paid person in the room. It's all psychology in chat shows. He was the smartest and quickest person in the room. No one could outwit him. Pure charm and warmth. Now I would sit in his audience. It was meticulously produced. Not a moment wasted of the audience's time. In and out. Perfect. He made it look so easy because despite being a chat show host on TV he was a comedian who worked LIVE audiences. THIS IS THE KEY! Working LIVE gives you the skill to ad-lib any situation, experience gives you the confidence to pull it off. He was the master. I knew my decade of shitty shows would eventually pay off without even knowing it, if I were just given the right opportunity. The art of <u>GREAT</u> conversation is a muscle. It's hard to make it look so easy. You have to work tirelessly to master the craft. What a shame nowadays that Letterman is deemed a 'pale, stale, male, gammon' with <u>no</u> boxes ticked. No MSM career post 2020 other than on-line. We should hold our heads in shame. His warm-up man didn't do a lot but what he did was perfect. Years later I did warm up for ITV. I tried to learn from the best. Magical times.

I would regularly fly between Michigan and New York City into LaGuardia, minutes from Manhattan. It was like getting on a 75-minute bus ride. ID, but virtually no security, you could fly every hour to any city in America and think nothing of it. Hop on, hop off like a bus. Not anymore. Those days were over post 9/11. That evil day destroyed easy air travel forever. The world would never be the same again. Also, after 9/11 prices rose disproportionately and schedules were axed. Nothing was as easy or fun anymore…....identical to post Covid.

I remember watching the towers collapse at my friend Barbara's house in Leicester. I found it profoundly moving and beyond epic. We'd met at Century towards the end where she co-presented a late-night agony aunt show with a darling and hysterical DJ called Paula. This was one of my first 'you couldn't make it up' moments. Paula had her demons with the barman's apron and hit the headlines after she spilt the beans over someone having horizontal refreshment at the Christmas Party! I believe both were married. I remember the front page of the tabloids 'she's a Barbie doll with fat thighs.' So funny. I pissed myself..........but the fella's wife didn't. Snort. Years later at BBC Stoke she hit the headlines again whilst off her tits on-air having a 'partay' at 2pm on-air ('partay' was her catchphrase). It became the worst example of a presenter given the mic rope to hang her herself LIVE! It was hysterically pitiful to hear twenty minutes of 'Pissed Paula' being allowed to throw herself under the radio bus. Not a single colleague or boss ran into save her from herself. It's sad. That tape was even ridiculed on 'Have I got News for You' – by the BBC. The very people who allowed her to do it. Hilarity and belly laughs, of course. Paula was always nice to me. I understand she's still on the BBC. Good for her. Having the last laugh is cashing the cheque – even if you sell your soul to the mouthpiece of the .gov devil. Aunty is the only broadcaster in the world who loves to self-flagellate and would allow this to happen. I saw it at Radio Nottingham when a brilliant but troubled DJ was an alcoholic and would endlessly end up injured or turn up late. They laughed in the office and allowed and enabled shameful addiction to continue. Any opportunity to whip and humiliate themselves, destroying the little credibility they have left, is taken big time. It's almost as if the staff hate their own employers as much as the BBC discompassionately despises them.

Anyway, Barbara and I sat mouths open at what we saw in New York. I don't know why I took 9/11 so personally but I was consumed by it for weeks. The enormity and tragedy were horrific. I ended up flying to NYC six weeks later to record a documentary, twenty-two years old with no budget or team. I created the best show of my life. 'How New York Recovered' was an optimistic but real insight into how those in town coped and got back on their feet. My cousin Concetta flew in from Detroit just to be with me. We both adored New York. Those two buildings were so iconic – and now gone but still smouldering. It was incomprehensible. How could humanity be so evil? New York has never been the same since. I arranged interviews in New York but spent three days at Ground Zero doing 'vox pops' talking to anyone who had a story. It was so recent that the dust was still in the air. We now know so many people ended up seriously ill with those toxic particles causing cancers. The impact of 9/11 is still taking lives decades later.

There was an eerie silence and taste in the mouth next to that beautiful tiny St Paul's chapel - which remained miraculously untouched. A beacon of hope, said to have survived due to a giant Sycamore tree that was planted in its graveyard. Over that week, with the sounds of New York City behind me, I interviewed firemen, policemen, grieving relatives and even survivors who simply passed me by purely by chance. "Hello, I'm Alex from the BBC" – even I have to admit that back then those six words were powerful and people knew exactly where I was from. People believed they could trust the BBC back then. Since Bashir, Huw

Edwards and Savile – I'm not sure anyone would stop other than to pick up their kids and run off quickly. In fact, you may well get rotten tomatoes thrown at you for wasting their time and infecting their personal space with infectious noncery. In fairness the horny boss at BBC Leicester gave me time off to record this and even offered to cover my expenses. Listen, I was a mere apprentice, and the sixty-minute programme was ropey in places. But you have to admire the pure tenacity and audacity of a working-class kid who in five years had gone from Hospital Radio to independent producer and presenter for BBC Network Radio. All recorded on a mini disc player powered by batteries. How times have changed. Now all you need is an iPhone to reach 500,000,000 on YouTube via your own laptop.

My voice was still a mess and needed work, BUT the pure energy and content was only to be admired. Over the Easter after 9/11 that hour special was aired on nineteen BBC Local radio stations plus on independent wireless across the UK. If the BBC had made it, it would have needed twenty journalists, weeks of pre-production and a £100,000 budget plus travel. I did it for £2,000. I sold each bespoke hour for £100 each. How naïve hey? I didn't care. Whilst I was in New York I interviewed Ozzy and Sharon Osbourne and the kids. I went to their showbiz studios on Broadway and had a great time chatting. They were at the height of their popularity on MTV. This became very normal. Their kids Jack and Kelly were not even teenagers. We just sat like old friends. They were terribly gracious and patient. How privileged was I? I also had the smarts to request an interview with the

Duchess of York who had been due in Tower Two just an hour after the first plane hit. She was in the car and on the way to The Twin Towers when it happened. She kindly agreed to give me fifteen minutes. She told me the story that she saw her charity's doll 'Little Red' on TV. They presumed it was a baby's toy. It was in the window of the 90$^{th}$ floor of Tower Two at her New York offices. It had miraculously and incredibly survived. What an amazing story and privilege for me to have that conversation. I didn't flinch. BBC Leicester played it out on Drive Time as an exclusive prior to the special. They were over the Moon on the scoop. This sort of thing became increasingly just my average day at work. Looking back now I see how crazy it was for such a young lad to take on such mammoth productions. I just saw it as the natural sincere and right thing to do. I loved telling stories and this was the biggest story for decades in global history. It touched me greatly. I do hope that my compassion came across on-air.

Shortly after that I did LIVE cover shifts at BBC Leicester on weekends, but it was like wading through drying tarmac. Such ponderous, dull, soul destroying, fake 'nice' radio and phoney baloney content. I couldn't wait to leave this pitifully outdated waste of public money from day one I couldn't work out its function. This is no reflection on the staff, all very nice people – nice doesn't have anything to do with talent! A breed of insufferable journalists without an entertainment bone in their precious bodies. I didn't have a bother with any of them just like Radio Nottingham, but, Good Lord, it was like Nursing Home FM.

I did not want to have their contempt or be this boring, patronising and condescending. Well, let them get on with it in their corduroy cardigans. I'd had enough. I had to go. No one could believe I'd resigned from a STAFF BBC job intended for life with an £8k 'turn up' bonus. It meant NOTHING to me. I needed fun and sanity. I couldn't wait to leave fifty shades of grey flat shoes and blouses. There're only so many interviews you can hear about colostomy bags and cystic fibrosis! I couldn't take it. It was Suicide FM, even worse today I'm told! The old lube loving boss of Century FM wrote and said "I wondered who that upbeat and charming presenter was on air this morning? It was you!" If only I'd gone to his creepy parties and tugged his man sausage – I could be doing mid-morning on some geriatric internet station today. NEXT!!!

My future for the next decade was set. Network specials were so exciting to me. It was my unique niche, no one even attempted to compete and it paid the bills. A bit like VoR since my sabbatical – no one has had the balls, energy or commitment to give it a go. Better still I could work from home. I was twenty years ahead of Boris' WFH lockdown shit. I invented it! So, I now technically had two proper jobs – gigging and my radio specials. Anything else was a Brucie bonus. This is when I dropped another rhino sized bollock! I let my ego say 'YES!' – ignoring my brain saying 'NO!' Within days of leaving BBC Radio Leicester, I had a call from the boss of Mercia FM. This iconic Coventry station was only an hour away and they were interested in me doing cover. Uniquely they had an 'early breakfast show' 3am – 6am. Early Breakfast? Other than milkmen and hookers who has their coco-pops at 4.30am? It was effectively over nights, but I didn't care. He promised me promotion to breakfast within three months (never believe promises) and he kept his word to be fair. This fella was called Lewis and he went on to run Heart, a brilliant brand for big boned millennial women who love Chris Martin and Gary Barlow. No doubt he could spot talent and I was chuffed he gave me a shot. It was just what the doctor ordered. No snooze interviews, just pop and prattle on smiley FM. It was my first Top 40 gig and I wanted to see if I could be a disc jockey.

To be honest Coventry is about as exciting as Leicester. It's sort of the boil on the arse of Birmingham. I didn't care it was only an hour from Nottingham - 25 minutes at 2am! It meant I had all day to gig and take a nana nap in the afternoon. This schedule was actually easier than Breakfast which destroys your life entirely. I'd be home by 7am and sleep until 11am then get on with my day. Perfect – I could avoid shitty daytime TV dopes and fakes. After a couple of months, they wanted me to be 'on-air producer' to beef up Breakfast which was piss poor. Mercia was BIG but played endless Beyoncé and Justin Timberlake as I recall. It played havoc with my acid reflux. I used to sit there listening to 'best of the 80s' on my Walkman bleeding out the Blue and Take That cack on the Mercia loop. I was totally incongruous to these formats. I talked for two minutes max per hour. Enough to make you choke on your own tongue. I still hadn't learned my lesson. I hated it but it paid for my holidays. I declined the offer to move to Breakfast, it wasn't fit for purpose and I didn't want to associate myself with it. To be fair this was the very last point in Radio where you could pick and choose - so balls to it. After the Sky co-host shambles and bore fest on Century, I didn't need to sit next to another morbidly unhealthy gob on a stick to laugh like a pathological hyena at their torturous attempts at whimsey.

On the back of this three months, I had a new 'cool' demo where I was slapping on my 12 inch and pushing up my knobs to Girls Aloud and J-Lo. Liam was great about me leaving and I got identical shifts covering daytime at Wyvern and Chiltern on the back of it which suited me down to the ground. Just like BBC Radio Leicester, there was no big fall out or goodbye – I just disappeared quietly and thanked God for small Mercia's!

I immediately buggered off to Greece for two weeks with my friend Jenny and kept a 50/50 balance of holiday and work through the entire summer – which I've more or less sustained ever since. Twenty-three years old and I hadn't been affected by public life or changed at all. I was defiant. Nothing on-air outweighed or out tempted me from fun, travel, friends and family. I knew it was a very silly way to earn a living. It was all just shifts and giggles. One day I'll grow up and join the 'real world' – but not yet. This level of nonchalance pisses my colleagues off to this day. I of course couldn't give to hoots!

This was another difficult time as during Mercia my dear Uncle Ken was diagnosed with Motor Neurone Disease. This is the most evil of any condition that I've ever seen. Your loved one literally watches themselves waste away in front of your eyes. MND is violent in its attack. You hear a lot about it on TV now, but back then it was virtually unknown. Uncle Ken was my dad's twin and they couldn't be more different. He was the coach for Hucknall Town FC. This is a red flag knowing how many similar victims of this odious illness who all seem to have been very physical throughout their lives. It's called Lou Garrick's Disease in the USA after an American footballer, amongst so many others, eaten alive by this incurable 'seven-year' disease from the world of sport like most famously Scotty in the UK. It's almost as if the body has been pushed too far physically. What do I know? I'm not a doctor. I really loved my uncle Ken, but a bit like my sister, we had very little in common until I was an adult. As a kid we really didn't resonate – other than our mutual devotion to Nana, his mum. However, there was always a massive respect. To see him wither in front of my eyes was soul destroying. It's an horrific and appalling illness. Uncle Ken would be dropped off at mum's house so that he could still be at our Wednesday family tea, which we'd done fifty-two times a year since I was born thanks to Nana's tradition. As months went on, he kept falling and tripping until he was unable to come at all. I would pick him up off the ground and watch him fight for every breath. His illness ironically made us very close. He married Linda when he was in his sixties. She was a hoot, enhancing our friendship. I loved spending time with them both. Linda had a gorgeous Shih Tzu called Kato who I adored. Prior to Kato I thought a Shih Tzu was a zoo with no animals. Who knew?

On what I believed would be his final Christmas mum and I had a huge row over what to do. For the first time I said I couldn't be at home and would drive to Ken's bungalow in Clowne for his comfort. Ken couldn't get up our stairs to use the loo. It's all so unedifying and undignified. I knew in my heart it was the right thing to do. I had to do it despite the argy-bargy and ruining our Christmas. We debated it from arsehole to breakfast time for weeks. It was so heartbreaking for mum and dad as they were best friends. This was hopeless. Mum just wanted a 'normal' Christmas. The reality was unbearable. She was destroyed by her bro being eaten alive by this savage disease. I didn't handle it well. I hadn't got the dexterity to explain why I knew I had to be there. I knew he wasn't well enough to travel. Finally on Christmas Eve, dad called Linda to say that we'd all be together at theirs' where he could relax. I was over the Moon. It was perfect. I was right, Ken didn't make another Christmas. Sometimes you just have to dig your heels in, right? Thank God I did. I'll never forget that magical day.

Over Easter my phone rang with an inconsolable Linda who was hysterical. She'd come home from work to find Ken dead in his seat with Kato sat resting his head on his lifeless body. He'd literally fallen to sleep. We're told it must have been peaceful as Ken hadn't moved. A small consolation. It's a test isn't it to navigate life's highs with the devastating lows. This one was massive. I'd been there for Ken for years as had all my family. This was a dagger to the heart, especially for dad. Linda wanted help NOW, inconsolable, waiting for the ambulance but I was fifty plus miles away! I sped up the A610 for the worst night of my life. There he lay on the floor with Kato next to him as I walked in. 999 made her put him on the floor. Dreadful. As you probably know, I'm a doggy man and my heart bled more for Kato than myself in that moment. Kato's dad had passed away and in failing health himself at fifteen, I couldn't wait to hug the dog – but Linda first. What do you say? No words can help. Finally, the undertaker came and with true compassion took Ken away for the final time.

My stomach is in knots re-living and re-telling this story. I haven't thought about this in fifteen years. It's still gut wrenching. Linda came into Ken's life through a mutual friend called Robert. He has passed now, as has Linda. Fack me they're all dead! Take me now, this is too much. I'm like the fooking grim reaper of publishing. Anywho…....Linda was a little bit too much for some people as she was confident and great fun. I'm sure people say the same about me. I loved her for being so house proud with an air of Mrs Bouquet. She was loud, OTT at times, a party person (great cook) and liked the finer things in life. Ken had a few bob, but I have to believe her intentions were as sincere as his. I don't care. I grew to love her regardless – and little Kato even more. We really had some great times and I even went on holiday with them to his place in the Canaries. I'm so glad that as I grew up, I made time for Ken. Like my dad, a truly great, honest gent. But it gets worse. Much worse….

That night mum and dad left after a little food, which we all pushed around our plates. I offered to stay with Linda and tried to offer a tiny bit of comfort, not only to a grieving wife but also to a dog who had lost his dad. If you're not a doggy person you won't get this, but these little fellas get to you! I'd been Kato's uncle for almost a decade and whenever Uncle Ken and Linda went away, I was his best mate. He couldn't wait to stay. Best cuddles ever. He slept under the duvet at the bottom of the bed in the winter. He snored like a trucker with a flat nose and bulgy eyes identical to Kay Burley……just less aggressive and defensive. The night that Ken passed, before we went to bed, I cuddled Kato on the floor in his basket as picking him up wasn't easy for a Silvertop Shih Tzu with arthritis now far too fragile to jump on a bed. I kissed him goodnight and gave Linda a hug, both of us crying and I went to the spare room to pretend to sleep. At 4am Linda ran into my room hysterically shouting that Kato was having a fit. She screamed so loud with devastated desperation. I'll never forget it. Haunting. I ran into her room to do 'something' but I was useless, I lay on the floor for more than an hour with Kato, stroking him before he settled. Linda was inconsolable. She got in the bed in the spare room as she couldn't bear to return to her own bedroom knowing what all of this meant. I just cuddled up next to a grieving doggy that had, after his dad's death, literally lost the will to live. I later had this exact feeling when I interviewed the ambivilacious fella from One Direction. Very light on her feet!

At 9am I carried Kato to the vet. I knew what was coming. Linda wouldn't go. I had to make the decision myself. Alone I stood there balling as the injection went in and Kato slowly went to sleep. How the fack was I going to tell Linda? I literally felt an electric shock from my toes to the tip of every hair on my head with exasperation.

I drove home in floods, drained and dazed by the last twenty-four hours. Linda greeted me on the drive. She knew. In one dark 24 hours she had lost her husband and her dog - her two best friends. How could life be so cruel? She was now totally alone. This was the darkest day of both of our lives. My father had lost his twin, mum adored Ken, my sister in her beautifully demure way remained stoic but broken and none of us knew what to say or do. I can't be doing with platitudes. This is where family comes into its own. The night Ken passed I had a show at Tibshelf Village Hall. I think it is still the only show I've ever cancelled (with two hours' notice) in my twenty-five-year career. I had no choice. Family comes first. My dad is such a hero and never faltered or allowed his despair to show. He had an indescribable connection to his brother so how could his life ever be the same again? I can't even begin to imagine the pain. I'll never forget how brave he was for us all. What a man! Only recently do I tell my old dad that I love him every time we speak. He needs to know!

Kato was in the footwell of my car in a box, Linda was on autopilot and now the plans began for the funeral. The next day

Linda wanted to say goodbye in the funeral home with Ken laid out. She did something I struggle to forgive even now. I'd made it clear I did not want to see Ken in a coffin under any circumstances. I wanted to remember him in the nineties as the fearless and awesome athlete that he was. He'd come home drenched in sweat having run miles. Another RED FLAG for MND. I drove her to the funeral home and she said, "will you walk me to the door?" When I got there, she did a disgraceful thing and pulled me in by the hand, embarrassing me into silence and forced me to accompany her into the centre for ten toes up. So naughty. NEVER do that to another person. Classless, even at a time like this. Grief is so personal and not a competition. I've seen the very best and the very worst in people over death. It's amazing how differently people react. I did forgive Linda, she wasn't herself, but I'll never get that vision out of my head. Today I would have the confidence to refuse but back then I was too polite believe it or not. I had of course been surrounded by a lot of 'stiffs' in BBC Local Radio – but this one hurt. Another one of those tough life lessons. It's times like this you wish you were a heartless orphan!

The funeral came and went. An amazing turn out which was a celebration. More recently I find any excuse to be busy for funerals. I literally book a gig in for free to get out of them. Can't stand them. It's amazing how people disappear when illness lands, yet out they pop for a vol-au-vent and sausage roll with talks of endless fun times before asking about the will. With Nana and Ken no longer with us, the family was never the same again if I'm honest. This is all getting Les Misérables isn't it?! Empty chairs and empty tables, sums up life for us all. The passing of Ken and Kato profoundly moved me. I'd never seen such unthinkable illness take someone so quickly whilst they watched themselves suffer. Equally I'd never seen anyone dead before, other than Nana. MND is evil and wicked, that's the worst of it. If they were bonkers and in a care home you can almost cope, but knowing they're living this corrosion in real time is heartbreaking. Life goes on, right? Of course. We have no choice….

By now my two cousins Lee and Ross were growing up and I used to love to take them on trips to the seaside and days out in the car. I remembered how fun this was for me in America with my older cousins, so I went to a lot of effort to make regular plans. Two weeks after Ken passed Ross was in the back of my very cool £10,000 Punto with a red roof (just like it's owner) – and he said "you're getting old, you've got a bald patch" – I laughed it off and thought he was being funny. Being an early twenties male, I couldn't stop thinking about Ross's 'gag' that I might look like Grant Mitchell by the weekend, so when I got home, I did the double mirror trick to have a look. There was a two-inch round hole of bald skin to the top. This was not male pattern baldness, but I knew it was not good. Within two weeks my whole head was covered in holes to the point I couldn't cover it anymore. I had to shave all of my hair off. Only then did I realise that having ginger hair is better than having no hair at all! I was beside myself. Inconsolable. I didn't look like me. No one could believe it. I'm normally far too hirsute to wear a baseball cap and I looked a right Bobby Dazzler in a dear stalker. My whole life I'd made jokes about having a rusty roof (and a damp basement). It was galling to lose it all and be a slap head overnight. In one foul swoop of the clippers, I'd gone from a matinee idol (I do little in the evenings) to a Notts Corrupt Police henchman. Oh, the shame and indignity! I had to move away! The embarrassment was literally unbearable – so I did.

I went to my doctor who couldn't be sure but thought it was alopecia. It eventually spread to my entire head – gone overnight virtually. Everyone was worried. Playing the 'big man' was over. I couldn't hide this with a bobble hat and a few one-liners. I was the new Gail Porter but no one wanted to see my naked fat arse on the side of Big Ben……or small Ben for that matter! This was my bodies way of telling the world I'd had enough stress. It was a clear reaction to losing Ken and having to put down Kato.

Two massive angels in my life haven't been mentioned yet and they are mum and dad's two best friends - Sam and Dorothy were fantastic – I adored them for a variety of reasons. Both were schoolteachers and a lot of fun to be around. So smart and interesting. Both were amazing cooks and had a huge dining room to entertain. It was so grown up and sophisticated as a kid to join them for their fabulous home cooked meals when generously invited for a Saturday night soirée. I thought 'I hope one day I'll be able to do this' and I did. Most importantly they shared my love and passion for music. They'd known me all of my life. They could see I was a card. I think they like my unique spirit. Sam was so concerned about my hair loss he paid for me to see a Harley Street specialist. I was right, I christened my new Harry Hill head as Alexpecia. Sadly, there is no cure or treatment. It is what it is and fate would determine if it would come back.

I was beside myself; my identity was gone. I hated performing bald, I felt naked, not funny and soulless like an anorexic Matt Lucas…. just less lefty and annoying. I literally felt I'd lost my USP and character overnight. Even I didn't recognise me anymore and I certainly didn't want to be seen by punters LIVE, so it was time for radio to call again! Fortunately, Alexpecia doesn't affect your voice so no one on radio noticed. Isn't it ironic that when I got fed up with radio the LIVE gigs saved me, but now I needed 'anonymity' again, the wireless would spare my blushes until I hopefully recovered. Strange things happen for a reason they say. In fact, three back-to-back radio gigs came up whilst I was follicly challenged. I was used to the old chestnut 'we think you're brilliant and would love to work with you.' By 2005 I'd worked out this was a euphemism for 'we'll pretend we love you, sign on the dotted line and we'll change you.' I'd become one of the coerced battered wives you see on the news at ten. You may have gathered I'm not really big on change. I haven't spent my entire life dedicated to my act and learning my craft to have 'know it all' dopes in suits tell me what is and isn't funny - especially when these drones couldn't pull a laugh out of their droopy and highly stretched arseholes. The only people who decide 'funny' is the audience. Full stop! How are these people even qualified to comment.

In life we're tested and literally what doesn't kill you does (eventually) make you stronger! Often, we don't know it at the time. These gigs were a baptism of fire. The best thing was for me to go far away, pray my hair would grow back and then return LIVE! At this point we didn't even know if my hair would come back – ever. If it did it would take months……for some it's game over. A new station was launching in South Wales called Scarlet FM. The owner sold me a lie from day one. It was part of a group of stations along the south coast and based in Llanelli. The irony is that just eight years later I sold out a club twice in this fantastic little town with VoR LIVE! They assured me that they were going to spend money on the launch and I would be supported. I didn't really care as I just needed to escape home. It was fabulous timing and the money was fine. I'd been given a glowing reference from a man I met at Century who later said "that guy's a star, one day I'll be as big as him" – weird thing for a fella to say who was already doing the job for decades but I took the compliment and I was grateful.

We agreed a contract and I rented a house in Burry Port. This place was famous for Amelia Earhart landing the first transatlantic flight from Canada. I loved it by the coast. So relaxing and beautiful. One day I'd love to retire to the sea. It brings back memories of family holidays and days out. These days it's an overflow sewer of course. It was like stepping back to the 1970's. Nothing was modern, the people were salt of the earth and time had literally stood still. It made Mansfield look like Monte Carlo. I treated myself to a new bed, washer and sofa to save schlepping it from Nottingham and off I went. The terrace house was nice but I hated being away from home. I wore a cap and no one knew any different so didn't care. I was finally totally at ease. I felt like a drug dealer in a cap – they thought I was trying to be cool. Such is life! I should not have trusted the boss who was a typical radio snake. He wanted a launch presenter to make a stink knowing there was no budget to sustain my modest pay packet further than a few months. What a shithouse! I should have stayed in a B&B and just taken the money and run. I was being set up to fail, but little did this haemorrhoid harasser realise the second I was follicly blessed I'd be off anyway. From day one I knew I was being facked but I didn't care. I'd invested in Sky so I'd got Boobstation from midnight regardless. The 'radio station' was in fact a caravan/portacabin at the back of a school in Llanelli. I'm not working you from behind – my garage has more glamour and safer foundations. I couldn't believe my eyes. It was laughably shit. BUT I was just grateful to be on £30k and away from glaring eyes and little old ladies spitting on their hanky and polishing my bald head. Instead, I was now working for a bellend polisher in the arse-end of Porthcawl! I said to him one day, "what do you say to the Welsh boys on your mucky Welsh dating websites?" He said "Clydebank and Prestatyn!" This was still pre-social media so I didn't have to worry about the medicated jealous nutters on Twatter back then. I could go about my business in peace. These days it would be impossible to pull off such a stunt. The Wigatha Christies would out you by teatime.

On day one at Scarlet FM, they finally revealed I was the <u>only</u> presenter on the station and the rest would come from Pembrokeshire. I was literally the only man in the shed on wheels. The creepy and slimy boss would never be seen again. Not kidding you. This odious balloon knot licker headed for zee hills in a dark web of deceit. Total stitch-up from yet another boss who I've since learned has more skeletons in his closet than a Halloween party. They never intended this to be a stand-alone station. They simply needed a gobshite to launch it. So, every day I was walking the tight rope to being sacked, once I'd caused a big enough stir. It was only a question of when. Knowledge is power! You gotta be a step ahead. Why can't they just tell you the truth? Man up! I bet they've had a lot of 'men up!'

As ever the local press couldn't wait to pounce on me. What is it with Journos from tatty rags jealously destroying others who actually have talent, a career and ambition? I of course milked the headlines. Shushy! they think this stuff is damaging! I learned a decade ago to court the press, milk the free publicity and own all negativity as it makes people more curious and intrigued about you. Nothing drives business like controversy and curiosity - ask Trump! The public aren't blind and daft. They'll decide if you are or are not worth tuning in for. I made the odd front page for 'distasteful' gags and comments, which I repeated LIVE on-air every twenty minutes, and told the audience, "so now you don't need to waste 50p on that chip shop toilet roll, do you?" I'm told they were furious. Listen what's good for the goose is good for the gander! All pathetic journalists want is reverence and respect. Whoopsie, they've come to the wrong guy. The paper went mad 'how dare he?' I dare, trust me. The next day they got five locals to slag me off in a two-page centre spread. I thank you. Money can't buy PR!

Within days, I had the retarded editor hook line and stinker. They would write about me at least three times a week to 'close me down.' Blimey history keeps on repeating doesn't it! Every gag they deliberately misinterpreted for another moronic headline. Trump is right, you can't believe a word you read in the papers. It's fake news as it's their agenda and opinion of a story – that ain't impartial! They're a disgusting breed who pick a side and it's almost never the right one! A righteous breed of know it all's who in my experience are totally devoid of all humour, joy and humanity and have a closet bigger than Schofield's broom closet! And worst still they live like pigs, have no class, and lifestyles that could make headlines in their own papers far outweighing those they're trying to disgrace! Point a finger, and three point back, dear! Oh, they don't like it when you look at them! Sickos – but fabulous for my PR. I learned to play them at their own game and by 2012 became hunter turned gamekeeper. My deposit on my house was thanks to the fake news press - a medium that will be dead any time soon! Newspapers are the dinosaurs of the media – more redundant than Matt Handcock's agent. I wouldn't use the Guardian in a litter tray! One day I did a gag about the front page exposing a 'dogging' beach for people on the other bus. Police had arrested two men enjoying horizontal refreshment in the sand (that's got to chafe) so I read it out on air followed by a few over the top camp old gags. The officer said, "you're going down" – one of the fellas said, "well move the truncheon out of the way then." I did a good five minutes "have you got crabs?" one asked "no they're lobsters, it's posh round here." Copper said, "I'll bang you up" he said, "we haven't even had dinner yet!" etc etc etc……..

Once again, I'd tickled the tiger. The police turned up at the station investigating a report of a hate crime against people who are light on their feet. Can you imagine?! I'M NOT JOKING! As God is my witness. Never mind press and parliamentary paedos……this is a priority! Nothing has changed in two decades, has it? These people are devoid of life. It's a game to wipe you out. Thankfully the two twelve-year-old officers saw the funny side. Guess who was on the front page the following day in 'DJ Police Shame.' You just have to rise above it – almost as if it was a MSM set-up in collusion with the local cuntstables to get me sacked. Even back then I only saw the police and press as laughably stupid. You <u>cannot</u> take either seriously.

This went on for three months and one day the weasel who hired me sent his pitiful Happy Shopper line manager to stutter his way through why it's not working. 'Yes, it is.' The truth was the show was 'a breath of fresh air' – God even I'm sick of this line now. My 'fresh air' normally ends up smelling like an abattoir after Ed Balls has dropped one. I'd served my purpose, now I was off. I was relieved. Scarlet FM was going nowhere. South Wales obviously wasn't as bad for home sickness as Kenya but it wasn't nice. Four and a half hours to Nottingham was impossible weekly but I did get visitors which I loved. Sam and Dorothy came, mum and dad, Jenny, friends Pauline and Eileen who all gave me the chance to tour the stunning South Wales coast which I have to admit did feel like the end of the earth. There's a beautiful train ride along the sea front. There're dolphins close to the shore, magical. Incredible natural beauty. Pembroke is so lovely. I did get to explore South Wales and for that I'm grateful. Other than that, it was a fixer upper. I needed to get back to my people.

As for that duplicitous dufus, he sacked me with immediate effect on the three-month anniversary to the day and guess what... they NEVER had a live presenter on the station from Llanelli EVER again. It was now just simulcast as part of a network of stations. "We're not paying off your contract" he said. I replied, "We'll see about that!" This is the crappy tactic of media Mogadons who have to waggle their willies and piss all over you – "Are you threatening me" clay balls said. "No dear it's a promise - I'll see your woeful arse in court" I said. Despicable. This is not rare. Most presenters just walk away because they want to work again without controversy or a reputation for being difficult. I never had such insecurities. This is how bosses get away with relentless sexual abuse. I couldn't care less. A deal is a deal. I think it's odious to treat people like this. Even as a twenty-five-year-old lad I wasn't having it. Charlatans the lot of them. Well, it's time to go to make my debut in the Magistrates Court!

Secretly I was relieved to go home, I hated being away from my family and friends. I phoned the landlord, and she was amazing. It was re-rented in a week and I sold EVERYTHING for £1000. I didn't want any of the stuff. I just wanted my life back. I win. The girl who moved in was returning home from university and literally got a new home for a grand. It was my pleasure. I couldn't wait to go back up the M5. Best drive of my life. The lefties bang on about 'mental health.' No wonder so many give up and end up rocking in a corner, medicated or tossing themselves off an NCP car park with a piece of rope between their sphincter! BTW, you won't find any 'pro' in the biz who doesn't have horror stories like this. Few will admit the truth publicly as they want to be in the 'gang.' They can keep their glitter ball I'd rather be on the dole. Theatre and TV is equally as bad if not worse. It's brutal. I don't pander to liars, cheats and bullies.

The good news was that nearly four months had passed. Ken and Kato's passing was fading in ferocity and thank God my hair was slowly growing back. Firstly, colourless and then a month or so later back to my rusty roof as if nothing had happened. That Christmas I went back to touring in Nottingham and nobody knew the difference, an absolute miracle. Things happen for a reason, right? Thank God my hair came back – I'd have had to have my posters reprinted or wear a merkin! Also, you gotta have a gimmick. My hair made me stick out and memorable. I now count my blessings every day (follicly). They say Alexpecia is brought on by shock and stress. It's hard to argue. Repeat after me, 'ginger hair is better than no hair!' A couple of weeks later I filed papers at Cardiff County Court for breach of contract. I wisely self-represented. ZERO legal costs. I was smart. Legal is a swizz. 99% con artistes, self-serving and entirely profiting themselves. You win and lose at the same time all to bankrupt yourself to buying them a new kitchen in the wig and robe profession. Balls to that, I did it myself. Months later the day arrived and they hadn't filed a defence and I could have my day in court. It lasted twelve minutes. The weasel boss sent his stuttering yes man to the court who was literally clueless. "Why haven't you paid Mr Belfield?" the judge asked, "I don't know" answered the dope. Hopeless. The sheer arrogance to turn up without an excuse let alone a defence. A quarter of an hour later I was in my car with the full pay-off for the get out plus my costs. Ahhhhh Now I get it – three months of shit and £10k to go on holiday with. I win. I truly don't know how people can be so heartless and shameless. Pitiful but very common. Do twats have a conscience? Asking for a friend…...

The next two gigs didn't end much better either. Why on earth do we put ourselves through this crap? The next cab off the rank (wank) was even more preposterous. BFBS (British Forces Broadcasting Service) in Germany. Oy vey! I don't know how these people find me, but they do. 'We want a star' – no you don't! You want a compliant, homogenised yes man. Here we go AGAIN!!!!...

I went down to their HQ just inside the M25 in a tiny village called Royston Vasey. It was ludicrous, worse than the BBC for over staffing and a budget that would make Al-Fayed's eyes water. Not one had any talent. It was all so formal and deathly dull. Think Sunday Brunch on Channel 4. Why did I agree to go? In my head I thought it would be exciting and also noble to entertain the troops. Jim Davidson was in the back of my mind with all of the unbelievable work he's done around the world selflessly entertaining our heroes for decades. This couldn't have been further from the reality at our military's radio station. It was another monolith that had not moved on. It looked, felt and even smelt like 1970s BBC (think Savile's cigar and shell suit) and the bosses were identically as insufferably corporate. Autistic to the core and not willing to change. I lasted two days but the argy-bargy that ensued was extraordinary! BFBS budget is mind-blowing. In a 24/7 digital world I'm not even sure it serves <u>ANY</u> purpose sending radio DJs to places like Afghanistan, Iraq, The Falklands or in my case, their biggest base in Germany. Why does it matter? You could pay for two soldiers for the cost of shipping out one Smashy or Nicey. If you've ever seen 'The Book of Mormon' – I'm 'that' guy. I hoped for Orlando or Barbados and ended up in Hanover! The money was good and like Africa the package was even better. They gave me a house, a re-location budget and then did the most astonishing thing – they had professional removals people come to the house and hand wrap <u>every</u> single thing from ornaments to knives and forks, no joke. This was then packed by four bemused fellas who stuck it all in a lorry along with my car (yep, my actual car) and off they drove to the land of frankfurter. I was gobsmacked. They then flew me in two weeks later, with my life waiting for me unpacked in a home which I'm told cost about £6,000 – <u>of your public money</u> given to the removals people. Outrageous.

By now mum, dad, sister and friends realised I and my career were clearly never going to be ordinary or without controversy. The dramas always landed eventually but I never flinched. I just picked myself up, went on holiday and found the next gig. It was exciting. Maybe one day I'd write an autobiography and tell someone about it. I doubt I'll ever have the time. A bit like Pleasuring His Majesty - I cannot take this seriously and can't wait to get out, carry on and take the piss mercilessly out of my kidnapping and hostage situation. My constitution and strength are and were unwavering. It was another long goodbye to family and friends but somehow this was just another 'tara-a-bit' and like Kenya and Wales it would be over before the Christmas turkey and its parson's nose had defrosted. I wasn't wrong either. Little did we know I'd be home before the boxes had even been unpacked properly in Baden-Baden! How did I fall for this again? You cannot be hired by one person with vision and then managed by dopes with the personality of a root vegetable a few hundred miles away. I flew out of East Midlands direct on a Fokker 50 with KLM. I was collected at the airport by a lady boss. They're breeding! She was big boned, bubbly and exceedingly ordinary. Think that vicar woman from Gogglebox. She kindly drove me to her home for dinner and it was great. A lovely family. I then spent a couple of days settling into my three bedroomed home ten minutes from the MOD base. Once I'd moved into my new abode the piano set up first of course, then the bedroom, then the kitchen. It was depressingly average but spotlessly clean and of significant girth – a bit like my gentlemen's area. I made it my current abode and would go down the bar with the lads and their families. It was swinger's heaven. I never left my barracks without a pack of wet wipes don't you worry about that. These military wives bang like a barn door……..so I'm told.

On Monday morning I went to the Hanover barracks, passed security and realised this was my dress rehearsal for prison. I'm convinced the two regimes are identical. It's all about control, compliance, blind faith, reverence and bewildering respect. You'll never win trying to beat either corrupt system. Arguably though, prison in the UK is a holiday camp compared to the army - oh and the luxury we're in isn't extended to cannon fodder in the military never fear. I went through the locked gates and more locked doors and my heart sank. Honestly, I feel freer in jail than that hostage dump. It was cold and heartless, just like Clive Myrie sitting in Huw Edward's swivel chair. I was never going to thrive, be happy or grow in such cold antiquated and regimented conditions. Why didn't I learn my lesson in the Welsh caravan?

Yep, this novice Gobshite had done it again. Another gig totally unsuitable but I do wonder now if this was all about my learning curve and education? Everything happens for a reason, right? How many more times am I going to say that infuriating platitude. I didn't go to Uni – I'm not a Lib Dem wanting to chop my cock off – but all of these 'experiences' did give me infinite experience and ultimately backbone and resilience to make me the man I am today. I sat down in the manager's office where he played the very same demo I was hired over. My demo tape was the best (or worst) bits of my now ten-year career. This Gollum looking suit went through link by link telling me what was and was not acceptable. No joke – 60% was distasteful to him. VERY bad start. These guys made me puke. I couldn't hide my palpable contempt. This wasn't my first rodeo. I literally couldn't take it seriously. At what point in hiring 'known' talent do you accept you can't ask the dentist to have a look at your wife's cystitis? It's like marrying a big boned bird with blonde hair, palatial thighs the size of a 56-inch TV and on the honeymoon say 'Now can you please turn into Victoria Beckham.' Who in their right mind would want that? Not me dear! Get another kebab and chips down you dear!

I DON'T GET IT! To me this is like hiring a plumber and then asking him to sort out your electrics. Ridiculous. But this happens daily in showbiz. It was very personal too. These sauerkraut megalomaniacs don't understand how personal this stuff gets. One shithead at the BBC once said, "why do you use that silly voice?" Silly voice? How very dare you! A bit rich coming from a TV and Radio presenter who pretends to be married but spends his nights in Manchester pizza parlours on Grindr popping into hotels to nosh off a desperate trucker! My vocal gymnastics is a comedy vehicle to make a gag funny, you senseless fruit! How do you explain this to a retarded pen pusher and corporate sardine? Impossible. I knew I was doomed and I hadn't even done my first link. I went on air at 2pm that afternoon feeling crestfallen and deflated BUT 100% gagging for laughs and approval from the punters – that's <u>all</u> that matters. But I wouldn't bet your housekeeping on it - that I'll still be here by the time the kettle's boiled! This became my default position. I intended going out in a blaze of glory don't you worry about that! I knew it was going to be a car crash – so nothing to lose. Here we go! I wasn't even twenty minutes into the show when the studio door slammed open and a little Hitler pounded through screaming "no callers, we don't do callers." I beg your parsnips? What the actual fackdupery? I mean where do you begin to argue with this foolishness? "Oh and no jingles!" it spat at me. It was over, I wasn't willing to go through this insanity again. "In my office at 5pm" the vile, nasty, talentless, brainwashed bore chuntered. At 5pm I said goodbye on day one and left the studio and literally left the building. The next ten minutes of my life was like a scene from a movie. I swear on my mother and Doddy's life this is 100% true. Hooley Dooley, you won't believe this…….

I wasn't going to any debrief or meeting about my act to be humiliated by this third Reich gas inspector. I walked straight past their dungeon in case he switched the oven on to re-heat his bratwurst! The spiteful BFBS management control freaks, now in a pack of three, started chasing me down the corridor. "Allleeexxx" – like Diane Abbotcus on smack. I started to run for my life. I felt like Tom Cruise in Mission Impossible. I went through a door to the stairs and they started to run behind me – I shit you not! This was ludicrous. I genuinely felt I was running for my life – so silly now but it got dramatic. I was in a barracks/prison – where was I going to go? I just knew I did not want to say one word to these turds but if I could reach my car, I was safe. I'd lock the doors and they could fack right off. I'd sleep there if necessary to avoid ingesting their halitosis that could ground a flock of Luftwaffe. I don't think people realise how sensitive turns are and how profoundly we'll fight to protect our acts. We're not programmable machines like a jukebox that can change content on demand for a fiver in the slot. Balls to that. I was done. Just because we're gobby and rock solid on-air doesn't mean off air we're hard as nails. It's called an _act_ for a reason! I just kept running! I could not engage with these military morons and Reichstag imbeciles under any circumstances. I felt exactly like Bruce Willis in Die Hard; would I save the 747 with my wife on board before those terrorists crashed it? (Not being too dramatic, am I?).

As God is my witness, I ran out of the huge Army building and dashed across the forecourt to my car. I frantically unlocked it, my heart now pounding, desperately wanting to escape these arsehole assassins. The door opened. I jumped in. They were yards away and BOOM – central locking worked! My only victory would be _not_ to say one word. The relief was palpable. What now? I promise you, the big boned lass with a face that looked like she'd had an incident with a shovel and a sack of burning coal literally prostrated herself over the bonnet like a stray great tit in the Dartford Tunnel. Right hand up to the Bigman this is true! Like a scene from an armed robbery in New York City in the fifties – this daft cow screamed "In my office now." I mean, I ask you?!!? Who do these twats think they are? Respect? Reverence? I think NOT! Bollocks to her – I'm off! The glue on my laminated pass hadn't even dried and this low rent Rosemary Shrager was ordering me to the chambers like a school boy. What next? Sending me to my bedroom like Ann Frank?

I truly could not believe my eyes. Now I had a choice. Give in or drive off. Like a Tuk Tuk in the Maasai Mara with a bull elephant on the bonnet, this was not going to be easy. I started the engine and shouted "MOVE!" – she didn't. "Get in my office now Alex." What a piece of work! "I'm leaving, phone my lawyer, now move you blancmange sized bison buffoon!" I replied. I started edging forward slowly. The jumbo thighed mammoth still thought this was a joke. I revved the engine and she finally moved. I sped off like a scene from the Fast and Furious and made my way to the security gate. This heifer literally wobbled behind me waving her arms like a scene from the Vicar of Dibley when the salad dodger chased the ice-cream van and fell into the puddle of crap. Security let me out and I had freedom. Phewww! I drove straight home and started packing. I was done! WTAF. You couldn't write this – well I am......

An hour later the RMP (Royal Military Police) popped round for a chat. I welcomed them in for a cup of tea. As we <u>now</u> know, you NEVER open the door to the bizzies, let alone answer their corrupt questions to the cuntstables. We sat in my lounge and they couldn't believe my story. I also reminded them that I was not military and they had no jurisdiction over me. They asked to see my contract and were very nice. I'd used Gordon Astley's trick from Radio 106 and had already emailed my (pre-written) resignation to London which I showed them informing them in no uncertain terms what a shithouse of ineptitude I'd endured and that I resigned on day one. So, they had as much power over me as the mainstream media have over Trump! "I'd rather retire or chew my nipple off without an anaesthetic than ever set foot in that hideous radio station again." I told them. They agreed parting company was best. "How could you hire me and then send me to managers who were to radio what Katie Price is to parenting and safe driving?" By now, ten years into my unbelievable career this drama was only to be expected. I was neither shaken, stirred nor upset let alone surprised by my 007 escape. I called mum and dad and told them to put the kettle on. Dad laughed. They were thrilled I'd be home for Christmas and not remotely phased by this lunacy. They knew BFBS wouldn't (and couldn't) last but politely let me 'follow my dreams.' Not once have they ever said, 'don't do it.' Maybe I wish they had! I wish I'd got this on video. Comedy gold.

Another dear friend in my life was a peculiar but hugely loyal pal called Justin. We'd been at school together and he was an oddball, different, unique and ostracized by most because of being a one-off. They just couldn't work him out. Justin had the kindest heart and was one of the funniest people I'd ever met. He famously described a teacher – to her face – as having 'a brain like a sieve and a brassiere to match!!' Who thinks of that at twelve years old? He adored his grandparents and didn't care about being cool. He didn't like Puff Daddy or Fats and Small, he kept his grandfather's legacy alive with his penchant for Elkie Brooks and Matt Monro – quite peculiar for a teenager in the nineties. He was so generous with his time and loved to live vicariously through my ridiculous career and success. Justin would literally drive me anywhere and I'll never forget his kindness. We all need a selfless friend like this.

By now I was flying to America two or three times a year. He thought nothing of driving me to Heathrow having a coffee in Costa at Terminal 5 and driving straight back home alone. Who would do that? I of course took care of him with petrol money and dinners but what he loved was being my road manager and ultimately LIVE roadie. He delighted in driving to clubs all over the country or to theatres to interview stars. He'd carry and set up my gear and was my eyes and ears. This business is riddled with loose lips. What people say when you leave the room is astonishing. He truly was a rock, confidante and a good mate. I picked up the phone from Hanover in <u>Germany</u> and he answered and said, "you need a lift home already?" We laughed so loud. "You won't believe what these daft cants have done big man…..." – What a friend! The next day he hired a van and drove all the way to Germany BY HIMSELF to collect me. Unbelievable solidarity. He loved the drama, dined out on the car chase story and we laughed all the way home making it a truly one-off adventure that could only happen to me. What is extraordinary is that Justin thought holidays were a waste of money and had never left the UK EVER! He just loved living his 'quiet' life and taking me here and there and hearing my stories. It took almost a day all in all to get home. He loved it. This was his fortnight in Mauritius! I was naturally over the Moon to be home. Thank you, Justin. What a mate! We've lost touch in recent years after he became a cuntstable for Notts Police. You think you know a guy hey?…….

As ever BFBS tried to shaft me on the contract. Nothing new there. I sued and they wisely made it go away. What a bunch of characters! After Justin signed for the police in 2010, he changed completely. Unrecognisable. Almost as if he'd taken an arsehole pill. Like the light went out. His spirit was drained from him, and we just drifted apart. I can't be part of that skullduggery as I saw the dark cloud of the institutional cloak of brainwashing entirely strip him of all his common decency, moral compass and senses. That's what friends are for! I'm sure by now he's got tattoos up his neck, fist bumps instead of handshakes and calls everyone 'fella.' I shudder. Secretly I know he was weak and lost. The Army, Police and Civil Service Serpants empower and coerce lost souls into feeling important. You sell your soul the second that contract is signed. I didn't want any part of his new mafioso life. At the same time, he changed his name by deed poll. Curious hey? A new fake identity for a new fake life. I wish him well.

So, I was once again back on the road touring, in fact no one had even noticed I'd left. I'd learned not to cancel the diary 'just in case.' No flies on me. I did a short stint on 'Touch FM' in Coventry - the competitor to Mercia who I'd worked for years before. This station was unremarkable, but I did get off to a good PR start when I phoned a florist LIVE on-air to have a wreath delivered to our competitor's Breakfast Show! It was not personal. It was a cheap gag for publicity. The message read 'Wishing you good luck in your new careers.' They didn't see the funny side. The local paper splashed the story on the front page. 'Shock Jock 'dead flowers' threat shocker' – oh grow up! Where has the fun gone? Judging by that pair I'd be amazed if they didn't roll my rhododendrons up and smoke them.

This one did make me laugh and I had a hoot on air milking it. My punters loved it. A good old-fashioned tease that OUTRAGED the dreaded lefties. Again, I wasn't managed by the Australian head-hunter who signed me up. I'll never learn, right? Radio was in intensive care by now and I had to learn my lesson. By now I cared even less than the bloodbath accountants stabbing the life out of the wireless medium. Money ran out and they became networked so off I went AGAIN! No bother, it was only fifty minutes from home so this dosh kept me in Vodka and Cherry Max for a few months.

Whilst I was at Touch FM, I'd been made aware that Chris Evans on BBC Radio 2 had been given a new sound and blow my bloomers this flame haired freak suddenly had a very familiar sound. With identical gospel sounds, a jingle appeared with the lyrics "rise and shine sleepy head, jump right up 'n' get out of bed" – the identical riff I'd penned a year earlier. This went on and on. Chris was nothing to do with this, but his jingle producer put a video out bragging 'it just came to me in a flash – the words just appeared.' Look, we're all pilferers of prized ideas but for the love of God don't claim it's yours if you 100% clearly nicked it. I made a YouTube video with my jingle next to his with the producer bragging it was 'easy-peasy.' What non-creep would ever say 'easy-peasy' anyway – gives me the collywobbles! Two days later my phone rang from the lawyers of Chris's production company. "We hear you're going to sue us, there's been a mistake and we clearly can't argue those are our lyrics or original idea." They knew they were facked. As you'll see with court, you can't win. A fake sorry and politician's apology can be bought for £250,000 from what I've seen so rollocks to that. They agreed to remove the video of the hack stealing my glory. They said they'd put an apology in writing and I said I'd consider my next move.

Obviously, this is annoying and revealing but honestly, is it really worth the stress and costs to win a few quid in court? There's no material damage. Copyright is incredibly hard to prove regardless - a bit like disproving the notion that you made some crackpot loony tune suicidal, how do you prove you both didn't have the identical thought – or at least prove who had it first? I would have won a moral victory but lost thousands for a pyrrhic victory no one cared about. Only a prized sanctimonious, supercilious twat would go to court to lose money to score a goal. Instead, I walked away and spent my money on Vegas strippers. I WIN! The video about that jingle remains on YouTube today! Another row was with the freakishly plain looking and marble mouthed Dynamo. This lanky streak of piss is to entertainment what Rylan is to dentistry. I put up a video exposing his plagiarism of the world class illusionist Criss Angel. The shit hit the fan. Showbiz and his team couldn't believe I had the audacity not to like this Herman Munster with a magic circle – red raw apparently!!! I don't care I say it as it is. I was thrilled to hear Dynamo had disappeared in 2025. Not a moment too soon!

This is FINALLY when my career got EXCITING!

Whilst all of this malarkey and foolishness was going on around me, I still had an air of nonchalance as I simply couldn't take the industry, let alone the people in it seriously. I wanted to crack radio but I always knew my forever goal was much bigger and exclusive to the creeps, window lickers and crackpots who litter this unhinged and delusional craft. My plan would ultimately save me from any shenanigans by dick head wireless bosses. Even in my early twenties I knew managers and producers behaved with total impunity. It's a mafia of goons who are so ruthless they'll do whatever they have to do to protect themselves – covering up their litany of cockamamie schemes. In all forms of showbiz, you're a commodity to be used and disposed of the second you've served your purpose. Ask Caroline Flack and Liam Payne. There's a huge price for fame. There is no humanity, decency or compassion. This explains my infinite contempt for these trumped-up entertainment and media mobsters. Working for yourself removed <u>ALL</u> of this bullshitery. It would be the only thing to set me free. I was now <u>ME</u>! Loved by my punters but

HATED by the Ketamine loving luvvies, twirlies and fruit fake media mafia. The TRUTH hurts!

Whilst at Century 106 I met a dear friend called Jenny who I adored spending time with. She's one of the few people I've met who didn't piss me off – ever. I would like to think I'm a generous person but I know that I'm set in my ways. As I've got older, I've learned what I like and don't like. I would never enforce my peccadilloes on other people but I won't eat in crappy 'ping ping' microwave restaurants. I'll sit and have a drink and eat properly afterwards for example. You do what you want but don't torture me with your flights of fancy. I'm not going on holiday with screaming kids getting on my tits when I can go to Trump Doral in peace and I certainly won't sit through a show that's crap and boring simply to be polite. In the old days they'd say, 'he knows his own mind,' these days you're Putin's twin for not suffering fools gladly and you're on a terrorist list. Jenny was the first person who truly got me. We laughed at everything, never had an argy-bargy and when we'd had enough of something I'd say, 'right we're off' and she'd say, 'thank God for that.' I guess we were in sync. I still can't understand why people put up with mediocrity. Life is too short. I've left holidays halfway through if it's pissing down. I can't see the point of being miserable somewhere you don't want to be when you can be back home in your own luxury as happy as Larry or pissed off in comfort. Who is Larry BTW? So many questions.

Every penny that I earned I saved to travel and enjoy life throughout my twenties and thirties. Why? This made me very happy, fed my mind, lifted my heart and created wonderful memories. Savings and pensions are for shortsighted fortune tellers. Jenny only lived in Ripley. We were totally different people. She was an accountant by day, I was a knobhead by night but the alchemy worked. We went to Vegas and New York countless times. Spain, Egypt, Turkey, France, Cyprus, Canaries over and over again, three or four times a year. She visited all of my radio stations (before I was fired) and we laughed every time I got another gig 'how long will this one last?' Jenny died in 2019. I miss her terribly but I'm so grateful for two decades of incredible memories. Life can be terribly cruel. With her and Matt – can you see why my perspective is entirely motivated by live for today!!!

## Chapter 8

## London, My Big Break and High Court!

On the back of the new Scarlet FM and Touch FM material that I'd collected and edited I made a new much punchier demo added to the guff from Capital Kenya and my freelance work on BBC Local Dignitas. One day out of the blue the boss of Capital Gold called me. He was a much cooler type of boss, totally different to the rest for some very good reasons - namely he'd made it and had nothing to prove. He was finally the real deal, having worked with Chris Tarrant at Capital London during the heyday of radio as well as other legends stretching back to Kenny Everett. He made me feel very comfortable and for the first time confident. Andy said he could hear something unique in my cack. WOW! Could this lead to London? Well, not yet. He had local/regional stations across the UK and he needed six weeks cover in Birmingham on Breakfast to try me out. I couldn't believe my LUCK! I could drive in from my home and my schtick would finally be heard across the second city to a potential audience of five million plus punters. Meanwhile I had no costs of moving house and I could gig in the evening.

I have to admit for the first time in my life I felt totally at home at Capital Gold Birmingham. A boss who got me and directly managed me – THE KEY! It was a very friendly station to work at and £150 a show! Everyone thinks you earn millions in radio – trust me you don't, entertaining two care homes for one hour each is still way more profitable. But, to me that was a fortune. I didn't care. This show was a hoot. Radio pay hasn't gone up in twenty years. Same in nearly all departments of showbiz. Back then though £750 per week was a huge amount of money to me. Honestly, I'd have done it for nowt but don't tell my accountant.

Even today I have that millennial malarkey 'imposter syndrome' – a euphemism for 'my dad worked ten times as hard for half as much.' Again, it never sat well with me. Anyway, this gig I loved. I worked my cahoonas off to do the very best shows I'd ever presented. Located in the same offices/studios as BRMB it felt BIG! Radio should be sexy – it should be showbiz – it rarely is. For the first time I loved the music. Every song was truly a mega hit. Queen, Elton, Rod, Motown, 60's class, 70's camp and some 80's floor fillers. I bloody loved it. Uplifting and toe tapping. Not any hand ringing Adele or suicide watch Lighthouse Family. After eleven years of learning my craft, it <u>FINALLY</u> felt right. What an apprenticeship! I was prepared and ready, no messing about. This gig was the mother-load. It was still enormous across the Midlands and the switchboard was full. I was in heaven. Mama Cass 'It's Getting Better' out of the news, 'Killer Queen' next and ELO to follow. You can't fail! I was not only allowed, but actively encouraged to take the pish, mock the brainwashing, brain dead and afflicted plus ridicule those controlling this septic isle, which was all loved by the mainly 50+ audience – my favourite. No fart head whippersnappers allowed. I hate these prats more than box tickers and ANYONE who has a pronoun on their email signature. Get it in your thick head nonbinary is impossible and gender neutral is a mental illness.

I could tease and wind up the punters on their way to work and everyone loved it. This is exactly what BBC Local should be – but fails. Andy, the boss, was over the Moon and by week three the call of my life came in 'Would you like to move to London?' – Holy Mother of Jesus on a Penny Farthing – MY DREAM CAME TRUE AT TWENTY-FOUR! FINALLY! By the time the six-week summer cover ended I'd signed the contract for my dream show. 'The Late-Night Revolution' from 10pm Monday to Thursday and Saturday Breakfast from 6am. Honestly, this was singularly the most exciting time of my life, on Capital Gold Network – NATIONAL. For years I'd be travelling once or twice a week to the capital and it never got old. I still to this day marvel at the grandeur and class matched with mayhem and deafening excitement of Sickdiq's Crapital. Guess what? I'd now be working in the most exciting building in the country for radio – CAPITAL, LEICESTER SQUARE.

I'd be working for media goliath 'GCap' – later changed to Global who decimated local commercial radio when the boss admitted 'we can't find thirty good presenters' so he fired twenty-nine DJ's and networked one (TV totty) from London. Talent was irrelevant, it was all about national sales and reducing costs – the talent being nothing compared to building and infrastructure. Remember, it's show <u>BUSINESS</u>! Now almost everything is networked and there are virtually no opportunities to learn, develop and grow. You won't work if you've not got over a million Tik Tok followers which is nothing to do with your ability to broadcast. I was so lucky to get a last bite of the cherry and the education of hard knocks to hopefully storm it on national radio.

You have to FALL to rise as I've learned throughout my Humpty Dumpty career. You couldn't take on such a legendary gig without ten years of relentless radio diarrhoea to help you cope.

There was nowhere to hide. It was make or break. London was EXCITING and I lived in the moment. However, radio money was amazing in the north, but distinctly average in London even though I earned £20k more. I wanted a beautiful home where I could enjoy and share my success with everyone around me - this was more important than the gig itself. This was 2006, prices were already INSANE. I looked at a few two-bedroom flats and I found a gorgeous new build at Canary Wharf. I couldn't believe my luck, £1,800/month. What the actual fack?!?! You could buy a house in Nottingham for £1,800 + council tax. I'd barely earned £1,800 a month after tax for my entire career. Council tax in E14 was more than a week's BBC wages. Good Lord, who would ever want to live in London?

Whilst I was looking for my pad Andy put me up in the Selfridge Hotel on Oxford Street. Can you believe my luck? I was there three weeks living like a king before the flat was signed over. I even got a free set of 5* towels (shushy) which was very fortuitous. It's £300 a night, least they could do is give me a flannel. (I await the bomb squad in the STI van from Notts Corrupt Police to raid me for stolen goods!) I'd got a great deal with Capital Gold. They sent a car for me at 5.30am Saturdays and a car home at 1am during the week. This was the smartest move in the deal. Saved me a fortune! Again, I was the last generation of DJ to get such 'perks.' I still do not know how people afford to live in London. The first hour at work covers your travel and the next six hours to eat and survive. Pointless. By the end of the day you've earned 75p. Ridiculous! So, it was perfect. For the next nine months I was blinded by happiness on air. BUT off air and in the back office... guess what!

I couldn't believe it had happened again. Andy (after I'd started) allocated a pitifully inept manager to 'oversee' my programme. He was old school music radio and didn't realise his days were numbered, way before mine. He had an odious assistant who was truly the most vile and vitriolic waste of a wage I've ever encountered. 'You've had a letter who is it from?' said Mr Odious. There was a megalomania about these people akin to nonbinary Extinction Rebellion fantasist. I've never given a shit about office-politics, I only care about my three hours on air. This pisses them off even more. In fact, as my colleagues will confirm I never go in the office EVER unless under absolute duress. I learned very quickly to avoid unnecessary banter and be busy when they called. I don't do meetings, no thanks, 'I've got a gynaecological appointment, sorry about that.' I don't think I went in the office more than twice during my entire stint in the West End. I'd book all interviews after 5.01pm when they'd slithered out the door.

I genuinely LOVED the 'Late Night Revolution.' Music and stars 10pm - 11pm and a phone-in 11pm – midnight. I was 'King of the Cabbies' – a massive barometer of your success and genuine popularity with our people. Unlike anything I'd done before this station was massive! Covering Manchester, Birmingham, South Coast, London and more – it was as national as it gets. I'd joined for the launch of Sky 0121 and DAB making it even bigger and easier to listen to. Now you could hear it in quality – unlike dodgy AM – cute, but not fit for purpose. Back then there were powerful PRs who understood the power of the radio star. Video didn't kill us BTW, accountants did! I basically had my dream come true and no one said no to anything. If a star was available – I was on the list, why not – a national platform, they couldn't lose. It was intoxicating. The scale of the station finally gave me a platform to shine. Cleverly I had a deal that I owned the copyright to the stars I interviewed out of the studio so I could still flog network specials to the BBC. Owning your own gear is paramount! I knew this would end one day, so as always, I needed all of my pans still simmering outside of Capital. Another bonus of being 'networked' is the invitations you get.

I was the Bonnie Langford and Chris Biggins of 2005 and would go to the opening of an envelope but only if I could guarantee an exclusive interview with the star. If not, it was a no. I refused to do red carpets though. I draw the line somewhere. It was a content goldmine. With working in the heart of the West End, everything was within walking distance and a stone's throw from the studio. I used to look out of the window and think 'I've made it' – I had! My own West End Show! All I need now is a big opening and clever lighting.

I settled into Canary Wharf on the 19th floor of a new build block of flats in the Docklands. I LOVED IT! This lifestyle was sexy. I'd never felt delicious before. Twenty-five was a good age to be me. I was growing into my face and finally 100% comfortable with who I was and more importantly what I don't want to be. I was more driven by my principles and integrity than ever and now had a huge platform to stream from. I also for the first time in my life started to get fit in the gym. My mate Loza got me some diet pills to kick start my thunder thighs. I was hot for a salad dodger! When I first stood on the talking scales it said "one at a time please' – that <u>had</u> to change! It's amazing how easy you can get laid when you have a national radio show and penthouse pad. Ladies tell me during this period I went from a two out of ten to a three out of ten. None taken!

You'll remember my love of aeroplanes, well now I had a bird's eye view of the Heathrow flight path one way, and London City airport the other. My flat (apartment) was relatively small by northern standards but a palace to me. My biggest joy in life is sharing these incredible opportunities and I could now make London accessible to friends and family who ordinarily couldn't have afforded to stay over. I had a spare room for waifs and strays to pass by. Mum and dad used to stay a lot and I'd always get a plus two for opening nights for my visitors for lovely nights out. Friends could stay and it was a joy to give them access to my privileged bonkers world. To them another world. I'm not being disingenuous, you cannot feel like this in Mansfield or Coventry sadly. I'm not going to lie. Nobody rushes to see you in

Swansea. Our once great Crapital still has majesty – just a shame Sickdiq has since destroyed its class. London is truly its own country - unrecognisable from 20 years ago. You can go to the opening of something every single night. I'm not a big drinker and don't stick half of Columbia up my nose so I was never bothered unless someone I loved and respected was there. I now had the power/influence to get my press tickets when the press and D Listers weren't there. I'd simply say "I'd love to come but I want three tickets on Friday." They had little choice if they wanted national coverage. That's what PRs get paid for – reach not volume of reviews. Finally, I could avoid the mentals of press night. I win!!! To share this lifestyle though was brilliant. After a while you realise it's a tortuous, pathetic and vacuous world leading to very dark places. For me it was 100% content and great gossip for the show. I'd now got my dream gig and could use it to work for me on my terms. Phew!!!

I did agree to go to a Savoy Oscars party one Sunday night. As I walked in, I took a Champers off a tray and the other twenty collapsed all over the poor cow on the door. Oy Vey! Being a Champagne Sipper simply isn't for me! I was mortified. I said "I'm awfully sorry, I'm more Timothy Taylor than Veuve Clicquot!" Ouch. She was clueless and very moist. Nasty business. I made a sharp exit before I bumped into David Tennant or Steve Coogan. What a hideously terrifying thought – enough humiliation for one night. I was on a flight to LA once and Coogan asked to switch seats with me. It was all very Partridge. I agreed after he signed a photo card from North Norfolk FM. I met some truly lovely people at Capital. Before me on-air was Dean Martin a fantastic music jock. We became life-long mates. After me was a true old-school character. He'd often roll in late and like all 70's stars had an aloofness that I admired. He was on 1am – 6am five nights a week, enough to push anyone sensible over the edge. He'd often be found having a cigarette in the studio years after it was strictly banned. Two shites he did not give. You've probably got the drift by now that this game is dangerous and toxic. If you're not strong it's designed to reel you in and destroy you. It intentionally wears you down. I remember the 'station manager' dope calling me one day saying "your show is the second least important show on the station." He was referring to Breakfast being the biggest and the later in the day you go the fewer listeners tune in. What he hadn't realised was before long I'd bucked that trend and had a switch-on at 10pm. I politely reminded Gormless Graham that he was right but "it's national radio and at 10pm at night I still have a bigger audience than most local or regional breakfast shows put together at peak breakfast." He was speechless. I wonder where this level of passive aggression and bitterness comes from. Wonder if he'd produced Savile in the 80's?

I was later told what 'Radio people' (50% nonces/49% head the balls) don't like about me is that they can smell that I don't respect them or fall for their flawed personalities and dysfunctional warped lives. I won't play 'the game' to get on with blind reverence. Turn it in. Brown nosing is not in my constitution. Once the whoop-de-doo of listener reaction starts this infuriates them as it undermines their authority to belittle me. Success removes their ability to condescend. My only conclusion is once again, jealousy. They secretly wished they had communication skills and not sat fingering files all day and sending shitty emails to provoke a reaction. Undermining authority is my biggest hobby and thrill as you know.

Within the first month the stars were dropping in ten to the dozen. I got to interview Carol Vorderman every few weeks. She was on EVERYTHING and hot to trot in 2005. I think she won 'bum of the year.' Of course you won't find a bigger arse in post Covid! I later worked with her at Loose Women. Despite my recent parody of Carol Vordernorks – much deserved – following her fixation with social media selfies, I respect her talent. She's a pro and always the smartest person in the room. Her new hideous lefty ranting leaves me cold but in a LIVE studio she's second to none. Her Labour rants are puke inducing. I'd stick to taking two off the top and one on the bottom if I were you love! Another confused TV Totty who can't work out if she's Gretta on CNN or Kelly Brook on Babestation. I was once watching Cazza on Countdown and I got aroused – seven letters!

There were other regular guests too like Piers Morgan who I loved to chat to. It was a wonderful time. Back then everyone had books, DVDs and CDs – all gone now. Ironically Piers was a newspaper hack back then and wasn't known for doing my style of gob-shittery like today. Notice he's gone very quiet on Meghan lately to avoid being accused of stalking her…...those ranting days have gone. Always loved our joust. What a pilchard he's become embroiled in all his jibby jab, Captain Tom and phone hacking PR disaster and nonsense. All rather backfired. From GMB to Talk TV and now YouTube. Ouch – how the mighty fall. I thought YouTube was for 'underground losers' like me??? Nope, it's the new Meka (bingo) – I was once again ahead of my time. A level playing field now my friend! I'm honoured to have known Piers before he became MOM – Morbidly Obese Morgan. Too risky to talk to him now in case he falls on me. Equally I got to know Eamonn Holmes very well who in my view is the benchmark for TV News Class. I always loved chatting to comedians such as Alan Carr, Catherine Ryan and John Bishop new on the scene. In fact, I later did 'Sunday with the Stars' on City Talk in Liverpool where John was my warm-up 2-3pm. Small world.

Another regular was Katie Price. At her prime she was a genius marketing machine with books, perfumes, clothing and any other pink tat she could flog. I was fascinated by her pure audacity. With seemingly no talent but bucket loads of intrigue and press, it seemed like the public would buy anything with KP associated (including her nuts!). She was a great talker and fearless. She certainly didn't worry about my various interrogations. I'd probe her more than her 17 husbands at one point. I have to admit a bit like Kerry Katona, I knew it would end in tears – too many wedding cake tiers I suppose. I'd be ruthless doing my cross between Judge Judy and Oprah on these people. Car crash but fab for ratings. Selling your soul to the mainstream media (the devil) is a very risky business! Kerry does finally seem to have sorted herself out, but Katie is a worry to her mother. Katie is another car crash waiting to happen (literally) and what do the media do? Sit back and wait for her next (literal) meltdown. If it wasn't for Harvey, she'd be in the cell next to me. Vorders and Katie are what I call 'filler' guests as they just wanted to promote their product for a chat but occasionally you get offered legends and this NEVER gets old! One day in the spring the phone rang from a record company, and they asked if I'd heard of Andrea Bocelli. Heard of him? I adore him!

I was introduced to him by my cousins Concetta and Maria in Michigan years later. One Christmas 'that voice' was blaring through the house with 'O Holy Night' and I was hooked. People don't realise that I have an eclectic taste in music, like the rest of my life nothing really makes sense, I guess! I love Amy Winehouse, Billy Joel, The Chiffons, Meatloaf and Bocelli in equal measure. My favourite classical piece is 'Concierto De Aranjuez' on the Flugelhorn or 'Léo Delibes' the Flower Duet from Lakmé. Both are better known as 'Orange Juice' or 'the British Airways theme tune.' Respectively they're palatable for the masses but hugely moving masterpieces too. The best LIVE shows I've seen were Elton in Vegas and the Royal Philharmonic doing Elvis. I just love musicality. An orchestra is so moving to me - it's like a fireworks display in my mind. I see music as colour......a bit like language, it's totally exhilarating. I can't be bothered pissing around with whacky jazz rifts or the dreaded twelve-minute drum solo. I could never see Springsteen. Who's got five hours to waste listening to that lefty racket? I'd take one of the sticks off his drummer and make him the conductor! Anyway, Bocelli's tone is magical. He gets the game to remain palatable to huge audiences and makes sure every record is mainstream. His 'PR story' is genius for putting bums on seats. Judging by his girlfriends and wives I've got a feeling he's more visually blessed than the white stick implies. Katherine Jenkins and Russell Watson are also masters of their craft – two other artistes I've loved interviewing over and over again throughout my career. Alfie Boe is vocally flawless but always seems awkward in his own skin when interviewed. Sensational voice though and a joy to listen to live at the Royal Albert Hall or even at Westgate in Vegas where I recently saw him. It's a shame when he sings with Ball the two voices have the blend of butterfly and a chainsaw. Pitchy as a fart. Michael too has been kind to me over the years with six-hour specials for the BBC. Sadly, when I hear him on Radio 2 these days, I want to shoot myself in the knackers every time he says 'my lovies' – beyond fate! I've been in love with Katherine Jenkins for a decade – an untouchable and incomparable sublime talent. Russell Watson is a hero and a friend I couldn't admire, respect or adore more. What a star and British triumph. These turns are my very favourites.

You won't believe it but cousin Connie was a mega fan of Bocelli. She was flying in from Michigan the day before my interview with Andrea, to stay with me for two weeks and could now join me for this thirty-minute exclusive chat. Andrea doesn't really do interviews, so it was exciting. It's very rare I get excited about a celeb interview but this one was special. They'd arranged for me to do it at BBC Broadcasting House (the nonce factory with the paedo statue on the front) after Steve Wright had finished for Radio Two. I adore Steve Wright, so it was an added bonus to say Alo and share a mic. I walked in the studio and there he was. Pure class. Mr Bocelli, waiting for me. We needed an interpreter for the chat, but I have a feeling he understood every word. You see I have no interest in Brad Pitt or Taylor Swift. Crap guests like nearly all politicians. I've always tried to avoid 'actors' too - a ludicrous arrogant breed generally who are not interesting and take themselves far too seriously. I love talent who can link a sentence – and are willing to talk openly with sincerity. These in-depth specials are still deep in my heart as my best work I've produced. To be able to put them on YouTube years later for the world and their fans to enjoy again is fantastic. In thirty mins I probably talk for less than five. It's all about THEM. I make them shine. I take great pride in this work. The art of the interview is VERY simple. SHUT THE F UP. Ten second questions – two-to-five-minute answers. If it's the other way around, you're just not very good! 99% of anorak radio DJs can't do it. Too busy reading their next question and not listening. I cringe at half the dopes on TV who try to interview. Have you seen Robert Peston? Oy vey! Parky would be turning in his grave at The One Show. It's all Clearasil and trainers – stick to virtue signalling and box ticking. Leave chatting to grown-ups and pros who are passionate about it!

Other unique chats popped up like Frank Sinatra Junior at the Palladium. He died a while back, but it was the nearest I got to his dad. Again, I never get bored listening to Blue Eyes. He was the master. I adored him. His phrasing is spectacular! His pitch wasn't perfect but his diction and delivery were sensational. I got to interview Sinatra's MD recently in Vegas, Vincent Falcone, what an honour. I also saw Frank's warm-up Don Rickles who I adore. There'll never be better days in showbiz than this generation. What a voice hey? Sometimes (deliberately) slightly off, it made each bad salad…...I mean sad ballad so much more powerful and authentic. My favourite ever interviews are the comedians, entertainers and singers because they spread such joy. The BBC's obsession with cancer, doctors and featuring starving, depressed and poor perishing pensioners isn't for me - far too downbeat. Some believe it's the 'real world.' I don't particularly like the 'real world' nor want to be in it. I'll stick to my own world with my own people and simply block out the stinky drains who bring us down with endless negativity and remain with my head in the sand. I truly believe the world is waking up to the 'victim boohooers.' Me, me, me – poor me... pour me another one. Oh please, stick on some ABBA and Spandex and try smiling. Don't get me started! It's a shame Benny and Bjorn weren't called Steve and Dave or they'd have had to have been called ASDA!

It was during my time at Capital Gold that I ran into bother in the West End. I was kindly invited to everything. In fact, I'd been up more huge openings than Russell Brand in the nineties. Anywho – after a couple of months I realised I wasn't like other so called 'critics.' Good Lord I'm an outsider in journalism, radio and now theatre – why??? 'Reviewers' are a very creepy breed, worse than programme managers. I don't think I've met one who I would allow into my home. Riddled with awkwardness and a plethora of prescription (and other) pills, they make my shingles tingle. Producers are generally a mafia. Actors and twirlies are off their heads with insecurity and jealousy, and the West End obsessive fans seem all to be overweight, have pink hair, wear a pearl necklace and talk like Julian Clary awaiting the snip snip. Most peculiar. Seriously, I've never met a bigger bunch of misfits. This was never the case twenty years ago. It's a social media driven, 'nonbinary,' bipolar, heavily medicated, OTT, cringe fest that is all about attention seeking. The drag queen crap on TV has further encouraged this weirdo breed of desperately bizarre and worrying window lickers. Too harsh? Well, that's my review. My honesty and willingness to tell the truth was hated by PR's and the fruit loop 'SIXSTAR' obsessives. That's a show where they chop people's heads off – oh the halcyon days! They were so genuinely bewildered that I didn't need their endorsement and affirmation to function as a human being. I did not want to be in their Glitter Gang as I've said before! Little did I know, this 'noise' would be the making of me. Turns out there's a lot more traction in HONEST 1* reviews than 5* arse licking bribe endorsements. How are these so-called reviewers/critics qualified? It's just a title. These dreadfully pompous lot take themselves terribly seriously and are mostly (like radio bosses) failed turns who aren't good enough to do it themselves. I realised it was an elite bunch of born-again pricks who should be on a 'save the planet' committee or do a daytime TV chat show rather than pretending to care about the new cast of Phantom. I avoid them like the Monkey Pox. I just didn't like most of the crap that I was invited to sit through, so I walked out. It doesn't exactly make me Wayne Couzens, does it? You see, 'it's rude to walk out' – says who? Life is too short to watch stuff that bores you – 90% I didn't even understand. So, awkwardly, I started leaving at the interval and eventually sometimes even before. The PRs were outraged, I mean proper pissed off! This is another band of bullies who like 100% control 'if you want a ticket say something nice' – errrr – no! Fack right off! Slowly I was at war. It got very nasty and personal. Another mafia, who work like a mob collectively in the hope you'll need them before they needed you. Whoopsie. Times had changed. It was hunter turned game keeper.

Luvvies and twirlies were petrified by my honesty……well any honesty. They live in a trained and infantilised Disney World. Suddenly I came along with a full-length mirror. Trust me this breed are almost entirely wolves in sheep's clothing. Little did I know hurty words would eventually become an imprisonable crime in the UK to my cost and many others! They were personally affronted. I was the first person in the history of 'blaggersville' that didn't need or want to be there. It was my job and life was too short to sit through a snoozefest. Yes, a job. Not my hobby and social life. Boy they hated that! This ruffled feathers and forged a lot of rich saboteurs and a tribe of ambivilacious haters online who all sounded like Joe Lycett's bastard 50/50 son. Who knew that my reviews would become #1 on Google/YouTube and they had no other choice but to wipe me out in such a choreographed vicious, vindictive and calculated way. The truth has always been my only salvation but BIGGEST enemy. I'm now officially (at twenty-five) my own worst enema!

Luvvies will have you believe I hated everything. This is a total lie. The reason they hate me is because most of the time I predicted failures and closures and the '#BEKIND' community of backstabbers and bottom blowers couldn't bear to hear the truth. There's a pattern here, right! Many of these people are very sporty. A lot go on the crossdresser in the gym and others go up hill skiing. Many enjoy muff diving in the sea near Brighton. The reality was they're so delusional and blind that they ignored the hundreds of 5* reviews I proudly promoted and focused on the rare 1* car crash that touched a nerve. It's all about their narrative and agenda which has become the entire raison d'être of the radical left. It is political. They're nearly all brainwashed by the extreme left. If twirlies could afford a house, they would house several Dinghy divers, I'm sure. But haven't they suffered enough without being forced to watch 'The Sound of Music' on repeat and sleep under a unicorn duvet. The irony is my haters and most furious jealous critics were the first to tune in. They pushed me to the top of the algorithms as they couldn't wait to be outraged – thanks guys! Absurd right? I guess it's the same as the loony tune, medicated trolls, liars and saboteurs being the first to read THIS book - simply because they're secretly in love with me and obsessed. Bless them. They're already on the phone to the thought police over 69 pages. This will be a diagnosed illness one day. You can just hear the doctor telling them, "you have 'BD' (Belfield Disease) and there's nothing you can do about it Chunky!" At least they'll get PIP and can sit on their huge arses all day and listen to Elaine Paige on a loop.

I wouldn't only go public with flops, but I'd also fight the arrogant cowardly and pompous critic crowd with stuff that I loved. 'We Will Rock You' opened to hideous reviews. I loved the band and music. It was a fun night out for 'normal' people like you and me but the Uni Woke Toffs (who believed they owned and controlled the West End) thought it was low rent shite. It was! That's why I loved it. It has possibly the worst script in the history of the West End. BUT who wants Shakespeare? Ben Elton wrote it for the masses – as theatre was intended to be – as The Bard! My review made the original poster and fifteen years later I'm still good mates with some of that phenomenally talented cast. By 2018 I bought all of my own theatre tickets so that I never had to sit in a room next to any creepy and out of touch theatre critic, managers or producer pervs again. I'd rather pay to attend first night and beat them to the chase than be beholden to the mobster PRs and producers. Theatre (like radio and TV) believe they're a 'community' – pfft. They're in fact a cult of cover-uppers and control freaks. Seriously, less than 1% I'd ever associate with. Makes my skin crawl and my tits tingle with their fake duplicity and Judas like hypocrisy.

On air this gave me another edge and unmissable content due to my pure disdain. I never lied or exaggerated for effect. My reviews and shows were entirely sincere and authentic – that's why it worked and took off like a rocket. The punters loved it. Capital Gold was rocking! 'The Late-Night Revolution' was a unique party with the energy of a breakfast show. No Labi Siffre or 'Smooth relaxing hits' coming out of my woofers. After shows came down in town stars would often pop over to be my guest LIVE on Capital Gold. How cool is that? Handpicked – no shitheads, fakes or dreadful reality stars brought in for 'PR.' I produced, booked and greeted every guest personally. I promise you I've NEVER interviewed anyone I didn't believe was of interest to my audience. Hence why I've never talked to anyone from Love Island or Towie. No one – ever! Eventually as much as the West End establishment tried to shut me up and ignore me, they couldn't avoid coming to my review first to see what I thought (even if they deluded themselves, I was wrong). Could there be a better compliment? I suppose this sort of sums up my life and career. The incongruous mix of intrigue matched with malice to stop me saying the very thing they can't stop listening to. Most peculiar. I guess it's the Howard Stern rationale in America. The people who 'hate' him listen longer than his fans......they can't bear to miss what he'll say next......even if it's to be outraged. I'm told West End Wendy's pride themselves on being versatile – I presume that means they top and bottom. Very ambidextrous! They work so hard in the dance class. They can all get their ankles behind their ears!

As the weeks and months went on the gossip about my late-night show grew and grew so the ratings got bigger and bigger, as did Saturday Breakfast. The morning show 6am – 9am was a totally different kettle of fish. This was my topical 'nob gag schtick' with no controversy whatsoever. It was 'feel-good' and deliberately camp old malarkey and upbeat with my 'kerching' punchline humour that I still do today based on the morning's headlines. I love this stuff. A totally different craft and skill. I love the art of precision and hitting the jingles and intros, again it takes years of practise and a ton of dedication to perfect. My musical background really helps hit the beat. It sounds geeky but the art of comedy, punchlines and tomfoolery is all about rhythm. My musicality paid off in matching the songs with the gags seamlessly. That's what I mean about radio 'craft.' This type of fun used to be all over the dial but has been wiped out by humourless spectrumed programmers that would rather play Olly Murs and Coldplay back-to-back. Zzzz. I get it - gags are risky in this hypersensitive risk averse world. Dullness prevails now to protect the sales department. DJs won't say boo to a goose let alone FU to a corrupt politician or closeted charlatan TV fake for fear of losing their gig and being locked up for hurting someone's feelings. Few get a second bite of the cherry – ask genius Danny Baker. Obscurity is a second away when you're mainstream. I am proof of the consequences of sticking your head above the parapet and tickling the tremendously powerful proverbial tiger.

I knew I'd touched a nerve when my boss scheduled 'The Drugs Don't Work' by the Verve as my 8am opener - peak of the show. I wrote on the playlist 'is Suicide FM the new format?' Monday morning the phone rang with an explosive raging madman who insisted he knew what he was doing and how dare I undermine him and mock his genius? I facetiously agreed and asked if we could open next week with the funeral march and Celine Dion's 'My Heart Will Go On?' He slammed down his Diamonte covered Nokia 10. It's all a game. I later asked (on-air) after 'Everybody Hurts' how we could have a head of music who hated music and knew even less about it? I asked my punters to mail-in any leftover anti-depressants to 'The Head of Music, Capital Gold, London.' This did not go down well as you can imagine. Again – fury. I learnt a good lesson that these soulless twats do this stuff to trigger you giving them a chance to have a go back. It was water off a duck's back to me - I couldn't care less. I knew I'd wound him up and enjoyed the prick party. When will these dopes realise you won't out-cunt me. I'm shameless in defending my product and shows. The next time he deliberately scheduled The Verve I said after it "Anyone got a Valium, some Ketamine and a Nytol? – Morning – it's your Big Breakfast Capital Gold. I'd go back to sleep if I were you." It once again did not go down well. But as always made me laugh…...which is all that matters right? Bosses or bully compliance operatives have no button for this contempt. All they want is unending respect. I didn't care, I'd still got Andy onside (the proper boss) but I could sense he was being pressured from within to control me and make me comply by the two office Judas' who were feeling threatened. The success quickly created jealousy even by jocks <u>much</u> more successful than me. 'How can he get away with that?' Curiously, no complaints from the punters. Who knew?!

On Saturdays I was followed by Kid Jenson. Another radio legend with that fantastic Canadian lilt. He was a pro and I greatly admired him, but he was everything I didn't want to be. I thought we got on great and I admired his career massively, but as my figures rose (and ended up being the peak of the day at 8am) the mood changed. Someone within his show started sabotaging my celeb guests. Now this was astonishing as whilst I was getting the likes of Michael Ball, Dara O'Briain, Lenny Henry, Jo Brand and Bill Bailey – The Kid was getting Stevie Wonder, Elton and Rod. I ask you. Incomparable. He was <u>leagues'</u> ahead. I was literally no competition at all, yet there were dark forces working the bosses from behind to whip me into shape. If there was an A Lister in town – he got them. Full stop. I didn't even ask for this level of legend. Why fear a mere radio whippersnapper like me! Disappointing. Sad.

Other fun guests I got on were people like Jerry Springer. He totally got how preposterous his insane and arguably dangerous circus and asylum TV show was. Jerry was in the musical Chicago at the time and did his US radio show from our studios at Gold. That was the magical thing about working in Leicester Square, the people that passed through were amazing. I'd often share a lift with Ricky Gervais going to Radio X or Alan Titchmarsh going to Classic FM. I love Alan! Another star who I interviewed a thousand times over the years. We shared a car once from Nottingham to Leicester. I have such respect. What a star and brilliant broadcaster. It was an Aladdin's cave of talent with so many incredible stations pumping out the woofers from that iconic building. Proper talent. Not regional ego driven fakes. I did not expect the backlash at this level of broadcasting from icons as big as 'The Kid.' Sadly, I was on-air at the same time as Jeremy Kyle who I despise. I truly think his TV show is the most evil hour of deplorable bear baiting in the history of British broadcasting. Unlike Jerry Springer who knew his guff was low rent shite, Jezza appeared to believe he was helping society by mocking the retarded, ill and addicted. Shameful!

I get Jezza's woeful act and I understand it made him a millionaire – I do a similar thing myself with one unique difference, I make <u>funny</u> (not fun) out of the public. With Kyle it was utterly spiteful and humourless, just humiliating vulnerable and medicated reptiles and J Cloths for his profit. Sickening. I was not surprised that there have been three suicides (at least) on the back of that satanical show – which despite having his name in the title, he denies is anything to do with him. He was mean spirited preying on imbeciles who need help not national mockery in ITV's daily colosseum. He should be ashamed. I don't know Jeremy (and would never want to) but, from what I saw at Capital he's got an ego bigger than his bank balance and the charm of an anaconda. The notion that he sleeps well at night in his multi-million-pound mansion paid for via ridiculing the socially inept, often broken and damaged human beings is beyond my comprehension. The fact he was poached by Murdock for Talk TV says it all. There's only one thing more indefensibly unconscionable than Kyle and that's ITV, the advertisers and Foxy Bingo who sponsored that atrocity and were all complicit in that murderous format. 'Be Kind' ITV? Yeh, right. Hypocrites the lot of them! This is why I hate so much about the sanctimonious and supercilious dog shit scumbags in the media and theatre who will defend such excrement to finance their dubious lifestyles to which they've become accustomed. Deplorable abusers pretending to be holier than thou. Pfft. To think ITV paid Jezza off a million quid speaks volumes about their moral compass, sincerity and duty of care to that show's dead victim's families. Horrific.

Things started to go sour for me at Capital Gold 'upstairs' when my ratings went up and Capital FM's figures did not. In the race for late night success, Kyle (who was head-to-head with me) should have been leagues ahead – he was on FM. My increase was counterproductive for the sales monkeys upstairs. AM cannot take a single listener from FM – they're the cash cow for the entire group. Gold was no more than a contra-deal. Business is all they care about. They have no time for mavericks or loose cannons. There's a pecking order. Capital London was the king! Capital Gold was Prince Harry – put it that way! What I didn't know (wait for it) was that the 'bigger' plan for Capital Gold was to virtually get rid of all LIVE DJs and continue show fee free as a jukebox, identical to my demise at Touch, Scarlet, overnight at Century and now here. They were not looking for a new star, quite the opposite. I was relatively new and within six months of winning the ratings war on Saturdays and increasing the Late-Night share, this was not in the future plans for Gold and could in fact undermine their cockamamie scheme to close Gold down completely as a LIVE 24/7 station. It was harder to shutter if it was growing. Radio is akin to a leaky sieve and it didn't take long for me to see another career storm brewing. I was facked. Not <u>again</u>! Have you noticed BTW in all of these stories I've never been sacked for failure – it's always politics. I have crap timing. If I didn't have bad luck, I wouldn't have any luck. If I fell into a barrel of tits, I'd come out sucking my thumb!

Everything went quiet for a bit and I carried on bringing 'personality' and 'talk' back to Gold. Oh yes, they dropped Capital. It was now just 'Gold.' Get ready for a 24 carat rebrand. Remember – this was the station that SCREAMED entertainment thirty years ago. Why couldn't I have been born twenty years earlier? I was just too late. The ship had sailed, the business had changed and I was the last survivor on the Titanic. Now the bosses were simply moving the deck chairs in the hope they'd catch the odd lifeboat. I love my gag 'hoist by my own retard' – well once again I did my old trick. It's only my optimism that keeps me going.

But I was now getting a full switchboard on the phone-in and people loved it. Ironically, I knew it was curtains regardless of the mega phone-in mega success. It was all tongue in cheek and I'd find anything to wind up the nation for entertainment purposes only. Boy did it work. One night I had a 'fack' slip out from a caller and this was a huge red flag. Once callers know that you can drop one on-air, guess what, the rest will follow to try their luck. I was genuinely terrified as I knew this would be their bullet in the gun as we were regulated by .gov owned Ofcom. Without a 'delay/dump' button on late night radio it's a recipe for disaster. How could I be responsible? This is the biggest radio group in the country. LBC had a delay, but not Gold. It was only a matter of time. Despite the success, scale and size of the network I was alone. I didn't even have a producer or phone-op. Seriously. 'No budget.' Totally alone on network radio. It's unbelievable and unheard of. BBC Radio 2 give their presenters six to ten producers and three phone-ops/answerers – I had <u>NO ONE</u>. Almost sabotage in itself and totally irresponsible of GCap. They'll argue they trusted me implicitly. No safety net, this was indefensible and setting me up to fail. I was (stupidly) talking LIVE to air calls, I had no choice. It was the only way I could create the energy of the show to make it clear it wasn't set up. It's identical to Voice of Reason. The difference is at VoR I'm my own boss and there are no rules. I don't have Ofcom gagging me (just the corrupt Nottingham Corrupt Police).

One night I did my old (trigger) topic about under aged mothers. The Sun thought a fifteen-year-old 'up the duff' with triplets was their 'Nappiest Headline Ever' and a brilliant front page. I did not! I wondered if she was just a 'slapper?' Of course, some lowlife lefty complained to Ofcom and they slapped me on the wrist for the next fabulous hour of argy-bargy with very upset (and mostly big boned) knicker droppers (I mean single mothers) faking offence at my question. Of course, most of these women had eight kids and lady parts like a dropped lasagne! – Er – don't bother complaining about this book because we don't do refunds. Seriously their downstairs department looked like a wizard's sleeve after such clenching. Quite appalling. Anyway, I love the hype! Courting the PR off the back of these absolutely intentional pre-written stunts is my calling card. It's all a game to trigger ENTERTAINING calls and create theatre and pure wireless pantomime. So simple. Of course, the dopey receptionist woman (who happened to be an odious and manipulating box ticker and thought she was the Managing Director) called for my resignation. I called for her to have a lip wax and facial. Dreadful woman. Isn't it funny how some people (for their own agenda) just don't like me, having never even spoken to me! Vile. Miserable lazy cow – these types find me. Bet she listened every night whilst on the Ofcom website reporting her own station. Not a joke BTW. They're absolutely capable of such self-sabotage and stupidity. It appears this once young and pretty PA (piss artist) only worked at GCap for the free show tickets and Wimbledon hospitality invites. Nothing gets past me. Another one 'up to corrupt' shenanigans that this delightful lady of colour didn't want me to see! What this skullduggery did teach me was that I was once again vulnerable, alone and haters (I'd never spoken to) weaponized any opportunity to stab me in the front. My curiosity to this day remains – why do they care? These snakes must spend hours in the shower washing their two faces. Andy did have my back at this point and I carried on regardless surviving another day. Unlike LBC though, I was now at great risk without a 'delay.' In hindsight it was unforgivable that a network as big as Capital Gold allowed me on-air without this protection. I'm not even sure their insurance allowed it. It was only a matter of time before the shit would hit the fan.

Regardless of the BS station politics, my life was still cock-a-hoop privately. I made more and more friends in the smoke and made sure that my Nottingham clan were invited down as often as possible to celebrate and enjoy this opportunity with me. Life at Canary Wharf was like living in a movie. Mon-Fri it was rammed with bankers (rhyming slang) off their tits on coke enabling them to work their fourteen-hour shifts making millions in the UK's financial hub. By 5.30pm the entire place was completely desolate and often I'd have the entire underground shopping mall to myself. Seriously it was eerie! My beloved M&S Food was a five-minute walk and by 6pm £2 loaves of bread would be 5p and the 'yellow tag' offers were mind-boggling! On Friday evenings, when they knew nobody would be back until Monday you could literally get a five-course meal for four for £10. Again, on Saturday I'd saunter down there in the afternoon and have the entire place to myself. I got more special offers than a dinghy diver in Dover. None of my visitors could believe it! I'd send food parcels to Nottingham as part of my care in the community. Post Covid, I often wonder if the whole place is still 'working from home' – which was a proven euphemism for 'wreck the entire economy.' I'll get to that in the next book.

I carried on regardless awaiting my next career assassination. Showbiz guests kept flooding into the LIVE studio and one night Max Clifford came in. The now deceased and disgraced PR man was a fascinating talker whom I'd known for years. Max was a master manipulator and a hugely powerful man. We got him a car from 'The Pride of Britain' awards (ironically) and there he was at

10pm 'willing to talk about anything.' Andy gave me unlimited budget for cars for guests. You'd never get this today at £50+ a pop each way. Max cleverly gave answers to his own questions……a trick Boris Johnson mastered until exposed and ridiculed. Both men mastered the manoeuvre of truth and could pivot out of any reality cul-de-sac. Max was Simon Cowell's manager at this point and told me off air that Simon was on $18M in the USA alone! Even if Max was on 10% (I suspect 20%) that made Clifford a very wealthy man from that one client alone. Max had released his autobiography which was a Who's Who of who is that! Most famously there was the classic 'Freddie Starr Ate My Hamster' story which was splashed on The Sun – arguably the most memorable bullshit PR front page in history. A genius PR triumph that still lives on today. Freddie was a genius comic but totally wild. His demise over unfounded allegations literally killed him. He simply could not get over the lies and stain on his reputation. He foolishly bankrupted himself trying to get justice in the High Court. Repeat after me – <u>you can't win</u> in the High Court (even if you win!) Ask my shushy gagsters. Defamation is £1M+ if you lose, or you settle for £10,000 with a fake sorry which lands the claimant their own £300,000 bill. It's a lose lose for everybody……other than lawyers. Do you see the pattern throughout my book and life? History repeats itself. You have to learn from those who came before you. Freddie taught me a HUGE lesson I have never forgotten. Bitterness and principles can eat you alive.

Max was also working with James Hewitt and, in possibly my most explosive interview I EVER broadcast, Clifford proceeded to explain how James Hewitt and Princess Diana were 'dating' at the time of Prince Harry's conception. That clip has 100,000's of hits on YouTube today. The problem with a guest like Max Clifford is that it's easy to dismiss anything he says as self-serving promotion, but honestly, I believed him. Reminds me of my last pre-death chat with Jimmy Savile who had a lot of the same tricks. The stories Max covered up are far more exciting than the stories he published in very clever cover-up deals. He was frankly the captain of the seedy world of HMS Showbiz. It was his job to negotiate his client's skeletons to be swept deep under the carpet in return for another headline to barter and buy silence and cover-up for corrupt or criminal clients. Do you see why I have such caution and derision for the world we inhabit?

Since his arrest I've heard awful stories about the 'true' Max from the trial and even his close friends, but I'm also aware that there are two sides to every story. We know only too well that 'victims' should not be blindly believed; often victims are bonkers and off their heads with spite, malice and jealousy and simply want revenge. Some of them are simply fantasists and money grabbing, attention seeking liars. With Max I have reservations by his own private confessions to me in person. The tabloid world is breathtakingly corrupt, without any scruples or conscience, as we now know since the demise of the News of the World and revelations of indefensible phone hacking. In summary, you can't believe a word the mainstream media and press tell you – let alone from showbiz types. From my own trial I personally watched as the gonorrhoea drenched hacks left the room whenever the defence spoke – utterly crooked and completely biased to the prosecution.

What I do know is that Max was unbelievably well-connected and indescribably influential and powerful. I also know that 99% of my interview with Clifford could never be broadcast on the BBC. They wouldn't let you go anywhere near such scandalous and legally untenable accusations that Max was stating (to promote his book) as FACT. Regardless of the truth, the physical similarity between Prince Harry and Hewitt could just be a curious coincidence? Could Max's insinuation be correct? I'm just glad that Harry and Meghan pissed off to the US to invade their own privacy and are leaving us alone. I guess my only hope is that time will tell, and the truth will out in the end for Harry, Meghan and even myself! In 2005 I (and the rest of the world) knew nothing about Max's private life and was fascinated by his razzle dazzle career of celebrity management. Similar to my interviews with Rolf Harris, Stewart Hall and of course Jimmy Savile these 'chats' worked at that moment in time.

I shudder now at their double lives, but I'm not bloody Mystic Meg! What I do know after twenty plus years in the business is that there are many Max Clifford's around. There are even more Schofield's and Huw Edwards! The married, happy, two kids' veneer is a brilliant ruse for duplicitous, rich and cunning 'stars' to get away with their double (crossing) hypocritical lives! They literally 'kill' any story by bartering and negotiating their way out of publication by offering a 'better' story from a bigger and more famous client in return. Schofield got an extra year on TV after the 'This Morning Runner' story broke after he came out to deflect? PR razzle dazzle kept it covered for months until Holly headed for zee hills! This shameless and indefensible practice will never stop to protect careers and their management. There's simply too much money at stake on all sides. It's all a BIG game of chess. A seedy game of protection and a world where money talks. Max was the master puppeteer! You can run but you can't hide. The truth ALWAYS comes out in the end. Normally it's arrogance that opens the closet door…...even if it is behind locked doors at posh 5* hotels minutes from their house!

By 2006 I'd fulfilled my life-long dream of having 'my own West End show,' I'd spent a magical Christmas in Canary Wharf and the ratings were through the roof. But it couldn't last, through no fault of my own. DJs were a thing of the past. I'd got more whispers of a buy-out of GCap, the owners of the entire Leicester Square brands and A LOT of people were suddenly leaving in all departments from News to Sales in their droves. I've had this Mary Celeste feeling before. It turns out turkeys don't tend to vote for Christmas lunch – they much prefer the lefty, woke vegan version!!! Jump before you're pushed. The writing was on the wall……

I just woke up every day happy to be on-air and milking the opportunity including my car home. I was the last of the phone-in 'shock jocks' to survive but my time had run out commercially. This may sound soppy but to me it was romantic. I LOVED London, the theatre of Trafalgar Square and the Majesty of the Mall. Once a week I'd ask my driver to divert to Buckingham Palace at 1am, up through St James' and back down past Parliament and Big Ben to Embankment and along the Thames to my Wharf home. Every night we'd drive past the London Eye, I was furious when I found out Kia Cars had sold it to the Japanese rebranding it as the Jap's Eye is a PR disaster. I sat in awe. I couldn't believe my luck. A ghost town all to myself. I LOVED it! It's so exciting, a London no one gets to see. Knowing you'd just been talking to the Capital was exhilarating. All ambitions completed. Truly, I was a very, VERY lucky boy! I'd outlasted most of my contemporaries who were already working in Lidl or on benefits as their eyes were bulging out of their heads with bitterness. I was just so grateful for the chance to do the gig albeit curtailed by the box tickers and accountants. There's only one thing bigger than national radio - that's YouTube! How do you crack that global beast?

One day around Easter tensions were rising at Gold as we had new jingles and a new tag line. 'All About the Music.' HELLO. I'm not stupid! The fella gobshiting for three hours is toast. I'm no Mystic Meg but I was about to be on the bones of me arse again. We all knew that Gold would eventually become a jukebox – which it did without anyone being told. The days of 'big personality' creativity had vanished. The 'Bully Boss' was suddenly all over me. He started saying bizarre things, quoting lines from my show and even brought up my first link with a fella called Paul Coyte on Drivetime. Is he off his head? This pillock wanted a row. I was being baited again, but I'd learned my lesson. Kill a dick head with kindness. DO NOT ENGAGE! The day I started at Capital Gold I was on holiday in Valencia. My dear mate Giles had moved there with his wife and kids. I adore his family. I loved this city by the sea, similar in style to Barcelona. I was minding my own business on one of my many last-minute trips and was walking down the central park which was an old river turned into an endlessly meandering gorgeous garden. The phone rang and Andy said, "can you start tonight?" WOW. Weeks of negotiation and procrastination and now I'm on air in ten hours! I explained where I was "Well Valencia is only two hours on a plane, that's the same as the train from Nottingham" he said – Andy made a very good point. He offered to pay all expenses and there I was in the back of a London Taxi to Leicester Square six hours later. The fella I replaced was unceremoniously dismissed. It's never nice. You're an asshole before you even begin for replacing him. Don't shoot the messenger I've got deep vein thrombosis and jet lag from Spain! I've been here many times before. Andy wanted a '2 way' with Paul who was an old-school DJ on drive to promote my launch. I didn't feel any warmth from Coyte. BTW, he's apparently working for GB News now – that'll teach him! I'm glad GB News is doing so well, I hear Nana Akua is their big star. I told Tarquin when it launched that I bet it would take a queer to save that TV News disaster. Honestly, I'd never heard of him although he assured me that he was terribly popular and qualified. My very first line 'offended'

Paul and the entire team apparently - the bosses who had clearly ruminated on this for almost a year. What could I have said that was so shocking? Paul said to you "we're going to be best friends" – wait for it – "you replied, I'll be the judge of that, I have very high standards!" This was the horrific moment that offended these precious snowflakes. I ask you. What these pricks remember, (write down and later use in evidence) is beyond me! I couldn't help but laugh at such foolishness. Surely people can't be this sensitive?

A week or two later I signed my own death warrant with another unfortunate LIVE slip when a caller called me the C word and slammed the phone down. It was inevitable and I couldn't do a thing about it. I guarantee you it was a jealous disgruntled ex-colleague - punters can't be arsed with this malarkey. God bless them. I cut them off, apologised to the listeners and moved on. This is 'LIVE defence' and all that you're required to do by regulator Ofcom. This wasn't <u>any</u> defence in my case, it was the proverbial bullet in the gun to axe the show. Inevitably they were 'all about the music' and not about Belfield inciting radio genius, a mass debate, argy-bargy and ratings. Rebels were out – automation was in. Within months all but Breakfast had been axed. Everyone had gone. It was all planned just like Scarlet FM in Wales before. Seriously bad timing. The party was over for my breed and sadly I was left with a mop to clear up the dance floor and shown the switch to turn off the lights. As usual though, I had the humiliation of being blamed for something beyond my control for reasons which were absolutely nothing to do with me.

Days later they confirmed in writing they would not honour the £12,000 remaining on my contract. I was sacked with immediate effect. Oh really? We'll see about that

## The High Court Scam

Back then I was naïve. I believed the courts were about the truth and justice. I couldn't have been more wrong. As I've previously alluded, you can't win in court – especially in civil (non-criminal) cases. Let me explain the Magistrates and High Court to you. NO ONE WINS! The law is an ass and completely self-serving. It is set up to solely profit lawyers and lawyers alone. It's a sick game. I was owed £12k but that wouldn't even cover the court fees and filing the claim…...let alone being represented on the day. It's a sick joke that they claim justice is open to everyone. IT IS NOT. I took advice and it was clear that I was totally unable to prevent the caller swearing as the broadcaster hadn't provided me with a delay – the liability was 100% on GCAP. It's not as if I snuck in the building to do my schtick. They'd head-hunted and hired me to do it and allowed me for months to do the phone-in. However, to get this to court risked bankruptcy through costs in excess of £100,000 – all for a £12K win. Well, as you know I'm a man of my word and will do anything for the truth and justice. Even if you win you only get 80% costs so a victory wouldn't even break even. Some think this is pride. IT IS NOT! It's 100% principle.

For over a year the lawyers battled it out. Little did they know at this point I was renting and had no assets. To me I had nothing to lose. I self-represented and filled in the forms myself with occasional advice from a barrister along the way. They had a team of lawyers on £1000's per hour to fight back as a collective mafia. Why does injustice grind my gears and rile me so profoundly? Why can't I just take the punch and walk away? Well, that's thanks to my old gran and incredibly honest parents – I was brought up to believe right is right and wrong is wrong. Old school principles. You don't give into liars and bullies and you stand with pride against saboteurs who want to bring you down at <u>all</u> costs – even if you lose. Powerful media oppressors who thrive under 'go away quickly or you'll never work again' don't intimidate me. Sadly, the law doesn't work like that. You have to pay on account before a lawyer will answer the phone, let alone write a letter. All costs are paid pre-trial. It is purely a pissing contest of he who has the deepest pockets……and the chambers who can drag it out the longest with the most impressive willy waggling wig wearer. I was young and feisty and there were no consequences, but others have been less lucky. My dear mate Spanner Face – Katie Hopkins – (I call her Spanner Face because when I look at her my nuts tighten) - paid the ultimate price for the evil legal system and lost EVERYTHING. Katie lost a defamation case and was bankrupted. How is this possible? Well, even though she was only 'fined' £20k the costs of £1,000,000+ wiped her out. Vile, vindictive LAWYERS only have one ambition not only to win, but to wipe you out in entirety! They're identical to the corrupt police. I genuinely believe this from the bottom of my bottom.

I've wasted £400,000+ on lawyers to date – only possible by the incredible success of VoR. I truly believe it's a scandal that 'justice' (or self-defence) comes at such a ludicrous price regardless of right or wrong. This is not a level playing field. I chose to self-represent in this case as the alternative was £100k+ for a barrister which I clearly didn't have on £50K a year salary. Instead, I ticked a few boxes and paid the £350 listing fee myself. Their pre-action defence would have been £20,000 for sure. Ludicrous. To me the argument was simple. Nearly a year later I turned up at the London Magistrates Court for a three-day hearing and they had <u>eight</u> lawyers in camp frocks. They'd make fabulous vicars. There's a lot of this sort of thing about in Soho. Eight! I mean WTF. At £2,000 to £10,000 each day, that's a shitload of dosh. I look back now with complete bewilderment at what they hoped would make me lose my bottle and walk away. At the time I didn't flinch. My dear pal Matt Genever came with me on day three. He thought that me self-representing and playing the part of a barrister was hysterical. Good Lord, if only he'd been around for the farce and fiasco in 2022!

On the final day one of their woeful wig wearers came over and said, "what are you going to say about the delay?" I said, "you'll find out in court!" He said, "that's not in the spirit of the court!" What an arsehole. Must think I'm limp under the cap. What a bunch of characters these legal filth are!

As in recent Clown Court visits - I truly couldn't give two shiny shites about fancy costumes and ridiculous pomp and circumstance. Days before they offered me half the claim to walk away. I of course, said 'no' on principle. In for a penny……

After two and a half days it was over, but I did at least get my bosses on stand to confirm that I was not given a delay and therefore could not have prevented any caller saying anything. Individually they said I'd provoked the C word to which I replied in each case, "What can I say to you right now to provoke you to say the C word?" – both said, "you can't." The judge raised an eyebrow on both occasions! This was a ridiculous argument. The nasty bitter boss came on stand and I cross-examined him. I swear to God he was wearing eye liner. "You never liked me, did you?" I enquired. "No" he replied, "You never liked me from day one, did you?" – again "NO!" he replied angrily. I then had that glorious moment and snapped back "Well I didn't stand a chance then, did I?" "No" he confessed. In an instant I replied "No more questions. You're dismissed." I've never seen eight men in wigs look more shell shocked since the close of Act 2 in Les Misérables when they bomb the shit out of the barricade! It was a circus as are all of these cases. It's 100% theatre. It should NEVER be taken seriously. As if things couldn't get any worse, I had a retiring judge and it was his last trial. He couldn't care less and understood nothing about the nuances of broadcasting. "What does profanity mean?" the judge asked. Hopeless! How do these people find me?

It was months later when we got his decision after I had written to the court three times. It had literally been forgotten. Again, how is that a thing? They'd completely kicked it into the long grass (deliberately). The GCap lawyers didn't care – they'd already been paid and made their money. I believe he/they hoped we'd all forget and it would go away quietly. The Judge agreed that I was powerless to prevent the C word being broadcast and that my content was intentionally controversial which is the reason I was hired. That was kind of my point. At the end of the ruling GCap had spent £150,000+ on costs. I'd spent £3,000. Isn't it preposterous?! There was a costs order against ME despite the vindication so miraculously there were seemingly no winners. I got the train back to Nottingham and stopped at the County Court for a bankruptcy form, filled it in (didn't pay 1p to GCap and I swear on my entire family's life I NEVER HEARD A WORD AGAIN FROM ANYONE about the matter! Not ONE syllable. How insane is this system?

GCap spent £150,000 over a £12k claim and didn't recover a penny. Alas 'Do Little and Diddle Em' solicitors got their wanga. From the bottom of my bottom, I promise you this didn't change my life one bit. I'd cost them almost twenty times my claim. Job done. I was only renting so they couldn't do fack all. They knew I could never pay this bill and didn't even ask. They didn't even care – why would they, it came from those deep pockets of the media mafiosi straight to the legal mafia. WOW. A life lesson in stupidity that could only be exceeded by the witch hunt of 2020 costing MILLIONS to shut me up. This law is a disgusting, broken, corrupt institution to cripple the poor and allow the rich and powerful to bully anyone into silence and submission. Shame on you scales of justice. Fair? My hairy white arse. From this second, I had <u>ZERO</u> respect for the courts and the cabal that find and empower them.

The sneery lefties would say 'why bother? You didn't win.' Well, I didn't lose and the truth outed which is good karma for my soul. I maintained my position as a man of principle, honour and integrity regardless of the courtroom circus. This was a pissing contest not a court case. I didn't like the slight on my character or the bully boy intimidation. I couldn't care less about £12,000. I earned that back during my packed Christmas season. Principles mean more to me than money. I sleep very well at night and loved my second Court experience. What an education – it certainly taught them a lesson. Do not invest in the pantomime. It's entirely based on failed actors showing off in order to peacock their way to victory. It's a crooked game onerously set up to guarantee one winner – the legal profession. Even Vegas has more sincerity, morality and integrity than the British Court System.

## Chapter 9

## The Calm After The Shitstorms
## Work for Yourself

Life is never easy. Well, my life isn't! A decade in showbiz is like a lifetime in politics. All of this may seem very dramatic if you aspire to mediocrity but for me it was just my job and par for the course. Avoiding the vipers on a daily basis and fighting for your life seems the only way to survive in this turd infested world of radio and cesspit of showbiz whack-jobs, weasels and closeted fruits. Finally though I'd had enough and they can stick that in their pipe and smoke it. I had to admit defeat. Ten years of schlepping and battling troglodyte takes its toll. I was over the Moon to return to the comfort blanket of Nottingham with my entire friends and family at my fingertips. My world was in Robin Hood County then – as it is today. I'd dipped my toes in 'luvvie lake' and was happy to leave Canary Wharf with nothing but magical memories and my ambitions fulfilled. I'd been smart this time. Canary Wharf was a brand new fully furnished flat, so I didn't have all the drama of beds and washing machines to schlepp back up North. Not easy on the LNER – especially with all the strikes. You look a proper muppet carrying a chaise longue through King's Cross during rush hour.

Honestly, I was so excited to be home. It was so clear from day one that I was right to protect myself by coming home and being my own boss. I wouldn't waste one second trying to work out or comprehend the lunacy of this creepy business that can easily eat you up and spit you out like a pussy's furball. I had no negativity about London. Zero bitterness about Gold, I loved every second. I just moved on and looked forward. I simply wasn't on enough money to win in the capital. You're better on £25,000 in Notts than £100k in London. During my time at Gold, I still took holidays and went to America a couple of times. No one could believe I'd take a week off national radio to actually have fun. Such dopey logic – leave them wanting more! Audiences love to miss you - a break is a fantastic way of re-energising yourself and re-boosting the momentum of the programme.

So, to cut a long story medium length I was cock-a-hoop being back in Nottingham. So where now? Well, for the next four years I was back at the BBC doing hand-picked shows as a freelance as my own boss! I LIVED for my BBC local Network specials which were still selling gang-busters and indulging my passion for in-depth chats with fascinating people. Pre-twatter no one knew (let alone cared) about Gold or Scarlet legal shite so I carried on as is. I worked LIVE in the Midlands and continued to have a ball! I'd found my rhythm being BOSS FREE in a BS exclusion zone. Looking back, I now realise this was a truly magical time of zero drama, lots of travel and some of the best shows I'd ever presented with no pressure or gaffers playing power trip games and twisting my melon – man! Whilst at Gold I had been chatting to Tim, the boss at BBC Shropshire about work. He'd graciously taken all of my network specials for years for which I was eternally grateful. He was a fan who appreciated more than pop, prattle and the usual BBC local filler gobbledygook. He knew he needed to up his game to compete in a DAB market as did so many other editors. I had so much loyal support from so many switched-on bosses across the UK like Matthew at BBC Jersey, Tim at BBC Cumbria as well as Humberside, Bristol, Kent and Essex who took everything blindly. I hadn't met any of these managing editors which was weird, but they bought and broadcast everything on trust. Proper loyalty. Prior to Johnathan Ross and Russell Brand screwing us all over at the BBC over 'Sachsgate' no one cared less about compliance checks we just got on with it. After that storm in a teacup, you couldn't fart at the BBC without filling in a form and getting the neurodiversity manager to put a cordon and flashing beacons around you. I did <u>everything</u> from home which was magnificent. What a privilege to be paid to do what you love and have no management mincing about to ruin your life, spirit, will to live and fun. BBC Shropshire booked me to do a lot of LIVE cover work along with BBC Hereford and Worcester who were fantastic. I was their go to man for the same reason. I never let them down. No issues or drama whatsoever for over a decade. I look back now with amazement at the trust they gave me. I was often completely alone in these buildings, switching the BBC on and off without any fuss. No one blinked an eye even though I was only freelance. They wouldn't let half their own staff lifers set the alarm, let alone have a set of keys.

Within weeks I was asked to cover 'BBC Midlands' at the weekends across the network and did a posher version of the 'Late Night Revolution.' The smart BBC editors could see I was perfect for their new 'younger' grown up audience. Contrary to popular belief, I'm not a risk or loose cannon – I will craft my show as required. The days of gardening phone-ins were out and Wogan/Bruce style whimsy was all the rage. Add in my celeb chats and topical gags and I'd got millennium motherload for less than £200 a show. For four years I did my window cleaning round travelling the country popping in and out of a ton of BBC Locals. It was a joy. I loved staying in posh hotels and it was all tax-deductible. I couldn't lose. I didn't hear any negativity, I avoided all 'feedback' and talent were not unnerved by my presence as they knew I didn't want to stay. I was living my dream and could see a daily show was radio torture and wireless Groundhog Day. Quite appalling. The genius of this stability was that I could fill my diary months ahead and live well while work poured in. I could just mix and match as I pleased. Alchemy was mine for now.

Clubland was dying. The silver tops were shuffling off this mortal coil quicker than YouTubers were going to prison. Whippersnappers would rather stay at home and get off their tits on cheap ASDA cider or alcopops. There was the odd exceptional club that would be full which was thrilling but you could feel the numbers dropping and overtime more and more closed. A sold-out Embassy Club on a Saturday was rarer than a funny left-wing comedian on Have I Got News for you. Curiously the clubs and BBC Local Radio had exactly the same challenge. Times had changed. Their punters were in terminal decline as people had moved on. In fact, the world had moved on. Devastating for both. Social media was slowly taking off and old-fashioned values were being lost. Even my own pit estate community no longer regarded itself as such. A generation had passed and they didn't care about variety. They no longer recognised gag men comedians. The heart of the community – the pub – was also starting to struggle and the fabric of what it is to be British was becoming taboo. Religion played a big part. It wouldn't be long before Mohammed would be #1 boys name as it is at the point I scribe this epistle. The four closest pubs to my house have all gone and been knocked down for flats. Bit by bit our lives were unrecognisable. It's utterly tragic that these hubs for 'the common man' have been driven out of business by cheap booze in supermarkets and lazy millennials who would rather stare at an Xbox off their nut on weed than have a pint and a laugh in the Phoenix, Tavern, Grey Goose or Windsor. Football was no longer affordable you need to sell a kidney to buy the shirt......let alone a ticket.

However, I fell in love with performing more than ever before. I worked tirelessly on my stand-up gags and built more and more confidence over time standing erect with mic in hand. Unlike many of my colleagues who were jacking it in, I was still busy. I also found such warmth and community in the various U3A's, Women's Institutes and Church Hall gigs which frankly were a piece of piss and a relaxing night out by comparison. New senior communities (old cock villages) were springing up which paid the equivalent of two radio shifts and couldn't be more welcoming. Seventy-year-olds had changed. No more purple rinses and Dorothy bags – now it was jeans and the Beatles – not Jim Reeves. They were so lovely and I smashed it with ABBA,

Manilow, sixties, Elton and anything with a fantastic melody. I was shameless in giving them what they wanted. It paid off and word spread quickly. You have to know your audience and keep your finger on the pulse of our once GREAT Britain rotting corpse.

The days of driving to Blackpool for £100 to do 2 x 45 minutes were long gone. Total fool's errand. Petrol was simply too expensive. I worked local, regularly and relied on repeat bookings – all without an agent stealing 20%. For me it was all about lifestyle now. I was like the proverbial pig in shit. Anyone can get a booking BUT can you get re-booked every six months? That was my goal. Eventually I'd block off two weeks holiday every two months and use my money, well-earned and well saved to travel. I've been so lucky to visit most of the Greek Islands, all over France and Spain and visited my beloved New York and Vegas like popping to Scarborough. My USA trips went from two to five weeks in the end to enable me to review 30+ shows. My stars had aligned. Those were the halcyon days of travel. If you were smart and could book at the right time you could get to New York City for £200 and devour the seductive exchange rates. It was more expensive to go First Class on the train to London. These weren't 'pleasure' trips. I'd make sure I'd record interviews with the stars and then BOOM – write it off for tax purposes! I was the luckiest man alive. My travel was kindly paid for by the exchequer. Years of advice from Sir Ken had clearly sunk in. Then I worked out that 'Air Miles' enabled me to turn left where you get a flatbed! Plus, if you paid on Amex, every few flights were free. I couldn't believe my luck! I never looked back – or right!

This is working class smarts. In the end I never went cattle class despite only paying the lowest fare. No flies on me. I don't have a degree, but I do have a masters in common sense and beating the system. I make no apologies. Every penny I earned I put back into the economy, not up my nose. My mate once said he hated cocaine but just loved the smell of it.

Curiously I was better treated by Broadway and Vegas PR's than the lazy Brit control fruits in the West End. They'd bend over backwards in the states to give me access to the stars and tickets to see anything I wanted. In London they just bend over backwards - an offer I declined in favour of maintaining my dignity and not ending up with an exhaust pipe the size of the channel tunnel. USA PRs understood you can't win them all. They were sensible and knew that you can't like everything and some you win, some you lose. The only way to be credible was to love some stuff with more genuine passion than others. Brit's take this stuff so personally which is ridiculous. It's so incestuous. They were smart enough to keep me close, London (like radio saboteurs) simply wanted to wipe me out. In twenty years of working with marketing and PR agencies I've made two incredible lifelong friends - Alice and Charlotte. Two gems in my life today. They're both big players and from day one could see what I was trying to achieve. I cherish them dearly. I always respected the 'old school' PRs like Lisa and Amanda as they always had perspective. The new pouty lipped, caterpillar eyebrow, tofu eating GenX lot can do one. The PR circus makes my piss boil equal to anyone who puts they're 'reaching out' in the first line of their email. Keep your grubby hands to yourself. I can't even talk to most of them. I REFUSE to reply to their emails, with their 'he/her' bollocks after their nonbinary woke names. Imbeciles! Seriously these people are as dumb as a monkey on a rock. Not my cup of tea at all. I'll pass.

I had some marvellous opportunities that flooded in. I was invited by Venetian Casino to attend opening night of Jersey Boys in Sin City. This is a remarkable show. A perfect script and an even better litany of hits. I was offered an interview with Frankie Valli and Bob Gaudio which was such a thrill. They knew showbiz is full of crooks and shysters. Their deals were done on a good old handshake. Inspiring. One of my favourite interviews <u>ever</u> was with Dame Edna Everage on Broadway. I think Barry Humphries was a genius! It never gets old, even now, going through stage doors to meet an idol, legend or true star. I was so lucky hand picking the icons I genuinely wanted to chat to. I was lucky to be around for the openings of huge shows like Hairspray, Wicked, Hamilton, the Lion King and the incomparable Book of Mormon and Spamalot. The Producers was my favourite show of all time. Hysterical genius. I was lucky to work with both the Broadway and London original casts. It was a magical time for LIVE entertainment.

Interviewing is my joy and I think my forte. Comedians are notoriously tricky but my personal favourite as I love their artform as most have incredible minds. Most are not instinctively funny so it can be a challenge. Julian Clary is the best example.

In 'real life' he's intentionally not funny and frankly not even camp. It can be hard work opening him up – as the Nun said to the parson's nose. The job of an interviewer is to create entertainment. That only works if the guest is entertaining! Dame Edna was a different kettle of fish. He was in the Sir Ken Dodd category of legend in my book. He'd been there, done it and had NOTHING to prove. I was interviewing Barry on Broadway for a show called 'All About Me.' I went to his theatre and it was 'quiet.' Dame Edna came out and immediately addressed it…………'"Darlings those aren't empty seats, they're paid for seats left empty by those who died on their way to the show. Don't think of them as 'empty' – think of them as tombstones." Incredible! Just brilliant! God, I love this. Owning every inch of the stage, theatre and show, I watched in awe. A masterclass! Shameless confidence. An answer for everything – something I always dreamed of having.

I saw Barry in his 'audience with' show in 2022 in Nottingham but despite most of the Dame Edna sparkle having faded and withered with age, Humphries' raised eyebrow and knowing look was still there. Barry did an act. Unlike these creepy drag queens on the BBC, he left it in the wardrobe. These new drag nutters give me the chills. Horrendous. Neither funny or clever from what I can see with a couple of notable exceptions whose background is in comedy and cabaret – not lady shavers and penis tucking. They give me the heebie-jeebies. Just vulgar. Barry on the other hand was a pro. Why would he do a radio interview in drag? He didn't. Barry was magnificent. It was a true honour! He sat in front of me in a suit and tie and shut his eyes and did the chat as Miss Everage. Magical. What a pro. If only his contemporaries could learn from his 'slaying' speed of wit. Pure dexterity. <u>It was a true honour</u>! A fierce talent, miles above the rest. The world has changed. I'm an old gammon and neanderthal man. We didn't have drag creeps reading stories in libraries when I was three years old – I don't know how I coped?!

Another thrill for me was recording Andy Williams' last interview in the UK before he died. For decades he was an incomparable global legend! More recently I became close to Merrill Osmond and got to know siblings Donny, Marie and Jimmy very well. It's still such a thrill when you see their name on text. It never gets old. Had it not have been for Andy Williams it's unlikely The Osmond's would have been the global mega stars they are today. He was the Cowell, Norton and Ant and Dec of his day – put together. For me Andy was also 'Mr Christmas.' What a talent, what a legacy – what a voice. When you listen back to Moon River or any of the timeless hits you can hear instantly why he stood the test of time. The honour of sitting opposite someone like Andy never gets old. Sitting face to face with icons to find out what makes them tick, learn from their advice and most importantly celebrate their life is a joy and privileged honour. For nearly twenty years I've had this pleasure on a daily basis. I could ask anything. Being trusted to be in their presence is the greatest honour of all. Nearly all of these interviews are done alone on the talent's request. From Shirley Bassey to Petula Clark, I was so lucky to get an audience with exclusively.

Normally it's the hangers on who cause the trouble. Bassey's seat was too high, I was too close, the room was too cold – I heard it all. She came in and was a diamond. I did her at the Ritz – totally befitting her glamour and class. I loved the bones of her. What a set of pipes.

Possibly my best hour special I've ever recorded was with ABBA. I flew to Stockholm and was given forty minutes with both Benny and Bjorn separately in their respective homes. By now I'd mastered the art of 'less is more' and virtually removed myself from the programmes entirely. It's ALL about them – the opposite of Dame Edna or indeed Jonathan Ross's dreadful self-indulgent chat show. The skill is rapport and nodding. I'm so proud of that show. It cost a fortune to get there and stay in Sweden but boy was it worth EVERY krona (penny)! It all became very normal. My folks and family couldn't believe what my life had just morphed into. A brilliant combo of all of my favourite things.

At this point I started my newspaper career and would write the transcripts (copy) of these interviews and send them to editors who loved them. Stars hate tabloid journalists. They're cold, rude and arrogant. I was the opposite. Just like my BBC hour specials – this was my unique niche. In the case of Andy Williams, this life story interview was published as a two-page spread in the Mirror the day after he died. Because of my cheeky style I'd often get different stories to boring hacks who don't understand the minds of creatives. All of this archive is still on YouTube. I couldn't be prouder. I don't think anyone has an eclectic career like mine, it's extraordinary as I sit here reflecting and looking back. I've never flinched – there's plenty of room for us all. I just adore what I do and I think non-mentals can see that. These four years of network specials, LIVE daily as cover and BBC Midlands shows were extra special as I finally had the magic combination of travel, radio and LIVE gigs all in sync together. Vegas reviews and interviews took off as I topped Google search for almost everything. No one came close – that may explain why so many jealous losers were so determined to close me down! I was now friends with many of the headliners I'd met many times. I'd be invited to their homes for dinner and backstage for drinks. A wonderful privilege. I went to Des O'Connor's home for a chat and was invited to Cilla's penthouse in St James. This was a wonderful time in my life. I then indulged in my love for food, interviewing all the top chefs from Gordon, Jamie, Michel Roux and all of the current TV titivators of fodder.

Food has always been a huge part of my life. Restaurants are my favourite pastime to truly relax. I was now getting access to the best chefs (and their food). If I can review travel, shows, spas, hotels, casinos – why not restaurants? In the mid-noughties Vegas was flying and the obscene indulgence was out of control. A friend of mine who runs the glorious Eiffel Tower Restaurant told me that ten Chinese businessmen had a £10,000 bottle of wine EACH one lunchtime, took half a glass and left the rest. He comped the meal (free) and took the £100,000 for booze plus £20,000 (automatically added) tip and then shut the restaurant. The team celebrated this obscene waste and decadence and enjoyed the remaining £99K of 'wasted' wine and laughed their tits off all the way to the bank. But who paid for this? It was a time of corporate credit cards. No one cared. By the time of the banking crash in 2008 all of this ended and would never return. But for a decade in places like Sin City and Dubai, they were the Mecca of obscene wealth and shocking waste of other people's cash. During this period, I ate the best food I've ever seen in my life! They put caviar on cornflakes, scallops on a cheese sandwich and fillet steak was the new corned beef. From Joël Robuchon to Guy Savoy, they all welcomed me with open arms for a review and often gave a personally crafted menu for me to enjoy and photograph. I'm all for a posh meal but I'm equally ofay with popping to KFC and discretely fingering the boneless bucket! This got me thinking, if I could do it in Vegas why not anywhere else? So, I planned a trip to Paris – the home of gastronomy and the ultimate master chefs. Guess what, once again people were over the Moon to have me. My videos ranked high and sat on page one on Google and lived forever. Timeless. In fact, I don't think anyone has ever collectively beaten any of my #1 reviews. Google search is powerful and can make and break the hospitality and entertainment sector. I don't think I even understood the reach and impact of eyes watching.

Don't tell anyone but the key to my success is that I deliver what I promise. Lesser con artists 'get away' with blagging trips and freebies but are quickly caught out. I worked bloody hard to make my content creative at significant cost to myself. I always delivered the review - nicely packaged and quickly - on time and to a standard that looked like I had a team of producers. Often, I'd have my videos up before my guest had got home from work. That is impressive in this world of procrastination. Unlike 'old media' where if you miss it it's gone, mine would live on for years……. and now decades.

My dear cousin Harry flew in from Michigan to join me in Paris. We ate at some incredible places as well as going up the Eiffel Tower and seeing shows like the Les Folies Bergère and Moulin Rouge! All as invited guests. No longer did I need the 'BBC' three letters to open doors. My stats on Google spoke for themselves. At that point I'd had '12 million minutes viewed.' Back then I thought that was impressive. I travelled on Eurostar for the first time, another incredible feat of engineering. That big thing boring for years to get to the other side – not dissimilar to myself. Again, sharing this stuff with friends and family was always fab. We spent a week living like a king! I couldn't believe my luck. <u>Everything</u> was content. All of my passions became my reviews – how fortuitous is that. Hard work, but a hoot! To top it all we even stayed as guests of Paris Hilton – the hotel, not the porn star! Gobble Gobble.

One trip I made alone was extra special though. Sometimes you can't share things that blow your mind. I was invited twice by Canada Tourism to record two documentaries celebrating their incredible country. 'Press trips' are notoriously hard work but boy was I glad I agreed. I was in their hands. I won't do things in groups on holiday, let alone for a gig. Tortuous, so I agreed to film on the understanding I'd be personally escorted on the tour. The first trip was to Montreal for the comedy festival. A bit like Edinburgh these things are hit and miss. The odd gold dust and mostly forgettable crap. Comedians are tough to crack. Mostly morose, it wasn't ratings gold. Little joy for me – I'm not one for festivals. I used the comedy festival as a hook for the special and then spent all day seeing the sights. The irony was that I was better treated than the headline turns. Comedians are notoriously classless and cheap, but you know me, I like a hotel nicer than my bedroom, or I don't bother. They put me up in the Hôtel Le Crystal de La Montagne à Montreal. It was lovely. In fact, I ended up hanging out with Patrick Kielty after he moved out of his shithole into this swanky hotel. Over a beer we pissed ourselves at the irony that I had a suite in a 5* hotel whilst stars (selling thousands of tickets) were sharing some dodgy Airbnb flat with four other gag tellers and sleeping on inflatable mattresses. I do have the odd blow up in my bedroom, but that's another story. The 'press' title did have its benefits, that's for sure. This was all pre-Cat Deeley BTW and her trying to present This Morning. Watching Cat trying to be interesting and read an autocue is more painful than Patrick's stand-up (IT'S A JOKE!) Nice chap though. You see I can separate the two – the man and the act – most can't.

The trip began in style with Air Canada flying me out. They took fantastic care of me flying me out business class for 'Belfield on Broadway' for years for reviews and plugs. These were the good old days of PR. I scratch your back and you tickle my tits. I was picked up from the airport in a limo and taken straight to the hotel. As always, I didn't waste a minute and went to my first gig within minutes. With mic in hand, I popped back after to talk to the turn which was now perfectly normal – unless I didn't like them. This was the period my life got very awkward! Fifteen plus years into my professional career and I now needed backbone bigtime! Easier said than done. Only twice in my career has an act been so hideous I've had to refuse the pre-arranged interview – squeaky bum time for sure. One was at Edinburgh Comedy Festival and the other at Montreal. I can mostly fake it and find something positive – even if it's the size and quality of the programme or comfortable seating in the auditorium but these two stinkers were hopeless. I can't remember their names, but, two women in dungarees with nose piercings. I'm sure they later went on to be BBC middle managers or probation officers……but they weren't my type!

Montreal is a fascinating place. A legacy of Olympic monuments clutter the town. I was given a fantastic tour guide called Ruby Roy – isn't it funny how some names you never forget. She escorted me around for ten days and we had a hoot! I had an all-access pass to anywhere I wanted to poke around and we even went for a drive on the actual former formula one racetrack. This lady knew everything and was a joy to tour this Canadian gem with. A couple of years ago I flew in again for a cruise and it was even more special to re-live my visit to the Le Château Frontenac – a glorious historic hotel overlooking Montreal. It stands proud and majestic built in a better era of pure regal class. Akin to the

St Pancras in London it's an above inspiring monument. We have so much for which to thank the railway. My last night was in this glorious Fairmont Hotel. How lucky am I? My favourite thing was the hotel dog. He lives in reception and select guests get to take him for a walk. How amazing is that? He was the size of a pony. A Newfoundland Shetland I believe. He took me for a bloody walk. I didn't know whether to lead him or mount him! I can't believe my luck being given the opportunity to make all of these memories and record hours of new exclusive material. They can hold you hostage and kidnap you in a padded cell – but they can't take away the memories. They keep my heart alive. For me the comedy festival became irrelevant. Most turns weren't my cup of tea - in fact some were as funny as the war in Ukraine. I met the odd gem, but mostly comedians are socially retarded, awkward and don't know their real voice. I think this is why they do crap interviews. They're incapable of being themselves. I did catch up with a few great Brits like Jimmy Carr, Ross Nobel and Andrew Lawrence – that was cool. Often if it's not scripted and they're not 'in character' they can't talk. I think this is why so many of my comedy friends are intrigued by my 'free' style on-air. I have no fear as I'm just me. I can't be caught out because there is no script. It's an exhilarating way to 'perform.' Just 'Be You' – the two most important words in showbiz. Who can be arsed remembering a script? Ricky Gervais is 100% scripted. Not a single word is ad-libbed in his global stand-up 'play.' That's for Corrie and Emmerdale actors. It's reading and remembering. Hardly rocket science, is it? Toddlers at nursery can do it in the stable every Christmas. For me the joy is toying with the audience – Ross, Dara, Boyle (Frankie not Susan) are great at those electric, unique and LIVE moments.

Aside from comedy my tour continued and I was taken for a history lesson. Montreal is steeped in French Canadian drama – ask Celine Dion. The food was curious. A chef invited me to his tiny eatery for some 'authentic' grub. When he presented a delicacy that looked like a broken leg carved in half – literally – even I recoiled! I can do most things but 'bone marrow' - literally off the bone was a step too far. One man's luxury is another man's nightmare. There's no doubting though that the French influence gives a finesse and class that the USA simply will never have, but I draw the line at dinner time surgery. I put some things in my mouth over the years (ask Tess Daley) but this was a leg and step too far! It's so inspiring to see how un-yank Canadians are. Totally unique and uninvested by The States lack of 'je ne sais quoi' over the border, I do admire. I dare say most Canadians shudder at the USA. They certainly pity and mock them. It's like Martin Kemp and his less sophisticated popular brother.

For my next trip, instead of flying into Montreal they flew me to Halifax for a fly drive visit down the East Coast of Nova Scotia. This was prior to the iPhone so there were no iMAPS 'turn left, turn right.' I was heading to two glorious destinations. 'Peggy's Cove' – what a diamond that is - and 'The Bay of Fundy' for whale watching. I was cock-a-hoop to be back less than twelve months later. I'd been whale watching before, but that was after an incident in Blackpool with a big boned Biffa from Barnsley. Canada was far more impressive and a memory I'll NEVER forget. I was mesmerized by Nova Scotia's innocence, natural beauty, untouched and sincere magnificence. Stunning. They booked me in some beautiful tiny hotels along the coastline whilst I calmly meandered down south for just over a week. I loved it. Everyone was so excited to see me. They didn't have thousands of visitors in these hamlets with picket fences and so few people in town they knew everyone's name. Class. It was remote and often without any phone signal for days. What an expedition. You might have gathered I'm no Bear Grylls. I'm not interested in getting wet, dirty or eating 'Bush Anus.' Natural beauty is my thing, like Alaska, Norway and Kelly Brook. If only the NHS prescribed fresh air, countryside, beauty, walks with friends instead of anti-depressants and therapy - maybe the world wouldn't have a pandemic of anxiety and negativity. Anyway, that's not why you called…...

What was magical about this trip was that I would never EVER have booked it myself. To be given the opportunity to go clam digging was something I'll never forget. So simple but so incredible. Every town I stopped at were waiting for me. Brilliantly organised. It's up there with the Grand Canyon in terms of its impact on my heart. The scale of these places of wonder is breath-taking. The boat trips were so amazing. Akin to the Maasai Mara, the whales weren't forced to join us, they chose to and loved showing off. It was fun to them. Three enormous whales turned up. I christened them Gemma, Corden and Vanessa. I met so many kind and generous people along the way. One of those trips of a lifetime, only made possible by this incongruous, unique and bonkers job. My only regret with success is that these once in a lifetime experiences became more and more regular losing the impact through exhaustion. Travel is tiring. (Boo Hoo – I get it. This ain't a pity party I promise you!) I had to run from one sensational experience to the next. I wish we could bottle these memories and re-live them in quieter times and drink them in fully. I loved learning, growing and seeing extraordinary things and meeting incredible people. What a privilege. All of these memories have been captured for eternity in audio form on my website.

I've been so blessed to have had so many of those 'pinch me' moments over the last thirty years. The only reason these happen is because I made them happen and there was no one to sabotage or taint the moment. I fought for every opportunity. At this point I was under the radar and oblivious to my wannabee detractors. I promised myself I'd never have a boss again to ruin this peace and calm in my life. In between foreign trips I kept getting gig after gig at the BBC. Some Saturdays I'd literally do mid-morning on BBC Derby, afternoons on BBC Worcester and BBC Midlands from Shropshire at 10pm. How exciting is that? Better still, I only needed one new show which I repeated three times in the day. This became a well-oiled machine! One day BBC Derby called. They wanted to use me as the buffer in between a 'legend' and the new DJ. This happened to me a lot, often without being told. Smart programmers would use my nincompoopery to distract from an old-timer of decades on air before a whippersnapper took over to lose the entire audience in nanoseconds. They hoped my showing off in between the old and the new would soften the PR blow for the station. Very calculated. It was three weeks work replacing Alex Trelinski. I told them that no one would care by the time he'd driven out of the car park, but they knew best and wanted the Belfield Buffer! I added £25 to my show fee to put up with the shit. They happily paid and three weeks later the world had moved on. I was later told the reason I was given this task is because unlike my weak, feeble and flaky colleagues – I could take any crap or backlash. Again, that's the LIVE discipline and training from the school of hard knocks. That's showbiz. What reality check and kick in the bollocks hey for all 'legendary' turns. We can and will all be replaced. Poor Alex……. replaced by Alex and no one even noticed. What a fickle business.

Alex moved to Spain like my mate Chris Ashley. After decades on the BBC these legends and pros were unceremoniously let go for a 'new sound.' Yes, a shitter, less popular whippersnapper sound. I didn't care anymore. I knew the industry was bullshit and the lunatics were running the asylum. I took the money and ran. Complete contempt on my part. Just sad for these old boys who had dedicated their lives to Aunty. By Christmas I was doing three LIVE shows a day and fifty shows in the run. People ask why I've never done Panto? I would love to do Dick in December but it's £700 a week for twelve shows. I earned more in two days doing village halls. Maybe in 2026 I'll debut my much anticipated 'Jack and the Beanstalker?'

Since the age of fourteen I'd had Sir Ken's words ringing in my ears. 'SHOW BUSINESS.' Take the money, not the round of applause and 'work hard.' I never stopped punting for work. It's relentless. More work led to more gigs and crucial repeat gigs. The Christmas tour was always my favourite, but the pressure was immense. Even though some sneered that I wasn't playing the Palladium I took every gig seriously because whether it was a care home for fifty silver tops in an old cockery or New Year's Eve in a club to 250, people had gone to massive effort with food, invitations and the cost was massive to them. Regardless, I still earned three times as much as any twirly in panto land so stick that in your pipe and smoke it! In 2009 the worst thing happened on the 15$^{th}$ December – I got the Flu. Not man flu, proper flu! I'd done twenty-five plus shows but I'd still got thirty plus to go. I never cancel a show, but this floored me. I could have cried. This was a big lesson that I'M ONLY HUMAN. Most people get ill but when it comes to 'the entertainer' you're taken for granted and most importantly do not have a backup. They're NEVER going to find a replacement and you've screwed up their biggest party of the year. For two days I lay in bed motionless, tossing and turning……sometimes turning……and mainly trying to get back to sleep. That's five shows that I promised to reschedule. The Saturday night gig I just couldn't let them down as it was the second most anticipated night of the year after New Year's Eve. The weekend before Christmas is the biggest date and I was firing on a quarter of a cylinder and stuck in reverse. It was one of those amazing 'modern villages' for silver tops with one hundred plus in the audience, all paying attention, 100% invested, behind you all the way and their only ambition was to have the best night ever - so I couldn't let them down. Also, the money is phenomenal, almost a week's panto money for 2 x 45 minutes. I of course, always went above and beyond to impress - you mustn't be a party pooper. However, I had to do something I'd never done before – CHEAT.

Sometimes in life (and in public performance) you have to work out the bigger picture. I was seriously weak and ill. You have to do the wrong thing for the right reason. I shouldn't be leaving the house let alone wearing the big red suit and mincing along with fifty mods and rockers to the Santa Baby medley. The only way I was going to get through it was to do the show on 'track' which effectively means mime to the songs to enable me to have the energy and vocal strength to get through the comedy and variety schtick. At the end I always do '12 days' with props giving me a mechanism to get twelve punters up on stage to take the pish and pass fifteen minutes, totally unique to them with a tried and tested old gag that can't fail. Again though, all of this takes tremendous energy and concentration. I re-scheduled the 2.30pm for the following week and stayed in bed wearing a turban praying to the baby Jesus that I didn't lose my voice entirely. I knew if I could just speak, I could survive. This wasn't about me it was about not ruining these parties. Meds would give me the energy to get through it but NO VOICE = no gig.

So, I called the entertainment manager and explained it was 'fake it' or I'd have to cancel. They were over the Moon I was doing everything possible not to let them down. Honesty is ALWAYS the best policy, fibbing fools no one, I learned this on day one. If you tell the truth people will work with you. Trying to be a smart arse and pull a fast one never works. I dragged my miserable hairy white arse out of my pit, showered and put on my pretend smile, red nose and clown shoes. Within twenty seconds of walking through the door Doctor Showbiz kicked in, TITS and TEETH and off I went. It is amazing what the body can achieve through adrenalin, remarkable! I just didn't know adrenalin was brown until the finalé. As I've said before we're not owed a living and you perform every show as if it's your last. No one can say I'm not a tryer.

I take my end of the bargain seriously so now I had to pull it out of the bag. With the aid of a little audio jiggery pokery, giving me time to rest in between segments, I made it through. No one could tell. Not one person noticed I didn't sing LIVE. Makes you wonder why I work so hard when I'm well. By the way, if you think this is scandalous and cheating – the alternative is no show and disappointment. I remember seeing a MEGA headliner in Vegas who did the whole show lip synced 'on track.' He claimed 'desert voice' makes it impossible to do five shows a week. Are you paying to see the star or hear the voice? Basically, there's no moisture in the air – a nightmare for vocalists. In fact, in the West End, Phantom has certain notes on track and Mamma Mia! uses the same trick for various reasons during the heavy dance numbers. I suppose as long as the audience aren't disappointed the job is done right? All I know is that it saved my tour.

The show had to go on. This gave it an extra energy, and I was rebooked in twelve months' time. A rebooking is the only proof of success. As I did my gripping and grinning after the show to say goodnight after almost two hours, I collapsed in the car and didn't have the energy to say another word until the Sunday Matinée. I made it through the run – by the skin of my teeth. The point is that entertainers aren't paid for easy gigs that go right. You're paid for shows like this where you have to use every ounce of tenacity in your bones (and fifteen years of experience) to get through it alive and I did. Of course, the reality is by 10pm Christmas Eve my Christmas is over. I'm Rudolphed out. It's a shame but the reality of being a turn is by the time it's 'your fun' you're too exhausted to have any. The payoff is the kindness from those you entertain. After twenty years many of us had grown up together. We were friends and family. How lucky am I to have such amazing and loyal audiences! I guess entertainers are the party but sadly are never at the party. The turn's curse I suppose.

I have to admit that YouTube gave me my social life and Christmases back, for that I'm eternally grateful. That was the biggest blessing of all. For the first time in my life, I wanted to host and be at the parties.

## Chapter 10

## Man Up! Grown Up
## Becoming the REAL me!

Finding yourself is probably the hardest thing in life to achieve. I think you've probably worked out that I'm quite complex as a human being as my 50% torment and tease is nothing like the 50% private man who just lives for his family and friends and wants people to mind their own facking business. Showbiz adds a dimension to your personality that has to be managed. Ego is the darkest of your potential attributes and the 'do you know who I am' brigade are the most odious of all that I've met…..and something you would never want to be. Equally the 'I want to be an extra on Eastenders or Hollyoaks for nothing' just to be seen is equally as tragic. Ego is a part of every performer's personality to enable you to show off and have the confidence to do so BUT it has to be managed. The art is just turning up the volume on your personality and leaving the rest at the door.

I can promise you that I have never applied for any reality TV show any more than I've nominated myself for awards. Neither will leave you with anything other than disappointment, fake affirmation and a big head born out of something that is NOT tangible or real. These are the types who toss themselves off…...a bridge or car park. I always focussed on projects that were a perfect match for my comfort zone and talents. If I did 'Come Dine With Me,' 'Big Brother' or 'BGT' I would be edited to shit, mocked and ridiculed. Why take the risk? Ego would be the only plausible reason to humiliate myself on such shows. I'll pass. I always knew where my strengths and passions lie working LIVE which isn't reliant on producers editing with hedge shears or toe clippers. I was best at radio by a mile. If you think about it VoR is radio on TV. It's a filmed radio show so it's perfect for my skill set. Equally I love stage which I've worked hard at BUT it's a huge teeth-gripping pain in the ass – especially now at theatre level. I know I'll never be a great singer or comedian – I just put everything together to pull it off. Finally, when all of these really work seamlessly together you find 'your voice.' I've been influenced massively after twenty years of studying the art, but you use that melting pot to create your own product. By thirty I'd done thousands of hours of broadcasting and stage time but was only just feeling invincible in my identity personally and professionally. I'd always dreamed of being thirty-five which let's face it is the perfect age to get laid, woo and warm to visually impaired gals or birds with low standards. Only then do you have the emotional intelligence to 'be a man.' God I must have been shit in bed before then. I was so bad I wished I was someone else. Never mind multiple orgasms, I couldn't even get my taxis to come on time! What with low self-confidence, my micro man sausage, bingo wings and the personality of Timmy Mallett's bastard grandson – this is a hot mess! I must have had the social allure of fish pie smothered in stilton. I also found my political voice and confidence after two decades. No longer did I let my working-class upbringing shroud my contempt for lazy Labour excuses. No longer would my political embarrassment keep me quiet. I felt I needed to speak my mind, own my conscious bias and become a raving proud and prejudiced gobshite! I felt reborn…….

Finally in my thirties it all felt right and fell into place! I only wish I could relive my twenties knowing what I know now. I mishandled so many personal and professional 'incidents' simply by not being equipped to deal with what was going on. I know I could never have coped in jail in my twenties or thirties. Absolutely not. Every day I use my inner peace, calm and serenity to laugh at fackwits, take the piss out of inept civil serpants and most importantly NEVER react to any bait or manufactured shenanigans, designed to give me another black eye. Death also taught me so much. Nothing <u>REALLY</u> matters. We don't matter. And most importantly show business, with about twenty exceptions, taught me it CANNOT be taken seriously as almost none of us will be remembered or make any tangible difference. All that matters is love, being the best we can be and as the great philosopher Jeanette Krankie once said: "at the end of the day…...it gets dark!"

I was at that age where it all started to click – my neck, my back, my ankles……

I spent a lot of time travelling Europe, spending more and more time in Valencia, Barcelona and on the outskirts of Benidorm in Altea. I loved Greece and each January went to Sharm El-Sheikh for what they pretend to be 5* luxury. Trust me, when you spend the first three days on the toilet (clenching your sphincter with the same tension as watching Roman Kemp read an autocue) it's hard to find any glamour let alone indulgence. For a while I spent a couple of summers in Turkey until I realised only farmyard animals would consider the 'no flush toilet paper' rule anywhere near acceptable. One day the phone rang as I was by the pool in Egypt – I was sat next to my Mummy - and a boss from BBC Radio Leeds had heard of my success across the Network. By now I'd broadcast on nearly all of the BBC Locals in one way or another for nearly a decade and was very highly regarded. They wanted 'a new sound' for Leeds and I was 'perfect for the role.' Once again, they had all of my tapes and demos and more importantly first-hand endorsements from a lot of the stations I'd worked for who were chuffed to bits with my ramblings through my unblemished BBC career. I must make it clear that despite all of the dramas I've described in my career I had not had a single issue from 1996-2010 with anyone at the BBC whatsoever. I was as squeaky clean as Phillip Schofield's diary. Right hand up to the Bigman – I repeat – not a <u>single</u> incident. I was liked, trusted and respected. This is paramount in what was manufactured over the next year.

Foolishly I had the highly coveted 'BBC staff contract' dangled under my nose again and being the naïve prick I am, I thought what could possibly go wrong? I had totally forgotten my BBC Leicester experience of the pure depression being under their contractual mob like spell and maniacal control. They offered me two weeks cover on mid-morning for a very nice fella called Johnny I'Anson who was young and inexperienced but a thoroughly nice lad. The plan was for me to take over permanently if it went well as 9am was the networks new priority and this boss couldn't stand the current show. Being your average BBC management Judas, they didn't tell the staff but naturally they knew a change was coming. I was persona non grata before I'd even opened my big foot in mouth gob! I'd been told they were also hiring Martin Kelner (for the fourth time) to take over Breakfast. He had in fact been sacked unceremoniously and removed by the same senior manager (who openly couldn't stand him) several times before over thirty years and yet was regarded as the future of BBC Leeds by going backwards twenty years – bizarre! I like Martin personally but didn't think his show was any good. He's as sneery in real life as he is on the air. That's his schtick. He was given woeful content and spluttered out Cystic Fibrosis and 'inner thigh rash' articles through his gritted dentures. We got on fine and both had total disdain for the BBC and this hideous inadequate and inept hierarchy. The creepiness was very similar to BBC Radio Nottingham 10 years prior where bosses seemed to groom junior whippersnappers. This apparent culture of insidious harassment is almost as bad as the undeniable bullying from senior management and presenters. God, I hated that building, I wouldn't even use the toilet, someone told me you could catch 'it' from a toilet seat. I said 'you can't,' he said if you sit down before the other chap stood up you can. I'm not casting aspersions but it was like finding a needle in a gaystack, if they weren't ambivilacious, I got the feeling they'd sway in an imaginary breeze. Martin and I loved a beer and a dinner. I much preferred the real Martin to 'BBC

Kelner.' Great fun for his size and age. This has happened to me a lot where I prefer the person to the act. Like so many I only wished he could be as funny and genuine behind the mic as he was in the pub. This is a tragic BBC bred culture actually. They break the first rule of success – 'DON'T BE YOURSELF!' is their mantra! It just didn't make sense to me to take an irreverent satirist like Kelner and make him do boring BBC Radio chats about binmen shortages and the latest developments in anti-pile cream for your anus erectus! He hated doing them, mocked them and yet this boss was convinced it was the future of their station to re-employ his complete open contempt for the format. Neither of us in hindsight should have gone near this toxic, vile and pitiful station or management team all of which have now fallen off their mortal FM coil. My only concern was my three hours on air though – I learned that lesson <u>LONG</u> ago. A few weeks later the BBC Radio Leeds vultures descended like a rabid pack of lepers at a free for all lesbian food bank!

It was a car crash from day one. What on earth was I thinking? Old school, bitter, nasty, protected BBC mafia with their knives out like a Saturday night in Sickdiq's crapital city. I stupidly bit the bullet and signed a twelve-month contract – what was I thinking! Honestly, this was entirely born out of ego and laziness. For 365 days I wouldn't have to tour and schlepp all over the UK. A very ill-advised and devastating disaster that would cost me everything! Needless to say, this was the most hideously toxic atmosphere I'd ever worked in. It was ghastly, unnecessary and totally unprovoked. This was their culture. It seemed everyone hated everyone. There was no gay mafia here, much worse! A virtue signalling, box ticking, lefty, paranoid, jealous, front stabbing office full of talentless has-beens, freaks, entitled pen pushers and manipulating Mogadons. It was worse than David Walliams' multiple personalities! From day one producers and presenters tried to sabotage me mercilessly and others. They sold stories to the local press (which only made me bigger – I liked that bit in fact I sold a couple myself). They got more and more pissed off the bigger the show became. It was relentless. Never in my life was I more excited to leave my flat and go straight back to Nottingham at mid-day on Friday. It was beyond vile and the top bosses knew it. It was seedy with bosses shagging new recruits and bullying into social activities that mostly led to young BAs getting BJs and a free pearl neckless (BA = Broadcasting Assistant/BJ = Broadcast Journalist). This nest of vipers was empowered from the top who set the example. Pure vindictive evil – all overlooked by the endless vomits of so-called HR Celia Imrie's (with folders under their arms) who in true BBC style turned a blind eye from day one. 99% of this didn't involve me, but I see and hear everything! No flies on me.

My timing was also hideous for various reasons. Firstly, I was forced to sign a contract I didn't want. Instead of making me staff like at Leicester or better still offering me a freelance contract which I requested, they <u>blackmailed</u> me into setting up a fake Limited Company which they liked to call a 'service company.' I was then 'employed' by my own Limited Company as a presenter! My 'service company' was then contracted to deliver my services to Radio Leeds, leaving them with zero responsibility for anything – including sick pay or national insurance. It was a swizz and a scam. Of course we were employed. I turned up at the same time five times a week. I took the BBC to court over this in 2018, unsurprisingly they used their bully boy lawyers at RPC to prevent justice! The barrister that was instructed by Aunty and paid for by YOUR TV rape tax has since been sacked, disgraced and banned from ever working in law again. She lied to her own clients so not a surprise it intimidated, cheated and misled me on the BBC's behalf and instruction. Rotten to the core this lot I'm telling you! RPC attended Nottingham Magistrates Court and wanted my claim thrown out as it was 'vexatious.' By the most hysterical twist of fate, the very same day IR35 was plastered on the front of The Times over Uber and other similar scam contracts. The judge ruled on my side. Less than three months after my court case the government agreed that 'IR35' contracts were not lawful and over a hundred presenters in my exact position were given staff contracts and compensated immediately. Basically, the BBC shamelessly wanted us to work under 'staff' control and conditions whilst they didn't offer us any holiday, let alone pension. Outrageous! Dopey bully bosses believed I was their slave despite the contract clearly stating they were NOT my employers. The BBC's cockamamie scheme hired my company who hired me so therefore Belfield Enterprises only had one Chief Exec. Sorry about their luck. It was a massive scandal that typifies what gangsters the publicly owned national broadcaster truly are. This was 100% onerous and criminal to bully talent into it. Utter contempt for human rights believing they are completely above the law and can coerce and blackmail with impunity.

My contract caused endless rows with those upstairs because as you may have realised, I'm quite litigious and they'd dropped a major bollock in effectively making me my own boss. I knew my rights and they'd stupidly not put any holiday clauses in the deal – because they weren't allowed to – so I'd just bugger off for a week or two whenever they pissed me off leaving them seething. WHY? WHY? Because there was nothing that they could do about it! This entire contract was untenable from day one. In fact, it was a total joke. These bosses wanted to control my entire life on and off air. They couldn't bear that they didn't have 1% legal right to demand ANYTHNG! In fairness the boss did give me a few grand (of your tax money) to move to Leeds, so that softened the blow and bought a few nice meals, a chaise longue and two banquettes.

The show quickly became a huge success in fact it was the biggest show in seven years and beat Kelner on Breakfast after six months making all of the jealous and venomous institutionalised office haters even more incandescent with rage. There's a pattern here, right? I'm not going to bang on about how hideous that nest of vipers was, but it was nothing short of evil. This place did get to me. The endless pecking was excruciating. The more I made them look stupid the worse they became. Management was clueless but micro managed my every breath. I'd get on-air and completely ignore them. They knew nothing about radio, audiences or even how to manage. It was a circus. The Stockholm Syndrome of BBC inmates after ten years is staggering. It was like Jacko's Thriller by 2pm.

The vicious manipulations were relentless and it was a disgusting way to work and perform. I should have known from day one to walk out - it's my own fault not maydaying and jumping ship. Johnny was truly a nice guy and had been thrown under the bus publicly by an inept and heartless, clueless and classless management team who had a total disregard for his ego, let alone wellbeing. Nothing to do with me, but I was the punching bag for even more outdated, bitter and twisted BBC bores who hated that they were done, finished and disgraced whilst I was deemed the future and repeatedly quoted as 'local radio's breath of fresh air.' Of course, when I was on-air, they chose not to get my sense of humour – let alone schtick or theatre – my 'comedy bits' went completely over their dull, corporate and make-up free heads. Try some eyeliner dear, it might distract from your wrinkles and BO! I remember sitting in the Virgin lounge on my way to Vegas in the April and a boss called to wish me a 'happy holiday.' I said, "thank you." It said, "Bring me back something Vegasy!" I said, "What, like an STI?" I thought that was a good gag. It replied, "Alex we've spoken before about being totally inappropriate!" I ask you. What do you say? They called me on my private mobile in my time and still their megalomania led them to believe they had the right to control everything I said! To think that in court I was accused of being grandiose and had delusions of grandeur. Not moi!

Within weeks I had 'THE CALL' – "Alex your humour isn't working for us - you're banned from doing jokes." I laughed out loud. "I'm serious," this slobbering suit spat with total incredulity. What type of moron would say such a thing to a man like me? It said "from tomorrow you cannot be funny. We don't want it, that's not in our new format." We're back to booking a window cleaner to fix the car, aren't we? Insanity. Of course, I played stupid. I carried on identically. When they'd mince up to me in the studio spitting feathers with a hot poker stuck up their arsehole seething, I'd simply say – "sorry I didn't think I was being funny. Please tell me what you find funny?" They'd storm out. Then they started banning my jingles. 'I'm Dolly Parton. Alex is just like me he's definitely got his knockers.' BANNED. It was deemed obscene. Humourless androids! 'Hi I'm Carol Vorderman. You're listening to Alex Belfield a man who's just like me, he loves to take two on the top and one on the bottom.' What really pissed me off was their arrogance and contempt for their audience. 'You're not broadcasting from the market - they're riff raff and you encourage them' one trumped up führer quipped. That boiled my piss. Bloody cheek, these are my punters. When I left the radio station the private note from 'management' to staff said, 'Alex may well claim to have the biggest audience, but they are the wrong audience.' Utterly sickening contempt for West Yorkshire's finest. They despise the solid gold punters who are the backbone of my act…...and their licence fee! This became a massive part of my Clown Court hearing in 2022. The BBC simply would not accept my unparalleled and unprecedented success despite admitting my listening figures were enormous in comparison to anything they'd achieved in a decade. This is typical of BBC delusionists. The sanctimony and superciliousness reeks louder than their cheap perfume. I didn't know there was a brand called 'Tester.' One BBC fella who looked like Hilary Devay's drag act said he wore 'Come to Me.' The slut of a programme director's PA said "it doesn't smell like Come to Me!" I thank you! I'm here all week! OK, you started it! What do you expect for this price. Anyway, back to the script. These people truly believe their 'shit don't stink.' Teflon! They're so brainwashed even facts are distorted for their own agenda. It was staggering to hear this crap day after day in court about me being a flop when in fact I was their biggest and most undeniably popular success since Huw Edwards ran the BBC youth club in the 1980s!

Anyway, that's not why you called! I'd rented the penthouse at the top of the block of flats right next to the BBC studios in Leeds City Centre overlooking the market. It was £900 a month which I thought was a bargain in comparison to London. There were some very lovely times, all of these done in stealth. My guests would stalk in and out of my abode so the snooper's charter next door didn't pry and stick their brown noses in. I got incredibly close to one delicious BBC star in the region who used to visit me for let's say a little 'horizontal jogging' in between trying the one, two buckle my shoe. We actually had a few amazing trips to New York, Barbados and Vegas. She was the perfect spy in the camp who pretended to agree with the BBC bullshitery but would then come home and gossip proudly about how they continually conspired to set me up to fail. What a blessing being on the inside of someone on the inside of the Beeb! LMFAO! Keep your enemies close in showbiz my friend!

I have to admit, our secret sordid and illicit affair was exciting. They had <u>NO</u> idea. They're blind to the bleeding obvious. 'She'd never shag him.' Really. 'He couldn't pull a bird like that.' Little did they know! This is why I keep my gob shut about such private matters. Far more powerful (and sexy) to have the last laugh. Unlike her, this would not have gone down well downstairs – in Satan's national broadcasting dungeons! We actually spent my 31st birthday in the hotel at Le Manoir in Oxford. No one noticed we were both conveniently off. THICKOS! Blind to their own prejudice. This type of hanky panky does play to my naughtier side. I love that they all thought they were so clever. Every word was fed back. IMBECILES. Honestly, these people are as thick as two short planks. I win. My half an inch and a dozen wrinkles were chuffed to bits by the beautiful bon ami by a BBC babe.

My favourite balls up at BBC Leeds was when a top box ticking lefty with two hearing aids edited a <u>very</u> serious interview with the parents of an 18-year-old lad who was shot on his doorstep. This dope saved the interview at the wrong speed making this heartbreaking 'face to face' chat sound like Micky and Mini Mouse on speed. <u>No one</u> could understand my fury. 'She's deaf, it's not her fault.' That's like having a blind 747 captain and hoping for the best. MORONS.

I also had my three producers, all lady types (born with real fu fu's, not ones bought from a London clinic) who were great fun. Despite being clueless about radio, content, ratings or even who our audience was, they would pop over for prosecco and steak. Obviously these brainwashed, institutionalised poor devils had to play the game, but again were a great comfort to me knowing that I had eyes and ears on the inside and real fake showbiz pals for a year. They'd only ever worked for the BBC – can you imagine? I pitied them more than Joe Biden's carer. Their naïvety and sheer ignorance of the real world was staggering. I don't blame them at all, they knew no better. They had that victim syndrome where they were in love with their rapist, attacker or abuser. They absolutely knew how odious these dark forces and bullies were at the BBC but they themselves were openly complicit as they had to pay the mortgage so carried on regardless. It's a terrifying mentality. Nothing will ever change at this .gov protected monolith.

My lowest moment was Children in Need 2011. By November, my unprecedented success was sending the whack jobs off their rocker. Now they had a chance to humiliate and embarrass me. 'Would I wax Harry Gration?" How absolutely withering to that legend and local hero. Instead of using my talents for a variety show, they thought they'd humiliate and degrade me with these appalling 'challenges' which didn't work on radio – they were entirely visual. This total degrading stitch-up, like milking a cow on a farm which was apparently an idea inspired from my big boss's short period dating Savile down the road in Roundhay

Park. Stupid. I of course made it vulgar and riddled with inuendo – the very thing they despised more than my success. Listen if you ask me to wank a heifer LIVE at 10am, that's the risk you take! Despite raising a fortune through tossing off farmyard animals – the bosses were apoplectic at my smut. They started it!!! My '5-day challenge' culminated in a visit to the Bradford Bulls where I was rugby tackled by 40 stone of men which landed me in hospital. Yep, from milking fat cows to being mounted by two rugby goons they'd planned the whole thing without telling me. It was malicious and vindictive and summed <u>EVERYTHING</u> up. Two Pro players thought a LIVE assault was a good idea. I was virtually shanghaied out of the building by the sheer force. I was done. This was dark and evil. Even Katie Price would struggle to breathe under this amount of brain-dead manhood! Indefensible and shocking. I ended up bleeding and in hospital unable to catch my breath, talk or finish the broadcast. I later sued and got a pay out as the BBC didn't even defend the claim. How could they? It was sick, premeditated and frankly I should have filed a police complaint for GBH. This was no accident. Arranged by disgusting, bitter, jealous assassins who were too cowardly to fight their own battles so got two muscle Mary todger dodgers to give me a kicking in! This sums up BBC culture of bullying and passive aggressive intimidation. To this day this sort of indefensible crap happens all the time.

I loved Leeds as a place. The people were fantastic, and I'd made my mark but after Children in Need I knew I had to leave. I'm no victim boohooer but what that bunch of sick, no-talent losers did was vitriolic and systemic bullying as the court case exposed. They literally wanted to beat me into submission on air. Didn't happen, in fact, I became more outrageous for my remaining few months on air – I had nothing to lose. Being #1 on the station made things worse. I'd undermined an entire newsroom by being successful without them. I didn't need producers. I didn't need their shit content. I emasculated their entire empire. News doesn't get ratings, knob gags do! They hated that. Management was seething at my reaction on air and in typical BBC style they had no clue how to manage me so resorted to dirty tricks. My contract was up for renewal so I called their bluff and asked for a pay rise commensurate to my success. I knew they wouldn't pay. 'No one is getting a pay rise' I was told - another lie as staffers get inflation (at least) every year. 'OK I resign.' They couldn't believe it. Speechless. How dare I walk away from the BBC?! It was war. I resigned in person and in writing. What a bunch of disgusting characters and protected oppressors. I was threatened that if I didn't appear LIVE on Look North that night I'd be sacked. This is the modus operandi of scum sucking pondlife who can't bear the fact you're on more money than them. You don't know whether to put them over your knee and spank them with a scented bootlace or negotiate with these terrorists. Either way facts don't have feelings and my ratings were undeniable. I wasn't exactly on the bones of my arse and I was too old for a black eye so I'd leave these tosspots on tender hooks and pop off to Spearmint Rhino to see desperate Donna from Doncaster. They always say be nice to them on the way up so that they're nice when they go down on you. I think they dropped a bollock letting me go but they of course saw it as feathering their own nest and sparing their own blushes as I emasculated the newsroom further. Finally, the chickens were coming home to roost.

Next, I called their bluff and went BIG – and back to network. On New Year's Eve I did a six-hour party show called 'Belfield's Big Night In' on fifteen BBC Locals LIVE! It was brilliant! I played some of my favourite interviews from the year including Michael Parkinson, Chris Evans, Ken Bruce, John Cleese, Michael Palin, Graham Norton, Alan Carr and many more. This riled the jealous freaks further. I wish they'd keep their hair on, it's only wireless!!! I LOVE music so it was brilliant to playlist my own favourites. Mixed with LIVE callers it was an absolute joy.

What I did learn at the BBC over this year was all to do with their shameful and cockamamie schemes. The first was travel. BBC Travel centrally books all hotels, flights and trains from an outside company at a huge premium. I was still busy back and forth to London and the first time they booked it for me, it was over £200 standard class. Fack that, I'm too old and ugly to be stood up for three hours like sardines. I Googled and if I booked First Class in advance it was £60 return. I wrote a formal email to the bosses and they couldn't argue. I'd saved them £140 and I went First with a free meal and a couple of glasses of wine. From then on, I went First Class every time at a third of the cost to you - the licence fee payer. What kind of public service is this cabal and cartel? I was told never to tell anyone and she'd sign it off. How is this even a thing? I found this was identical with hotels and flights. Hotels (mostly 4*) were £100 more expensive than 5* luxury in Covent Garden so again I booked my own and saved THE TAXPAYER £1000's over that year of torture. I was staggered by their absolute contempt. For a decade later I made a fortune selling stories via BBC Freedom of Information to the newspapers. Every corner I turned there was waste. From lunch meetings with buffets at £30 per head to taxis booked but not used – no one cared. 'It's a job' - no it's not it's public money! It continues today, but I did chip away at their financial contempt.

Next the snakes upstairs paid for a salad dodger from BBC Radio 5 to 'whip me into shape.' This guy couldn't whip a meringue into shape – although, I bet he could eat a few! This balloon sized mammoth is a poor man's effeminate Eamonn Holmes without the class or talent. Despite the Irish lilt, he was charmless and a typical 'by the book' BBC homogenized paid Judas. He pretended to be a friend not enema, however he was sent into make me comply and put the fear of God in me…...which he did……….as I was petrified that he'd fall on me. I was having none of it. He started quoting my website – my <u>PRIVATE</u> website. "You can't say that" – oh yes, I can. "You'll have to change and delete it, that's not BBC policy." Oh, do piss off and shove a kebab in your pie hole! I couldn't wait to get out of the room. They'd spent a fortune sending him over from Belfast. I left him to his multi-pack of Walkers (that happened!) He's everything I'd never want to be on air. I remember him chasing folk without a mask during Covid and screaming at them for being so irresponsible. Hang on dear, you're 35 flaming stone, I think you've got far greater worries than the sniffles and a leaky bottom. Another supercilious, self-righteous journalist prick. Pfft. Not my cup of tea. Not sure if he sways in an imaginary breeze, but he gave me the chills! He was very polite and quietly spoken, but his 'light on his feet' approach to radio was as much use to me as a chocolate chisel. He was booked for four full day 'one on one' sessions. I never saw him again after the first one. Thank God for small mercies. He was last seen in the gents at an all you can eat Toby Carvery. Needs must! We had a mutual unpalatable disdain. He triggered my acid reflux bigtime.

Our time had come to an end after Christmas as I booked two weeks off to tour and the 'Head of Intimidation' hit the roof! "You're not having it off" one cardigan wearing woman with a moustache told me. The chance would be a fine thing! "Err, check my contract, I think you'll find I am!" It stormed off. I was right. The glory of my bullshit fake 'service' company was that I hired myself, therefore they had absolutely no control over me on or off the air. What an own goal hey? They HATED this! They presumed (like everyone else being 'freelance' with no paid holiday) that I wouldn't take time off. WRONG! I had more holidays than the rest of the station put together. In typical BBC style they believed that they owned every second of your life, every fibre of your being and every thought in your brainwashed head. No tar, not for me. It's satanic and creepy. I just headed down the M1 to junction 26. I'm far more relaxed and at home there.

The 'lifers' in prison remind me of these BBC drones. Hopeless. They're stir crazy, beaten by the system, feel worthless and have no idea whatsoever of the outside world. I had the temerity to question the way they did it as I knew they couldn't see the wood for the trees. I'm not saying I was a paragon of virtue but I knew these brainwashed Bettys needed to give their head a wobble. However, I also knew Auntie was like a leaky tap, I needed to be careful as everything I said is always taken down and used against me. It's truly pitiful. When you stand up to their insanity their heads explode. They're the epitome of 'my way or the highway.' I would never want to be them for all the ass plugs in Ann Summers! Hideously out of touch, hypocritical and a contemptuous breed who don't even know the law or their own rules. Most importantly they're mostly shit at their jobs and would never get a job commercially! Nothing has changed since my time at BBC Nottingham 14 years earlier surrounded by alcoholics, bullies and sex pests. My position was now untenable and pointless. I was #1 and they hated me more each day for humiliating them with my brazen tenacity and flagrant disrespect. Reverence has never been my forté. The pure laziness of my team was not only staggering but infuriating. At one point I had nine people working/interfering with my show. Seriously NINE! It was torture. There were only six segments, at least three of which I produced myself. What the cotton-picking colostomy bag of cack did, these daft twats do all day (other than cause trouble that didn't exist?). Please God, take me now! To justify their own positions, they booked meeting after meeting that I refused to attend unless they stated in writing why I was required. They gave up in the end. Good move! My favourite trick <u>EVER</u> was to walk into meetings I couldn't get out of, stand up and announce "can anyone tell me why I'm here?" Silence – so I'd walk straight out. They'd be tiggered and ready for a ballistic explosion.

After the local Gestapo failed to destroy my will to live, their next move was to bring in consultants from London. Oy vey – more pressure to beat me down and kill my soul. FAIL. 'I don't need a consultant I'm #1!' Their heads spun like a Catherine Wheel. Of course, the more they tried to destroy and control me, the more I wanted to succeed and be even more successful out of pure defiance. Devilment got the better of me and I couldn't resist having a little fun teasing these imbeciles and I'd be even more cheeky when they'd stand in the production booth opposite. I cut off a caller 'what a fart head' and hit the song! "You can't say that" one drone said. I replied "I just did, sack me!" It's impossible to control a man who'd resigned. Life's too short. I'd had enough. Nothing to lose and no facks to give. It was self-fulfilling prophecy at this point. The negative forces I encountered on a daily basis were depressing and ate away at my un-merciless optimism and determination to care. The quite appalling and relentless bullying – dished out entirely by women BTW – was sickening. Not one man was involved. Why bother? My life was still amazing in Nottingham. I was still making great money LIVE and I had built a reputation with the national press that would ultimately buy me my first house. Sod 'em – I'm off!

The final straw came when a producer from the 'funeral hour' filled in for my producers Emma and Katie. Ten minutes before I was on-air my scripts weren't ready. I'd asked five times nicely for at least some of my show. It was constructed sabotage of course. At 8.52am I finally said "I'll do the show myself, don't bother. I cannot work with you again." I said it in a calm polite tone. This girl screamed in tears. Projection. Distortion. Deflection. Pivot 101. All hell broke loose. I didn't rise. 'He's a bully and made a girl cry.' Bore-off! It was the best show I ever did. At 9.30am she offered the scripts. I refused. All a game. Pure evil manipulation. They're sickos and unhinged psychopaths.

So, rule 1 of BBC Bollocks – you are not allowed to walk away. If you do, they'll destroy you!!! That's second only to Rule 2 – never take a holiday and if you do, pretend your home decorating. Mental right?

To this day I cannot comprehend the palpable vitriol, vindictiveness and darkness of that appalling Yorkshire HQ that I endured. After I resigned, they understandably could not have me on-air still growing. They manipulated my 'sacking' (even though I'd resigned in writing) and they naturally didn't pay the remainder of my contract. History repeating matrix, right? However, I'd won as I had my life and sanity back and I was straight back down the M1 to Nottingham for the <u>best</u> decade of my life.

Court records prove I tried to get justice for all of the unforgivable sewer of duplicity and abuse. It was impossible to fight the evil BBC external lawyers and the onerous and corrupt court system but I hoped that the truth would out. Sadly, rats stick together on sinking ships. Government mafias close ranks. Proper rankers. They always cover each other's arses until they are thrown under the bus. Thank God I was out of it. Revenge was inevitable. I'd made them look stupid and committed the worst crime at the BBC of walking away from my abuser. Their ratings went from the highest in a decade to the worst in history. FACT!!! The switch off at mid-day when I said ta-ra was like the side of Everest. Revenge was inevitable. Never forget that <u>EVERY</u> piece of evidence for my Clown Court trial was delivered in entirety by the BBC who orchestrated my takedown in cahoots with the corrupt Nottingham Police Farce cuntstables. Yep, the intention was in black and white from a BBC employee to 'close me down.' They didn't……until now.

I sued the BBC for breach of contract. OK, I admit it, 'I'M A MORON!' I stupidly still believed that 'the doors to the court were open to everyone' – THEY ARE NOT! In the same way the doors to the British Airways Concorde Lounge are open to everyone…...if you can afford it, you can go in! The BBC hired private barrister goons to represent them (at tax payer's expense) despite having over sixty internal lawyers on staff. Clearly their collection of internal lawyers, weren't qualified enough to deal with my damming accusations. They pulled a lot of dirty tricks, even press releasing that I'd 'left the BBC' when in fact I'd resigned from BBC Radio Leeds only. Look, these things may seem tiny now, and petty to some, but when you're a man of integrity and principle it matters! This was their malicious attempt to stop me continuing with my BBC celebrity network show. It was the girl who you don't want to shag any more – 'if I can't have him – no one's having him!' They threatened, bullied and banned my producers from seeing me and talking to me. I will say Martin Kelner was loyal and stayed in touch.

For transparency, I have never paid the BBC henchmen, gatekeepers and bully boys ONE PENNY! What I can tell you for free is that their top mob lawyer was proven to be a liar and was disbarred by the The Bar Tribunals and Adjudication - the LMS = Legal Mafia Society! Why are these people never held to account or thrown in jail by the way? Almost feels to me as a layman, that people in power and their puppet master legal turds are protected at the highest level and have total impunity. If you doubt anything about this, it's all there in the public domain. To think the very *same* lawyers, would be instructed to go against my friend and gloriously noble and brilliant former MP Andrew Bridgen over his defamation case against Matt Handcock. Most peculiar hey?! Total coincidence how birds of a feather appear to stick together!

Hindsight is our biggest friend in life. Oh, if we could all only turn back time just like Cher. Sadly, we can't as her plastic surgeon can confirm. People lie, cheat and bully. They're corrupt, protected and couldn't give two facks who they bring down in the process. We live in a sick culture that believes elevating yourself by destroying others will work. It does not. Karma is a bitch! This is showbiz sadly riddled with deeply unwell and highly medicated lunatics who will stop at nothing to protect their own woeful world. You won't meet <u>anyone</u> successful that doesn't have identical stories. I wonder who will be exposed and closed down next? Did I mention that one of my judge's wife was confirmed to have been given a job at the BBC days after my incarceration to Pleasure His Majesty. This was confirmed on her LinkedIn page and by the Guardian so it must be true hey?!

<u>The Best Decade of my Life</u>
BBC Leeds taught me everything I needed to know. Jealous loony tunes and spectrum behaviour is a pandemic in these buildings and you must not get caught up or be any part of it. It'll give you brain damage trying to work these crack pots out. Their actions can have profound effects all for their own deluded validation. You have to remove yourself entirely. I had FINALLY learned my lesson at 31 - 15 years after I first took to the microphone and arguably a decade and a half too late - that I'm not the sharpest tool in the shed! You can't claim I didn't give it my best shot though. I tried to fit in, but, no matter how high my ratings – I could not navigate the odious covetous scum that litter the media. I do hope it's not contagious! What that year did prove was my on-air ability to instantly draw an audience and collect a pocketbook of insider knowledge 'where the bodies are buried' (in terms of BBC financial waste, mismanagement, ineptitude and

corruption). This would profit me forever! This was a life changer for me………despite the literal bruises and pain to get here.

For years now I had been selling my celebrity interviews to the newspapers. I worked my arse off from 2011 to be one of the most successful freelance journalists in the country. Via Andy Halls at The Sun, David and Ben at the Daily Mail and Mail on Sunday and Paddy at The Mirror Group (The People and The Express) did a week ever go by, for a decade, that I didn't have a lead page spread or the occasional front-page splash in one of those newspapers. I'd work all week to get the call on a Saturday evening confirming if the stories had made it or not. It was exhilarating and exciting but also devastating when a decent story didn't make it. I was a machine. If I missed it this week, I'd work three times harder to get it somewhere else the next. It normally worked. My job was to churn out at least three good stories a week praying that one would make it. I did have some incredible stories over the years. It was big money between £500 and £2,000 for each story depending on where it was placed. I had hundreds of exclusives in the coming years. Mail on Sunday paid the best, next The Sun and The Mirror who would often compete and if all else failed I'd take The Express for a bag of chips. How that is still going is beyond me!

Just before I left BBC Leeds, they set me up with what they thought would be a car crash chat. As always, I turned it around to be one of my most revealing interviews of my career. One of my forty plus lady garden shavers and pouty lipped producers called me one afternoon and said, "we've arranged an interview with Sir Jimmy Savile and you're going along on your own to his flat in Roundhay Park." They laughed and said, "no way any of us are going." I thought nothing of it. Savile was an enigma, but I'd never met or interviewed him before. I thought no more of it. It was a decent scoop during a long winter's afternoon.

Honestly, he wasn't really on my radar. Rumours were rife, but to be honest he wasn't the only one. In fact, in my experience there are just as many creepy predators around today as there were in the seventies. They just hide behind even more powerful PR protectors than back then to cover it all up. It was weird why the BBC set it up this way. I didn't go to anyone's house during that year and had at least two producers to accompany/assist me on any 'OB' (outside broadcast). Anywho, off I went. The good news was that it was recorded on my own equipment, in my time – so it was my copyright – also part of the contract that they hated! I arrived at a dated block of flats on the edge of Roundhay Park and pressed the buzzer. "Now then, is that THE Alex Belfield?" – Jimmy's show had started. My interview came after Louis Theroux's chat in the very same flat. Again though, remember, few flinched when Louis' circus first aired. Everyone is a genius now, but at the time he was regarded as an eccentric 'one off' legend, not show businesses' most prolific predator. Theroux made fun of the freak show. I found Louis' insight fascinating and (I hate to admit) hysterical in places. Theroux is a genius at underplaying his chats. Very disarming and worked a treat with

Savile. He's smarter than all his guests, but loves to play stupid. Great gimmick!

The lift opened onto the very top floor into Savile's penthouse flat. "Now then young man," charming and every bit the 'Jingle Jangle' Jimmy I hoped for. He had his shell suit on and a cigar in his gob unlit. Bit strange but exactly the theatre from this showman that you would expect. Curiously his flat didn't stink of smoke either. Could this be another one of his fake props to seductively bring you into his wacky world? We went through to the lounge which had a stunning view overlooking the park. There was no way this man was going to disappoint and he knew it. This flat was nice, but not the home of a multi-millionaire! Kim and Aggie would have a field day! He knew exactly how to play the game and made me welcome. To 'normal' people it may seem very strange going to 'stars' houses and meeting them alone, but I'd done it for twenty years. Perfectly normal. From Des to ABBA and Cilla – it's just a job. I even went to Andrew Lloyd Webbers penthouse in Broadway. I wiped my feet on the way out don't worry! My reputation was unblemished. No one flinched. I respected privacy 100% until the mic was under their nose and then <u>anything</u> was fair game. Nothing sneaky at all. The bigger the star, the more normal it felt bizarrely. It's weird but there's an unspoken trust when you have a microphone. I guess it's a mutual respect. All of this is so silly of course. I wouldn't trust <u>ANY</u> journalist in my home EVER…. that's why I decline all interviews. Curiously, I've only ever been to two apartments where the ground floor lift rises to the top and opens directly into the person's home. One was Savile and the other was Cilla Black at her St James (stunning) penthouse. Now there's a millionaire megastar! Hers was another league! I adored Cilla! To me she was the ultimate showbiz icon and deservedly so. A legend beloved for all the right reasons. I loved the bones of her. Proof 'box ticking' is bollocks. If you're a woman of any age or class, you can make it if you have the <u>talent</u>. I couldn't be prouder of that interview. What a shame there'll NEVER be another star like Cilla or another generation of this level of all-rounder with complete devotion to the business.

So, there I was in the outdated and shabby 'Chez Savile.' We sat on the very same sofa as Louis and off I went chatting for over an hour about his illustrious life and career. OK – total transparency – in 2010 when this was recorded it was a radio masterpiece. He told INCREDIBLE stories. I laughed along and indeed egged him on to tell more. Here's why Savile was so compelling and BRILLIANT as a guest. The man was 100% believable. As God is my witness, on the wall opposite where I sat were hundreds of photographs, through the decades, that legitimised his stories and proved his connections. When he told me a yarn about 'the Duchess' (his mother) going to the Vatican to see the Pope – guess what - there was a picture of the Duchess with the Pope. He talked of Prime Ministers and Presidents – all on the wall smiling back at me. Most famously our now King standing proud with Jimmy – not just once but over and over again. This is seductive because he'd point to Sinatra and then tell you the story. Why would I disbelieve him? He told me bonkers tales of

Frank picking him up from Vegas airport and driving into the desert. Eventually they'd reach a casino on fire. 'Sinatra' pointed at the fire and said "they don't mess with me here." It's hard to know if this was fantasy, theatre or reality but either way it was a captivating yarn. He told me stories how he used to police his clubs in the seventies to 'sort out' lads who misbehaved in the basement. "You don't mess with the young ladies in my club, I'll break your face" he bragged. He claimed the police not only knew, but they actively encouraged and thanked him for his goon and mob services to public duty.

When I asked him about his faith and meeting his maker it became much darker as he told me he wouldn't be let into heaven. More manipulation, jokes or a confession? Who knows? "I won't get into heaven I've been tricky. If St Peter doesn't let me in, I'll break his thumbs" he said. That quote was the front page of The Sun the day after he died. What I do know is he was undoubtedly compelling and utterly captivating. I laughed along thinking nothing of his tales of John Lennon nicking the idea for his glasses during a chance meeting on a 747. The photo, again, was on the wall. Undeniable right? This cringe interview was not only fascinating but ultimately revealing about his remarkable life, career and achievements. My conclusion was that if you raise £40 million for charity the establishment will let you get away with <u>anything</u> - and I do mean ANYTHING! I'm not sure if I believe all the crap that has been written about him though. You can't libel the dead remember – ask Al-Fayed. There's no question he was odd, creepy, enabled, protected and empowered to commit his crimes. It's just pitiful that it wasn't until after he died that the accusations flew publicly. Something else that makes me incredibly uncomfortable. Proves my belief showbiz types will cover up for anyone until they're dead, buried or gagged. He was the world's greatest media manipulator, that's for sure. His freak show made Barnum look like Mary Poppins!

My interview was the splash on The Sun front page the morning after he died with a two-page spread inside. This interview was a tribute written up as a celebration of his life. Six months later when ITV (not the BBC) exposed his true character my interview made the front page and two pages again but this time in The Mirror exposing his 'dark side' through his 'jokey' confessions throughout my chat - published in full. What this tells us about the press is they are absolutely not to be trusted. They can take the same interview a few weeks apart, firstly painting him as a legend and hero and then shortly afterwards, based on identical material, damning him as a savage paedo and a disgrace. This is what they do in court – edit who they want back…...and who they want to throw under the bus! Eventually the BBC bought the interview back for a Radio 2 exposé. Ironic hey? It still blows my mind the BBC are still profiting and making entertainment from his legacy via sick documentaries and dramas about Savile. Woeful and sick. This interview lives on and so it should. Some dopes think I should delete it through shame but that's ridiculous. You don't delete history to make it go away and sweep it under the carpet. As much as I shudder at parts of our chat, I'm proud that I got the confessions I did. I'm not a soothsayer or mind reader. My job is to ask the best questions I can with the knowledge I have at the time. The lesson learned is that long form interviews are deadly. Talk for long enough and eventually you'll drop yourself in the shit.

One of the amazing things about my huge archive of interviews is that so many of my guests are no longer with us and these interviews became a lasting tribute. Many were taken way too soon like Dale Winton who gave a rare sixty-minute chat. Despite his campery and showbiz smile he had a hideous upbringing with a mum who took her own life. She was in showbiz and another victim of this evil game of success, money, beauty and popularity. Dale was clearly inconsolable about her loss and never recovered. It didn't surprise me when sadly I read about his passing. The human mind and body can only take so much. Only last month I heard parts of that interview played on a Channel 5 documentary. They neither asked my permission or paid me a fee. Showbiz – need I say more?! Dolly Dale was a hugely troubled soul as so many are. Such a price for fame as the crematorium roll check proves.

Another massive interview for me was Cynthia Lennon. I was granted a face-to-face chat and it was very emotional for both of us. Cynthia was incredibly vulnerable and I remember how profoundly sorry I felt for her about the abuse she endured from John Lennon. I could tell Cynthia was still in great trauma. John is one of those 'stars' who is untouchable. His fans simply won't accept his flaws and will justify and defend his behaviour regardless of the damning accusation about his treatment of women. She couldn't kick him into touch until it was way too late. It's amazing how some people are forgiven with blind eyes turned, yet others are never seen again. Lennon is an icon, but his behaviour was despicable. Who do we believe? Same as Michael Jackson I suppose. I for one know only too well how people will lie for attention and affirmation for their own ego. It's a very murky and cynical world sadly. The bigger the star and the longer time you have with them the more open wounds are revealed. I've had many occasions I feared I was out of my depth and crossing a line I didn't even know existed – Cynthia was one of them. She was too honest for her own good. She wanted to talk and the microphone lured her into a false sense of security…….all to promote a book.

When people write their autobiography it's 'fair game.' I once interviewed the great Les Dennis and he was upset I talked about Amanda Holden. There were whole chapters about her in the book. What was I meant to do? Pat Lakesmith, his manager, was fuming I'd had the audacity to ask about Holden. I say if you don't want to discuss it then don't profit from the stories in a book! I guess 'celebrities' play by their own rules. When Cynthia Lennon passed away The Express did a lovely two page spread from our chat. One of my greatest sadnesses is that the halcyon days of 'my type' of star are leaving us. Most importantly of all for me, Sir Ken Dodd, who I think about every single day. There will never be another generation like this. I was incredibly blessed to have caught the tail end of the very best days of modern showbiz before Instagram, mental health and hurty words killed everything. I was never interested in Tom Cruise types as they're too robotic and trained. I'd rather have regular 'real' chats with my type of people. I was so lucky meeting my heroes like Freddie Starr, Jim Bowen, Frank Carson, Jethro and Joan Rivers as well as theatre legends like Linda Bellingham, Ruth Madoc and Bernie Nolan who were all taken way too soon. I missed a few too. I'd have loved to have interviewed June Brown, Brucie, Savage, Babs and few others – but mostly I couldn't give a toss about 99% of the deluded self-publicists today. I have no interest in tweaking the nipples of their lives. They're dull, boring and quickly forgotten.

The World was my Lobster!
It was time to create a new life turning from BBC hunter to game keeper. Freedom of Information is an amazing gift to the public holding government agencies to account as they can't refuse specific questions about the cost of things we pay for. I would send about three hundred specific requests a year and they had no choice but to answer them. In the end they had teams of lawyers to try and not answer them. The PR cost was devastating to Auntie's untenably creepy brand. They were FURIOUS!! I published endless scandalous stories in The Mail on Sunday, The Sun and The Sunday Express who loved my exclusives week after week exposing their undeniable contempt for public money via the nonce factory rape tax. The papers loved throwing the Beeb under the bus as much as I did. What goes around comes around I say! Some of my stories were preposterous. The 'BBC Bristol

Fruit Basket' costing £50 a week with a pineapple for the newsroom. Millions wasted on 'early riser' payments to BBC staff and the obscene millions on consultants hired to advise managers how to do their jobs! Doh! My favourite consultant was hired at £1,000,000+ to save money. It's another world. Well, they started it. This is 5* journalism. I should be poached by Panorama! They want to hold us to account, well what's good for the goose.......

It was delicious to no longer want to be at the BBC party. I was done forever. Walking away in life and having closure is not easy. That is the curse of life and showbiz. We spend our lives wanting what we can't have and eating ourselves alive until we get it. Once you get it, it's nothing but disappointment, heartache and endless horseshit. I went back to Nottingham with a few quid in my pocket so started ticking off my bucket list. The then current Mrs Belfield (who I'd met at Leeds) joined me in Barbados to find out if January in Barbs is as cool as the myths claim. It was! For years I'd been going Sharm El-Sheikh. Funnily enough during my trip a year before, I ended up on global news. Egypt was in political uproar, but I didn't care, as long as I'd got my sun lounger and Mrs B had a penis colada in her hand. We flew in and an uprising happened leaving us barricaded in the all-inclusive resort. In recent years I need pills to have an uprising, but that's another story. Before I knew it, I was on BBC Breakfast with Charlie Stayt every hour, LBC, CNN, Sky and a ton of BBC stations including 5 LIVE. This went on for three days. I was still at BBC Leeds at the time and the bosses were loving the glory until I got bored and started describing the reality of an open bar, 5* buffet and my flip flops by the pool. I had an email from a management retard (called Fanny Schmelling) saying I'd brought the BBC into disrepute. I replied 'you signed a contract that I don't work for the BBC. Mind your own business, I'm on holiday. PS: I wasn't paid. They called me!' You can imagine, the gnarling teeth and seething scowl the size of a draft excluder as they were rehearsing Hitler's speeches for my return to the naughty step.

This epitomised my 'problem' with the mainstream media mafia. They're utterly humourless and devoid of all reality and levity. Zero sense of irony or incongruity. Anyway, I was done with Egypt. Too much time on the bog with the Shame-ill-Shites. I haven't been back since. Barbados on the other hand was a bit of class, but it's a bloody long way away and crazily expensive! I got a decent package (not personally - online reviews suggest) for us with Virgin and used my heavenly air miles to get an Upper-Class seat for the ten-hour flight. This is the life. I'd made it. Every time I'd sit in some buttock clenching meeting, I'd drift off to such fantasies. I was channelling Cliff, Dale and Cilla as finally we'd made it to the Skeggy for showbiz tarts! We had a fab time. I had a couple of ambitions to visit the Sandy Lane Hotel. And yes, there were several 'vintage' luvvies at the pool bar including the Lythgoe's! You can't beat 'old school class.' It had a stunning restaurant.

I just love elegance and a bit of old school glamour. Nothing I love more than sticking on my dinner jacket. Only yesterday I was wondering if there will still be a market for The Savoy, Ritz and Claridge's in twenty years? Will my generation pay for this indulgence? I fear not. To me these places offer a temporary exquisite insight into a better time. Total escapism. I've always been the same longing to dip my toes into these magical places. A total pit estate imposter, but I just love the majesty and decadence of these delights where vape sucking dumbbells are mostly banned. Well, at least Union Jack shorts are not permitted! Whenever my Americans come over, I love to take them to Claridge's for Afternoon Tea. What could be more gloriously British? Poo poo people say, 'how can you pay £50 for a sandwich?' These knuckle draggers should stick to Subway and leave the rest of us to a couple of hours of perfect service and total escapism. They'll spend £300 on a pair of trainers or £150 to see their football team but…………..each to their own! What I love is that nothing is too much trouble. I don't do drugs, hookers, smoke or waste money on the above – this is my titillation and buzz! As long as I can get away with it I will. It brings me such happiness to share this stuff with my loved ones and make memories with my besties. I was dazzled by the beaches in Barbados and had a couple of really beautiful meals. I can see what Cliff and Cowell see in it. It's massively expensive in comparison to Florida where I now go every January at half price. It's a lovely treat though. I never take it for granted. I work all year to get away in the dullest month after 30 shows in December. This one was special. For me (now especially) the dream of perfect blue sky is just sensational! Pure ecstasy only a flight away. The kid in me still enjoys the lounge and flight more than the holiday.

Travel has become my biggest passion by a mile. I had been going to Las Vegas for fifteen plus years and it was my second home. Sadly by 2017 the love was gone after the shooting where almost five hundred people were injured and fifty-nine were killed. I had landed the night before. I was based at Tahiti Village which I love and is within walking distance of Mandalay Bay where the lunatic shooter took aim. Just before it happened, I was at the now demolished Tropicana next to the concert site where the madman attacked. Fortunately, after the show I got a taxi downtown to my buddy Frederic da Silva's pad for a party. If I'd have gone back to Tahiti, I would have been walking past that massacre at the exact time he struck. What a wake-up call. We're all one wrong choice (by pure luck) from disaster. Frederic, his gorgeous girlfriend Delphine (at the time) and I have become very close over recent years. He's without question a genius and she's a stunning Cirque Du Soleil aerialist. I love their company and we've shared so many incredible memories on his boat, at his show or at dinner which we love. Fred's Bally's 'Mind Reading Spectacular' is still the best one man show on the strip by a mile. He's the ultimate perfectionist. My respect is infinite. To see my friend's poster on a bus the following day after the massacre with bullets through his head will NEVER leave me. To be in town and see the shot-out window from Mandalay Bay was devastating and still is. Fred and I spent three days walking around together in a daze. That day changed my life forever. My friends and family were also horrified as they knew I was in town and were waiting to hear that I was OK. So many were randomly caught up in it. There by the grace of God hey? Vegas is no longer a hospitality town and now doesn't care about ripping off its punters. The shows are rarely special - whippersnapper DJs are now the $500,000 a night-megastars - PRETENDING to play records LIVE – what's that all about? The magic has gone.

Vegas has been so kind to me over the years though. I'd become great friends with the greatest magician on earth, Criss Angel. For over a decade I'd supported him and he'd helped me with exclusive content in return. He's such a pro. 100% dedication. True obsession for perfection. I marvel at his brilliance, craft, dedication and pure talent. Truly the rock star of magic. There aren't many people I'd call a true friend in showbiz but Criss is one of them. I adore his family. We've been through so much together. He's not shy of controversy himself. The scale of his show is epic. World class. Remember, Vegas is not a joke. There are billions of dollars flying around and the consequences of pissing off the wrong person can be fatal! By now I had established myself as the #1 YouTube critic in Sin City, topping Google which is unbelievable. Criss was smart enough to see the rankings of my videos. Unlike many of the out of touch dinosaurs, he knew that search engines mattered – YouTube was king! We built up a trust. To have dinner and know wonderful Vegas headliners like Criss, Frederic, Terry Fator, Murray, Marie and Donny is just mind blowing. These people are at the top of their game. World class. It doesn't always go swimmingly. I got to know Matt Goss very well during his Vegas run. We had dinner and he was gracious with backstage access. We had an argy-bargy after he felt my 5* review didn't go far enough. Sadly, the ego of some turns outweighs common sense. He got over it quickly, but it proves how personally the very top take criticism – even from a Brit gobshite like me who gave a 5* review. What more could I do? Regardless, he's a very unique soul who I loved to interview and got to know over many years. Often, it's easy to go into a show blind. Getting too close can become VERY awkward! It was nice to hang out with him before his show. My sister was a massive fan in the nineties. Funny old world who you get to know in this silly charade.

What an honour to have such access in the entertainment capital of the world! It still has incredible restaurants and shows………but sadly, little is new entertainment wise. I feel that ship has sailed. It feels like we've seen it all. When I started, they built the Colosseum for Celine Dion who I've loved seeing many times. Since Celine though, who has that talent and discipline to do two hundred shows a year and sell 8,000 tickets each night? It's all been done - just like radio. I missed the halcyon days of variety, but at least I was there for the entire decade of the Vegas' explosion and luxury growth. The worst thing about Vegas now is 'dynamic pricing.' All of the casinos are digital, so the busier they are, the more expensive everything becomes – from a bottle of water in shops to entry to nightclubs. Mondays are half the price of weekends now. This airline/hotel room business model is now rolled out over <u>everything</u>. You won't see any prices in resort shops for this reason. Sadly, fine dining is now replaced with Gordon Ramsay burger bars – I'll pass thank you. Oh, Gordon was nice when I did an hour special with him. Chefs are show offs just like judges and vicars – it's all about pampering the ego to audiences......just in different ways. Imagine though going from being a genius and maverick master chef to now be serving fish and chips in Vegas for £30 a pop. Says it all right?! Urggg – I hate life since Covid.

I needed a new America. Florida for me was the motherload. Not Orlando – not for me…. it's all a bit goofy and dopey (think the hosts of Strictly!). Miami was about to introduce me to my new favourite trip of the year. January in the Sunshine State. I'm a smart lad, people might think I'm a few cushions short of a three-piece suite but you need smarts to thrive at my champagne delusions and lemonade wages. Years ago, I realised 'work out what you want and never give up until you get it.' I live like that today. I've always had to be a step ahead and shrewd with money as I've always felt my career is on the edge – as this book proves. Maybe my mentor Sir Ken's 'frugal' instincts had rubbed off just like his stage craft and comic timing? I worked out that just like airline miles, they had the same cockamamie scheme with hotels. I chose Marriott as they own the St Pancras – my favourite building in London (and the world) and a once magnificent place to stay. You have to stick to one airline, hotel or casino etc to benefit from these loyalty programmes. It's like the Nectar points for jetsetters. You build up points and before you know it, you're upgraded, late checkout, free wi-fi etc, etc

BINGO! So, every January for years I'd fly into Florida's atrocious Miami International Airport upgraded on the AMEX miles earned by paying for my previous trips. The more I travelled the less I spent and the more they upgraded me! Who knew?! Shushy, don't tell anyone or they might stop the swizz.

As you know I loved Donald Trump long before he was President. As a kid I watched him on Stern or Letterman. What a tease, what a wind up. What an entertainer, comic genius! It's <u>ALL</u> an act as his desire to walk off every stage to YMCA proves. Why do people not get <u>this</u>? HELLO!! Aside from the political schtick, Trump is a master at owning hotels. His golf course in Miami is world-class and not that expensive, in fact as cheap as a Premier Inn in London these days! BTW – my favourite drink in the USA, Vodka and Zero Root Beer – try it. It's the Marmite of beverages a bit like toothpaste with white wine! OMG! What a tonsil sensation. Anyway, that's not why you called……

Ninety minutes away from Doral in Florida is the most PERFECT town on earth called Naples. WOW! Palm trees, millionaires, the cleanest place on earth, dolphins, the sea and a pier create the most civilised holiday on earth! I'm not joking. If I had my dream retirement, I'd finish my days in Naples. If it weren't for family and friends, I'd go now. Back when I started visiting it was reasonable to stay there – of course Marriott Residence Inn for the points, full kitchen – right next to my favourite Italian shirt shop in the mall. The restaurants are divine and the people are incredible. My favourite chain restaurant is 'Brio.' Just like in

Vegas you can treat yourself to sensational stone crabs from their version of Tesco's called Myers or the Waitrose-esk 'Village Market.' Maybe it's the 80 degrees sunshine in January but I'm in heaven. Florida makes me feel alive. Totally at home. I can be me with no edge or pretence. For years I went for three weeks. Because of my job I can work anywhere online. I'm so lucky, I do count my blessings. This makes me very happy. No flies on me Chunky! I know it's a daft job and an infantilised silly life, but, none of us beat death so why take the run up to it seriously? Everything for me on holiday leads to the evening meal. I never eat breakfast or lunch out. I love local delis and supermarkets. On 5th Avenue in Naples, they have some amazing restaurants! For me though the golden shot is the ocean. I walk there every day passing the dolphins, mincing down the canals around the strip malls. It's paradise for me. This is me at my absolute most comfortable, relaxed and happiest. I wasn't born to be in a cold country, this is delicious, even shit days have an elegance that few summers achieve in Derby! Maybe it's just the halo of holiday heaven or the rosy glow of a lunchtime tipple? I know the weather can be deadly in the Gulf of America but what a pay-off for the other 364 days of glorious blue skies! One year it was eight degrees during a cold snap and the Iguanas (huge lizards) were literally falling out of the trees 'frozen.' Seriously, I'm not working you from behind. So funny seeing them all over pavements the size of Doddy four paws up! Eventually they 'defrosted,' woke up and carried on slithering around like a BBC paedo.

After Naples we drive through the Everglades to Key West. It's a breathtaking drive over the ocean (literally). We only stay a day or two but the Marriott Beachside is spectacular. Finally, I'll pop back to Doral and Trump for a few days before returning home. Beat that! I will pop to Miami beach (reluctantly) but it's not for me. All fur coat and no knickers! Too many druggies and whippersnapper clubbers. I'll pass. They have a gay beach which makes me laugh. It's like a straight beach but the sand is rainbow coloured and it's covered in crabs. Walking is banned on the pier, you have to 'sashay' like Alan Carr with a palm tree up his arse. America is too expensive now……blame Biden! Sleepy Joe has ruined everything. I always have a kitchen and washing machine so I can live a normal life. Works for me. Miami is truly tremendous, twelve lane roads and a melting pot of people who now can't speak a word of English. Bravo Cameltoe Harris! Pulling down Trump's wall has been a work of genius. More recently Florida is run by Ron De Santis who was magnificent during Covid. Since then, he appears to have been bought by the global elite and establishment. Very disappointing, sad even. The Sunshine State is untouchable for value in January. It's also the cruise capital of the world. For my 40$^{th}$ Birthday we went on a Caribbean Cruise. I spent 14$^{th}$ January on St Maarten specifically planned so that I could stand on that world renowned beach and 'touch' the planes as they land over the beach and ocean. Google it. My heaven – planes, sun, great company, amazing food and all you can drink booze. What's not to like. I'll never stop dreaming and fighting to fulfil my dreams.

Cruises aren't for everyone but if you pick wisely then it's an amazing way to see the world. It's basically the least stressful way of visiting the most amount of places in one go. I love it. It's like a floating Las Vegas, mostly full of yanks the size of a small caravan……often trailed by a ventilator and stick thin husband. After my Uncle Sam died, I took my Aunty Dorothy on a Cunard cruise around Europe. Despite being a floating care home in places, packed with well to do silver tops, the quintessentially English class was perfect. Such elegance that ladies of a certain age adore. A bit too much for me. It's so posh, they even get out of the bath for a pee. I saw the captain in the port. I said that's a very posh gold-plated watch, how did you afford that? He said 'I work for Cunard' – I said 'I work facking hard but I can't afford a watch like that!' I thank you!!!

I really enjoyed Silversea Cruise and Carnival aren't bad. I can't bring myself to book a P&O cruise – it just reminds me of a floating Pontins. Regardless, you can dress up nice and walk out full of eastern promise on nearly all the ships these days. In 2022 I ended up on HMS Stockings – I wouldn't recommend it. You can read about that in 'Surviving the Slammer' Book 3!

Back in Florida it's also a huge hub for entertainment. I was lucky to be invited to see Barry Manilow at the AA Arena. Shortly afterwards I recorded a life story interview with him in Las Vegas. What a prolific star. Such talent and a born entertainer. Above everything else I adore watching talent and all of these trips lead to LIVE performers and music somewhere. I still get a tingle and the hairs on the back of my neck go up when the band start. Electrifying feeling to me. I'm still a sucker for a show girl with tits and feathers up her arse. To endlessly see the stars and masters is magical. I saw Garth Brookes in Florida at the AA too – mega star. In Vegas it never gets old to see Elton, Rod, Celine, Cher, Bette Midler, Neil Diamond and even people I probably would never choose to see like Britney, Pink or Katy Perry LIVE. They're all such masters. At that level you cannot get there by luck. I'm so lucky that my hobby and passion is my job. I drink in their brilliance, learn from their genius and revel in their discipline and technique. Seeing the stars is still the most motivating and inspiring part of my life. Meeting someone like Manilow after his show is an honour and joy. To sit alone in what was Elvis' dressing room at the Las Vegas Hilton was mind-blowing to me when a dear pal Mark arranged for me to interview him back stage. I'm a very lucky lad. Barry Manilow to me is like a polished, professional and classy Gary Barlow (who can sing and play the piano properly). I'll always have an unending respect for the great piano men. I'd do anything to interview Billy Joel – what a sensational genius. I also loved seeing him live in Sheffield.

Like all the greats I've met, Manilow couldn't have been kinder, more generous or more honest about his spectacular life as one of the world's biggest stars globally. Incredible!

I never take my very privileged and bonkers life for granted. No matter the lows and bullshitery these incredible gifts and rewards for my dedication are the ultimate pay off.

# Chapter 11

## ITV, London & Becoming a Loose Woman

As one door closes another cat flap opens! When I came home from Leeds in 2012 a new chapter opened in my life, totally out of the blue. I was having dinner with my mate of twenty years Jane McDonald. I was talking about my next step. At the time she was a massive star on Loose Women and Jane kindly put my name forward to do some warm-up shifts for the show. Who would have thought as the BBC door slammed shut in my face the ITV cat flap would open. Warm-up is a very tricky beast and truly the hardest job I've ever done in terms of pressure. Your job is to keep the LIVE audience distracted and entertained before, during and after the taping or broadcast of a show. This is <u>NOT</u> easy. #1 – You cannot get in the way of the programme, despite being required to captivate and energize the crowd. #2 You must <u>NEVER</u> appear 'in shot' on the programme. #3 Make sure you <u>DO NOT</u> lose track of time – to the second. #4 You <u>CANNOT</u> compete with the show or steal/pull focus from the talent, whilst doing exactly that to keep the audience ALIVE. #5 Get <u>everyone's</u> name right. #6 Don't piss ANYONE OFF! It's a bloody minefield like juggling machetes. You're almost set up to fail. Fortunately, this opportunity was a joy!

Normally I'm so unlucky when I call those mucky sex lines, they can't talk because the slapper has got an ear infection, but this time I hit the motherload.

I loved this gig. For a start, it's TV - big and exciting with ZERO drama! You're part of a BIG machine, in which I only wanted to impress. I do not want to be a TV presenter. This was not an audition – the mistake 99% warm ups make. It was a great time for Loose Women with the dream team of Jane, Coleen, McGiffin, Vorderman, Lisa, Sherrie, Bellingham, Janet and Denise all gobshiting (often over each other) to the delight of an audience of mainly women of a certain age. Luckily, I knew most of the girls well from years of doing BBC Local dopey interviews. Where's McGiffin gone BTW? I love that loud mouth. She's like a classy Hopkins......but better dressed and less annoying!

I made my way to ITV on the Southbank and that iconic (block of flats looking) building was vast like BBC TV Centre - just more relaxed and fun. I presumed it was less creepy but we'd better leave that after the This Morning departures. Even decades ago the scale was totally unnecessary and redundant. A runner would collect me from reception, and we'd walk past the punters queuing on the left-hand side then I'd go through stage door on the right all the way around the outside of the building to the back of the studios. The building was tired but relentlessly sprawling with This Morning upstairs whilst Lorraine and Loose Women shared the same studio leading to a mad scramble at 10am to turn the two sets around. Next to us Graham Norton would film his show for the BBC and Ant and Dec were the mega-stars of Saturday night in the huge Studio 1. TV studios are notoriously tiny and disappointing. Loose Women certainly didn't have any glamour. It was almost as sexy as Ann Widdecombe's crotchless knickers! There is no time for glitz, but what was exciting is that every second is LIVE and there's no room for error. It's a five-day machine and there's little room for pissing about. If you drop a bollock you're out. TV is hard work. Bradley Walsh films a week's Chase in one day. You could argue it's like being on the checkout at Lidl churning it out......other than he gets paid £25,000 a day for reading an autocue and shaking hands. The great thing about Loose is that it's LIVE so it also meant we had to be done by 1.28pm so it was impossible to run over and miss the train.

The day before my first gig I was introduced to Ian Royce who was the BIGMAN at ITV for warm-up and did all of the massive shows like X Factor and Britain's Got Talent. He was nice to me but at 6'5' he enjoyed towering over you to remind you who was boss. His character was charmless and intimidating if you hadn't met his 'type' before. I believe he was a former cop. Interesting. I watched him from the audience that day and had no idea what all the fuss was about. He didn't tell a joke, didn't have any 'bits' and didn't even seem to be arsed to be there. What do I know? If your face fits........ Andy Collins is now the star warm-up at ITV and is far more up my street with high energy schtick and malarkey. He masterfully worked on Saturday Night Takeaway. He's a terrific turn and works his arse off unlike Ian who spent most of the show in the wings on his phone - I was gobsmacked. Akin to the creepy boggle eyed 'Mouth' at Century in 1999, – he taught me exactly what <u>not</u> to do. Each to their own hey? Jane was on the show that day so we went for lunch afterwards up The Shard (not many people can say they've taken McJ up the Shard!) – lunch was always far more interesting and fun to me than the gig. Seriously, what is wrong with me? I'd much rather have a bevvy with Jane and Sue than be working.

I kept my gob shut and learned nothing from Roycie. The next day was my debut. I was so excited I didn't sleep that night. They'd put me up in a nice hotel and I hadn't eaten since lunch as I was too busy writing and meeting up with London pals. This was just as exciting as launching on Capital Gold six years before. I'm still a big kid at heart. I was on one of my 'health kicks' with my life-long ambition to keep my weight down under 35 stones. I had completely forgotten to have dinner and I'd walked ten miles around London having the time of my life. That night I went to the theatre with my dear pal Alice to see some insufferable shite. It was boiling hot in the theatre and when I stood up, I knew something wasn't right. By the time I got to the front door for fresh air I went down like a ton of bricks taking a couple of passers-by and pensioners with me. Naturally, they thought I was pissed or off my tits. I hadn't had a drop. Alice explained and they wanted to call an ambulance. I'm Northern! Certainly not. Give me a sugar cube like Shergar and a glass of water and I'll be fine. My old dad would have been proud. This has never happened before or since. I apologise to the six foreigners and silver tops I fell on top of when I had my dizzy doo and collapsed. I was over the Moon I had an excuse to leave the revival of Funny Girl. I can assure you Sheridan Smith was neither funny or looked like a girl! She's so overrated the BBC ought to let her host her own show on Radio 2! We once had a huge row at the Palladium. A prolific and hugely powerful and successful producer called Michael Harrison allowed me to film her walk down in the finale of Joseph at the Palladium. I believe she was playing the Ark. The next day her agent called me accusing me of making her 'look fat,' I said 'it wasn't my iPhone that made her look big boned it was her costume and thighs.' Sheridan never used stage door during that run. Very wise. Mustn't scare the children! Her vocals took care of that dear! Anywho, back to me – is there any other? The next day I was fine. I got to the legendary LWT Towers about 10.30am and went in as 'The Loose Women Warm Up' collecting my 'ACCESS ALL AREAS' pass at security. I'd got some tracks and an intro and the sound guys were brilliant playing along. Jane was on again and she kept her eye on me from behind the desk. The audience loaded in about 11.30ish. That wasn't easy either. There was probably about a hundred in the audience but finding punters five days a week to fill seats wasn't easy without a cool guest. They'd often have to pop to the river and accost ladies with HRT patches to come for a sit down for an hour with the bribe of free air conditioning. Many of which were Chinese and didn't speak the language, then again when the likes of Sally Lindsay were on the panel it didn't seem to make any difference. Funny as cystitis that one. Not my type. I did my schtick and then I had to introduce the girls to great fanfare. You CANNOT get their names wrong – BIGGEST fail of any Master of Ceremonies. Thank God I didn't. You don't want to come a cropper on your opening line! The girls were fab, and I was off doing the best gags I've ever heard (yes, I'm still telling them today) and making the show feel seamless to the audience. It was exhilarating but very complicated. Even knowing where to stand was important. The job also entails getting the crowd to laugh, clap and react during the show – without cue cards. You truly cannot take your eye off the ball. Nothing makes me sweat in Showbiz (other than hearing Jason Manford sing) but that gig did. It was a work out. It's a tiny studio but had about a million tuning in. To think now primetime struggles to get that most nights. TV is doomed and on its arse. The ad breaks were electrifying working to split second timing. I was genuinely exhausted at the end of it. Warm up is such a joy to play at.

I worked on Loose Women for a couple of years on and off and loved every second. I just fit it in around other stuff. It was thrilling to be in the canteen too in between the three main studios. Studio 1 being the biggest and home to most legendary shows of all time. It was a Who's Who of who is that? The girls were always very generous and the likes of Janet SP totally got me. For me this was arguably the 'biggest' opportunity of my career. Despite having no TV ambitions whatsoever, I took massive pride in making sure I fitted in. Once again walking that impossible tightrope of 'owning the gig' but not getting in the way is not a bed of roses. Also, I realised that one complaint could end everything and this was the time that 'Cancel Culture' was brewing big-time. It truly is a disgusting game by the far-left, radical and mental loons to wipe out anyone they personally don't like and/or want rid of for their own agenda. Thankfully at ITV this wasn't an issue; in fact the bosses and producers couldn't have been more encouraging and supportive. ITV was uplifting and inspiring and felt like it wanted you to succeed, not to keep you submissive and in your place like at the evil BBC. It truly was exciting.

When ITV Daytime moved to the old BBC TV Centre at Shepherd's Bush, I did some shows there too. Another scandal - the BBC sold the 'donut' for flats but kept the studios…...which they now rent to ITV via their Private Limited Company (for profit) called 'Studioworks' – a <u>BBC PRIVATE</u> business! Don't get me started on the 'BBC Studios' farce – it's a national disgrace. Only the BBC could have the audacity to sell off all of the national TV programming treasure and family gold like Strictly, Top Gear, Antiques Roadshow, the Queen's funeral and virtually everything else other than 'news' to then profit hundreds of millions via a private company. Outrageous. Anyway, another ambition sorted to work in that very iconic building too. The biggest show I did was with Rod Stewart and Penny. To be in these people's presence is never normal and never should be. I'd just watched this legend at Caesars Palace in Las Vegas – now I'm stood next to him on the set of Loose Women about to introduce him. Now more than ever I realise how charmed and remarkable my life and career has been. I don't regret one second and I'm so proud that I've been able to step up to the glorious opportunities that I've been offered throughout my life. It's only possible because I dedicated my life to my hobby and craft and stuck at it for two treacherous decades. Delivering the goods was not luck or by chance. I'd earned my stripes by now.

The problem with most great gigs in showbiz is that there's little or no profit in it. Warm-up back then was £300 per show which for a lad from a pit estate is nearing a week's wages, but by the time you've taken out petrol, parking, train (and heaven forbid a hotel) I'd owe them money. For me this was always a vanity gig. Ego. Pure and simply done to say I'd done it and a day's fun pissing about in a TV studio with a load of gobby mates. Some people shag hookers, others do heroin – I love to hang around with trappy big mouths. Warm up is a full day's work by the time you've got the 7am train – about the most expensive time to catch a train – in the studio for 10ish and back on the 2pm train mincing in about 4.30pm. After a while this becomes pointless. I'd done it. Jane had left. I had nothing to achieve. I've <u>never</u> wanted to be the last one at a party. White City where ITV is now based, is a ball-ache schlep from St Pancras. I just couldn't be arsed. ITV was a gorgeous walk so that tickled my trout as I got free exercise and no medieval torture on Sickdiq's underworld train. It took longer to cross London than getting from Newark on LNER. Exhausting. My silver top groups for one hour were much better business, I'd leave home at 1pm and be back home by 4pm and have the same profit.

The shit the women would talk about was mindless by 2014. I got very wound up by the endless woke/box ticking crap the twelve-year-old producers would get them to chat about. Their mass debate got right on my man-chesticles! Even the girls got sick of the repetitive virtue signalling and politically motivated waffle. That was the way TV was going. By the time they launched Loose

Men, I had to jump ship. Vernon Kay should be ashamed – he talked more rollocks than his atrocity on Radio 2. Only ITV could do 'men's suicide' specials having paid off Jezza £1M…...for which his programme resulted in three suicides. I've lost count of the corpses due to Love Island. You couldn't make this crock of hypocritical shit up! TV execs don't care. Soulless. The world had changed. Talent was irrelevant. Even my mate Eamonn Holmes was out of favour at LW. Being male, pale and not a box ticking whale meant you'd have to bail or inevitably be kicked out and sent packing for sale. Loose Women fizzled out for me. There was no argy-bargy or fall out at all. I was travelling more and more, taking four or five-week trips to the States at the time and loving every second. This doesn't work for continuity with the bookers in TV who have to do the diary in between their GCSE's and going on 'Just Stop Oil' protests. Do you catch my drift? In the end I became the third cover. That'll do me. I loved every show and every second. I thank the ladies for being so kind and gracious, welcoming me to their daily gob-shite fest. It was lovely. It's gone off the boil these days without Jane and McGiffin. I say bring them back with Horse Face Hopkins as host and stick it on Prime Time! It can't be worse than the dirge and shite they shove out most nights in between gruesome 'real crime' creepy crap.

After Loose Women my magic mix of work and play went to a new level. By now I was VERY lucky to pick and choose. I was able to dip in and out and therefore nothing was ever a job. I was excited by the variety of everything booked in. My newspaper work was going gangbusters and more profitable than any radio or TV gig available. This covered all of my travel costs alone and over a decade allowed my savings to grow to build my future. I was more and more trusted by the editors and I was now doing exceptionally well with BBC exposé stories thanks to spilling the beans on their financial corruption which was seemingly endless. I eventually had a front-page story regarding the millions of pounds in extra money Aunty had bribed those with lady parts, who thought they should have been paid more, to shut up moaning and accept the same wage as those with penis. It was cat and mouse to dissect every press release from the nonce factory to find the scam and cockamamie scheme they were trying to cover up. I loved the joust. BBC bosses were apoplectic at my sheer audacity. Fury was growing throughout the BBC at EVERY level! "Who does he think he is?" My former colleagues were out of their minds with jealousy and self-protesting vengeance. They did EVERYTHING to stop my FOI enquiries and entire departments were set up to literally 'close me down' and hold back my exposing and revealing journalism.

Like I've said recently about VoR – if what I did is luck, easy or a piece of piss – why hasn't someone jumped straight on-air and stolen my crown and replaced me since my 2 years 9 months contract to write my six pack of books whilst Pleasuring His Majesty? As far as I'm aware no one has even been brave enough to even attempt it. It's all very well revelling and enjoying the highs, but can you pick yourself up IMMEDIATELY from the lows and carry on? That's the hardest thing about this business we call show. I've had to do this a thousand times as you can see. The reason I think I did so well is my tenacity and keeping my eye on the ball. You HAVE to stay focused on the audience and ahead of the game. You cannot give a second's distraction to the naysayers or your invisible enemies. I simply worked harder than anyone else. Pure working-class ethic. Get it done! I can only thank my incredible family for the example they set. There's no question it put me well ahead of the pack.

I spent every waking hour creating original content. My celeb interviews were getting more and more attention. Some of my favourite newspaper scoops include my exclusive chat with Noel Edmonds which went global. This hero of mine had seemingly fallen from grace after 'Deal or no Deal.' Noel had emailed me to use my archive for an online radio venture he hoped would succeed. It didn't of course. FM radio is dead. Radio on the internet is virtually impossible to monetise. We were speaking very regularly at one point. This was a total thrill for me as I admire him greatly. What a TV and radio maverick and hero! A bit like when Jim Davidson, Davro or Joe Pasquale call me now, it never gets old that these icons have become my trusted mates. Noel agreed to give me an exclusive chat and it sort of backfired (well for him – not me). He'd insinuated that 'negative vibes' encourage cancer and indeed positive thoughts could prevent cancer. He not only was talking scientific nonsense but became a laughingstock because of his beliefs and refusal to acknowledge the offence caused. He was ridiculed by Phillip Schofield on This Morning – oh, the irony! The moral to the story is beliefs are tricky. My old Grandad Colin <u>believed</u> you could have a wank on the bus. The three police men and a judge disagreed. I ask you. Why didn't Noel just backtrack? He's a millionaire mega-star – I guess he didn't care. The media naturally misquoted and manipulated this. It was a storm in a D cup for sure. I felt sorry for this formidable talent. Loose lips sadly cost careers in this cancel culture.

Shortly after, Noel appeared on 'I'm a Celeb' and was the first one kicked off. The public had turned. What a travesty. Decades of love and warmth ruined in one devastating career blow. Such a shame. I didn't judge him of course. That interview, like the rest is still on YouTube and you can hear it for yourself. You decide. Why can't he have his opinion and talk cack? I genuinely love and admire him. I've done a few chats like this. I did the first and last interview with DLT (Dave Lee Travis) for the Sunday Mirror. DLT was another Radio legend destroyed by Operation Yewtree – the campaign to encourage people, some genuine – a lot bonkers – to make any claim they wanted about anyone they thought they might have once met...or not! As you can imagine I'm quite big now on injustice and boohooers playing the victim for attention and in some cases reaping fame and financial gain on the back of distortion and lies. Disingenuous pigs band-wagoning government funded witch hunts. This breed should be locked up for being weasels. This generation of CVM's – Competitive Victim Manipulators - have set back real victims of proper crimes a thousand years. We will regret this dark period in law. I'm serious, if people lie to get others sent down, they should be named, shamed and given the same sentence to dissuade others from lying. It's all Tony Blair's fault. We should NOT believe victims blindly. Word of mouth and hearsay is not evidence. Oh, it was Kia Cars Starlin who was boss of the CPS (Crooked Persecution Service) at the time. I might have known! Don't mention Savile or Al-Fayed!

I genuinely felt sorry for DLT. As I know too well myself, the financial and personal cost of accusations is HUGE and can ruin entire family's lives. This interview took a lot of convincing, as do most of the big chats all ultimately booked and recorded on trust. We live in a PR world and no one wants to get it wrong. I'm so proud of my reputation for fairness and sincerity. Say what you like about me but I always allowed guests to say exactly what they wanted, unedited without interruption, even if I don't agree with them. I have a totally clear conscience that I have never stitched anyone up in my career. I've never done gutter journalism or been paid to cover up or distract from the truth with a 'better' story like 99% of this shady and unethical business does instinctively. Pretending to be holier-than-thou and righteous beyond reproach is a very risky strategy. You'd better be squeaky clean! It always comes out in the end. After my three corrupt Notts Police farce raids at least everyone knows I'm up to bugger all. I'm hugely proud of my newspaper work – hundreds of stories printed over ten years with no 'editorial' or compliance issues whatsoever! Nothing has ever been pulled.

## Chapter 12

## The Circle of Life

What goes around comes around and for everything that happens there's a reason……...so they say! As time passed in the naughties, three heroes left my world and more special ones arrived. As you know I love my family beyond words and live for spending time with them, especially the kids. I adored my old grandad who was a true 'character.' A line for everything and a fear of no one. Like my dad's mum, Nana, he believed respect is earned. I was a chip off the old block. After grandma died, he wasn't the same. How could you be after decades having someone by your side? My Grandad Ernie and George (the budgie) were best mates and I'd pop in twice a week at least to see if he was OK or needed anything. Grandad was an old-fashioned working man. He had four daughters and a son all of whom were unique. My Aunty Viv was a true legend. She had Grandad's disposition of impatience with imbeciles. She and he lived in the moment, were a hoot and loved a beer and the bingo. She was the youngest and to me the most fun aunty. Viv was a character. She was a foster mother and did a glorious job raising her kids. She and Den were heroes to me. Salt of the earth class acts. Love the bones of them. Her brother Uncle Ernie was so cool and dry witted. I love him and Aunty Sue who couldn't have been more lovely, kind and loyal of late. During Covid Uncle Ernie totally re-designed the upstairs of my home. Such a clever craftsman. I so admire skilled people. Aunty Sue became a club singer for years in the nineties and was well respected. She put up with all kinds of shit I would have walked out over. They made a formidable team. I adore my cousins Tracy, Emma and Alan. I'd do anything for them. My other aunties and their kids were a big part of my life growing up. I babysat my cousins Kyle and Paige for a while at school. Great memories. Now more than ever I'm so grateful for so many influences and so much love. As life goes on, we all take different paths. I know mine is bonkers and bizarre to most but I'm so lucky to have had grandparents that created so much fun, joy and love. Grandma Dora was a one off. I adored the bones of her. She lived for her family, the epitome of love and devotion.

Grandad was a proud and no-nonsense kind of man, but he had a wit I adored. 'I say' would be his eyebrow raising reply to any comment that bemused him when he smelt horseshit. He'd moved out of the family home into a warden aided flat after grandma's passing. These places are small for obvious reasons but also tragic as the next move is almost undeniably 'upstairs' – and I'm not talking about loft conversion. It's all unspoken, but just like my nana it's so sad moving legends into these old-cockeries. He did well despite his bad chest having smoked tobacco for sixty years, he didn't care, he loved it! Old school defiance. They knew no better. Grandad didn't fall at Normandy. However, he did once go arse over tit in Skegness after winning £50 at the Gala Bingo and getting tanked up. Once a week I'd take him food. At 1pm I'd agreed to pop round with fish and chips. The curtain was shut. Why was the curtain shut when I arrived? More importantly, why hadn't the warden checked on him? We'll leave that question for another day. I don't know if you've ever had 'that' feeling but 'I knew' before I put the key in the door. I just knew something wasn't right. I cautiously shouted his name. Silence. His bedroom was directly opposite the front door. There he was, my Grandad, this hero slouched over the side of his bed with phone lying next to him on the floor. What the fack do I do? More importantly I've just wasted £15 on fish and chips – they won't give a refund. What a bummer!!! I approached the bed slowly, but he'd been there a long time. Heartbreaking. Life is shit.

Calling my mum was the saddest thing I've ever done. How on earth do you tell a daughter that her father had passed? Next, I phoned my aunties who had various reactions. Some stunned and one begging me to try and save him with CPR. Great idea but as rigor mortis had already set in I felt it was somewhat pointless and a little too late. More chance of bringing the BBC back to life. Another seemed curious as to where he'd left his wallet. We all react to grief in different ways, right?

It's so strange that in these circumstances I became almost robotic via Dr Showbiz. A showman's autopilot, I guess. The skill and art in what I do is to remain calm whilst all those around me lose their heads. I'm virtually unflappable. It's the thing I'm most proud of in the slammer. Nothing phases me. Some may perceive this as cold or discompassionate. I've trained myself to deal without drama in the worst possible situations - this was definitely one of them. I did call an ambulance first which came before the family and they pronounced him dead at the scene and like angels laid him out in bed beautifully and peacefully for the family. They didn't need to see the unedifying indignity I'd endured. I didn't go back in. I'd had my fill of stiffs in Vegas strip shows – enough was enough. Hand wringing and clutching pearls is not my style either. Grief can often become competitive. I've seen the very worst in people at the darkest of times. I shudder at how some people react. Most importantly my old Grandad would have been furious wasting those fish and chips. I miss the bones of him. What a true character.

Another sadness came shortly after when my Uncle Sam was diagnosed with three cancers. My heart was like a volcano with all this illness and loss. I'd just lost my Aunty Marge and Uncle Tom in their eighties who were proper legends and two angels I adored. Marge was a matriarch and battleaxe, I loved the bones of her. Sam and Dorothy didn't have kids, and we'd been very close since I was a little boy. Sam was a maths teacher and supremely smarter than me, but he had a dry wit that I adored. He loved the news and was a no-nonsense guy, no fan of the new generation of woke terrorists destroying the very fabric of our once Great Britain. More like Grate Britain these days!

He hated shenanigans. Like me his propensity for foolishness was less than 1%. I remember once taking them to see Diana Ross at Nottingham Arena. She didn't have a full band and wasn't singing (everything) LIVE. Within ten mins I looked at Sam, he looked at me and we both simultaneously rolled our eyes, saw our arses and stood up and left. Balls to the £80 per ticket. Two peas in a pod. Rather go home and listen to the CD instead of the rip-off crap arena sound. I love that! A man who knew his mind. Both Sam and Dorothy were fabulous cooks so for years I would delight in having dinner with them every week.

So, when Sam found out about 'the Big C' it was time for me to step up, no problem at all. I understand why people are selfish and don't want to volunteer when times are tough, but that's not me. I was busy but who cares. Cancer is draining and negative. It's boring and relentless but it had to be done. It's in fact a different form of a prison sentence. Every morning, I would take him to the City Hospital for chemo. We'd do shopping on the way back. In the end he waited in the car – a very bad sign he was so drained having 'done' virtually nothing. You eventually recognise 'that look.' Life is cruel. Dorothy, who is astonishingly brave with MS for forty plus years fought on regardless and we got through it together. That's what family is all about. Teamwork. Thick and thin (that was Ant & Dec's original Club name. Not a lot of people know that!).

The indignity for Sam was inconceivable. He had a stoma at one point – a hideous de-humanising shitbag (think Covid PPE profiteers) for this crap disease. For a couple of years, we battled on through good and bad. He struggled struggling. Life is cruel. Shortly after the all-clear was confirmed, the cancer came back and Sam's time was up. My dad's best mate taken. How my parents coped with all this loss I'll never know. What strength and tenacity. Learnt so much from their stamina and stiff upper lip from the inevitable circle of life. First dad's twin and now this. Neither mum or dad moaned or complained once. What inspirations. My sister as always came up trumps at our time of greatest need but she had a baby and a full-time job. That baby, my nephew, was the ray of light that kept the entire family going. I was (and still am) besotted with him. I now promised myself (and Sam) to take care of Dorothy and I did. Big commitment but the least I could do. Almost a decade after his passing, I don't regret a second. I truly believe the more love and generosity you give out, the more you get back. The insight, laughs, knowledge and inspiration both Sam and Dorothy have given me will never be forgotten. Being a carer and friend of Dorothy was my honour and pleasure.

Of course, the best thing about the circle of life is the blessings of babies that replace the absent friends we've lost. I've never been paternal as my life is too busy but I've always loved toddlers – I used to go to nursery with them in the 80's. I truly don't think showbiz is conducive to having kids. Too many broken hearts along the way. Few dads in my game do a good job sadly. I don't want to be 'that' guy. I couldn't do that to my child. This game destroys families. Children shouldn't pay the price for my passion. Also, I mustn't have mucky kiddie fingers putting grubby marks all over my baby grand and posh Ladyboy sofa! My cleaner (Formaldehyde – lovely lass) would be chasing after them morning noon and night having a squirt and a wipe. She's busy enough as it is with Doddy's paws, the current Mrs B's prosecco glasses and my extensive personal grooming! Babies are boring but the joy I've had from my nephew, neighbours and God kids is INCREDIBLE. I live for them and would give up everything for them. When Kaiden was born it was a re-birth for everyone. The energy, love and warmth a baby brings to the house is indescribable. Way before Buba, I'd had lots of dear friends up the duff (nothing to do with me may I add dear reader). I love making an effort for birthdays and especially things like Bonfire Night, Halloween and of course Christmas. I'm a big kid at heart and I love planning get togethers – as big as possible. All I ever want to create for those around me is that feeling of pure love and community that my Nana created for me throughout my entire childhood. Nothing to do with money, it's about being together. Uncle Alex is on a mission! Memories are the oxygen of life, right??? It all began with my dear buddy Giles who has two beautiful kids I'd grow up with and babysit for. Next my bestie Claire had my gorgeous God son Sam and angel Oliver. I adore those boys more than words can say. The joy this family has given me is infinite. I adore Stewart and his amazing son Noah who is a true character. He's just had another bundle of joy who I can't wait to watch thrive. My dearest Anneka has been a beacon of hope with Reggie who appears to be morphing into me with his love for piano and relentless yacking. I speak to these angels daily. Now more than ever these little people are the lights of my life and beacons of hope. They're all about a decade old as I write, so now we can really have fun times. The fun and laugher of kids outweighs any standing ovation. I can only thank my mum and dad for my disproportionate sense of community and duty to others that they've instilled in me. What I do know about me is that I'm needy and thrive off genuine love. I'm done with fakes – I have an insatiable need for sincerity. Kids offer this in bucket loads. Zero pretence. They're the ultimate hope and future! Mum and Dad have been through so much over the years (as has everyone) but NEVER once have I ever heard them moan, self-pity or boohoo. I've brought them so many amazing and joyous ups – but also worry and ultimately the unforgivable anguish of being a political prisoner and hostage. They don't care. We have each other. I'm still their little boy. All I know, especially now more than ever is that I couldn't love them more if I tried. I'm so blessed to have had them holding my hand through the shitstorms and many luxuries of life that I've been showered with. The values of love and family will stay with me forever. Your parents and loved ones live in you – I'm a very lucky lad! I can blame them. After all, it has to be <u>all</u> their fault surely????

## I've Finally Made it – It's going TOO Well

By 2018 I'd had five perfect years career wise and I felt I'd achieved life's greatest glory – serenity, happiness and contentment. Nothing more to achieve or prove. The 'calm' was perfect. I had no ambitions left – just more of the same. No rows, no court cases and no shit heads pissing me off or telling me what to do. I'd found my groove. My perfect life is not for everyone but it ticked every box I needed to fulfil my dream happiness. I'd done so well with the newspapers that I'd put down my first ever deposit on a house. For me this was my ultimate goal that so few will ever achieve and maintain in showbiz. Over five years I'd saved up £50,000 and finally I had been able to buy a new build on a hill overlooking the village where I was born. I couldn't be closer to the coal mine that defined who my community is and who I am at core. It's now a gorgeous country park. I had no ambition to live anywhere other than Nottingham within walking distance of my parents, sister and family who, like most, never moved far from where they were born. I will never forget the pride I had watching my house being built and being able to take my proud parents to see it growing brick by brick. <u>NOTHING</u> I've achieved professionally will compare to the pride of owning my own front door at thirty-nine.

Being freelance is amazing. You get to write stuff off, work for yourself, travel, tell dick head bosses to 'do one' – but – when the bank manager says 'What are you going to earn next year?' You're literally facked. Now more than ever I realised the price you can pay for a life in entertainment. Few reap the rewards and the glory. It almost never works out or pays off. Most end up without a pot to piss in or can afford a window to throw it out of. They end up bitter, angry and tweeting bile from their mother's back bedroom, or slagging off motorists whilst Sellotaping themselves to the M4. Not for me. By now I'd survived twenty-five years being paid to do what I loved. I've never had to do a proper job. I think most 'turns' would tell you that this is the ultimate goal. I've been blessed with consistent work for 365 days a year for decades – actors often struggle to get five weeks panto – and that's only until their tits start to sag or their six pack fades. It's brutal! It's ALL about longevity for me.

In November 2018 when I put the key in my own front door, I felt ten foot tall. The irony that the mortgage was £500 less than renting a bungalow is utterly ludicrous and shows how absurd and broken this country has become. My three-bedroom house mortgage is £1,200 cheaper than renting the flat in Canary Wharf in 2005. Life rarely makes sense to me. I loved decorating it with unique bits and bobs – life's too short to be beige, bland and ordinary. The greatest thrill came when I could finally cook in my own brand-new kitchen and put a meal on the table for Team AB. To this day that never gets old - genuine pride. I'm a lucky boy to have been blessed with a niche that has kept me in gainful employment for my entire adult life despite the odd black eye - metaphorically speaking. What could possibly go wrong? I'd cracked it by forty!

No matter what I achieved, professionally, my twenty-year friendship with Sir Ken Dodd was still my greatest honour that reaped the most rewards. For me Sir Ken Dodd was still the king, the master and my greatest mentor. Since the age of fourteen Sir Ken had been in my life week in and week out. Now in his late eighties his health was failing but his wit, timing, spirit and love for the business was as strong as it had ever been. For two decades I had followed Ken around the country and felt part of his very small inner-sanctum, family and team. To this day I'll never forget the tingle when he'd phone. One of the biggest oddities in my life is that very famous people know who I am. It never becomes normal. I wonder if anyone else in the biz thinks about this stuff? It's normal now to have a tap on the shoulder from amazing punters, but when stars tune in, that's still very strange. For so many stars to become life-long friends is so mind blowing, a huge compliment, honour and very humbling! Ken and I rarely talked about showbiz – both of us saw it for what it was, but he loved and never gave up mastering his craft. He was truly inspiring.

Whenever I'd go to America, every single trip Doddy would have me call him from Barnes & Noble – the enormous book shop – and give him the titles of every book on comedy, jokes or writing on the shelf. "I'll have that one slim!" he'd say - he loved this. What do you buy a multi-millionaire of eight decades? Time and effort is the answer. It was a pain in the arse as I would buy them, box them, take them to the post office and send them to Knotty Ash. Often the postage was more expensive than the books themselves. 'HOW MUCH?' I'd send him the receipts when I got home and if it was £295.74 – that's exactly the amount sent back in the cheque. Sir Ken never changed. I didn't care. It's cute…...well it was Ken. He'd seen sixty years of showbiz shysters bankrupting his less wise pals. He didn't miss a trick.

Doddy was a mega-star who changed my life. Taught me not only comic timing but also comic structure. Of course, I'm just a nob jokey playing at it by comparison, but WOW, what a mentor to teach you the ropes. His genius didn't happen by accident. He was the most well-read man I'd ever met who never stopped polishing and perfecting. He was a genius and the biggest showbiz blessing and miracle of my life. The hours and hours we spent in dressing rooms was magical and precious to me. INVALUABLE! The repeated six hours I spent in the wings watching and learning from his LIVE performances were priceless. I must have seen him LIVE a thousand times over the two plus decades. Money can't buy knowledge, access and insight. For me the compliment was trust. 100% mutual trust. His confidence and serenity on stage was mind blowing. An Olympic standard turn. How does anyone remain so relaxed and at ease – this is what I wanted to master should my seafront audience ever appear. You have no idea how excited we were in 2017 to find out FINALLY that Doddy would become Sir Ken. What an electrifying phone call that was. Thank God it came when it did! Weeks later Ken phoned and asked if I would be willing to join him and his close family and friends at The Rubens Hotel close to Buckingham Palace to have afternoon tea following the ceremony. WOW! This blew my socks off. He could have asked anyone – but he didn't, he asked me! That honour will stay with me for the rest of my life. I think what Sir Ken liked about me is that I never saw his age. I talked to him on a level as the hugely impressive genius that he was. We would always rather talk about current affairs than anything else. This too developed my craft for debates and contempt for what we're told on the news. He opened my eyes. He schooled me on life and the importance of politics. He was a news junky like me and hated all the anti-British bollocks that the woke lefty lot are ramming down our throats.

I booked a suite at my beloved St Pancras Hotel the night before he became a Sir and the following day walked all the way down

Euston Road, then Tottenham Court Road, right after Trafalgar Square on to The Mall to Buckingham Palace. I shed a tear that day wondering how little old me had managed to sustain this life until forty. I prayed my family were proud and all the bullshit to 'make it' was worth it. Surely nothing could go wrong now – I'd qualified. I called Mum and Dad outside to include them in my very special moment. I was a friend of the greatest comedian in British history. How lucky was I? Lady Anne, who looked magnificent, welcomed me. I adore Anne and always did. Fiercely protective of Ken (which I love), Anne guarded him brilliantly (and rightly so). Few in this game do something for nothing, it took many years to build trust. Few just want to give. I can honestly say I never wanted a penny or anything from Ken other than his friendship and time. He knew that instantly. Anne took a lot longer to woo. Very very smart talented lady. One of Doddy's great lines when someone would try and pull a fast one – 'I'm too old for a black eye.' Sharp as a razor that one. His bullshitometer was off the scale. That afternoon was perfect. Surrounded by his family and friends, less than sixty in total, I was honoured to be Sir Ken Dodd's friend. A memory for a lifetime.

All those times breaking my back carrying fifty books to a post office in New York and Vegas paid off in loyalty. I walked back to the St Pancras Hotel that night on the phone to my nearest and dearest – as proud as punch. The following day I had the front page and page three of the Daily Mirror in tribute to my hero. I gave Doddy the splash he deserved. My exclusive quotes and pictures were much appreciated by Doddy who was the king of publicity even at eighty-nine. After this Sir Ken had a revival and did even more sold-out shows than ever. I was speechless at how he could turn it on. What an education. He had more energy than 99% of the dopes on these box-ticking BBC and Channel 4 quiz shows, a quarter of his age. Comedians? They lack one quality Ken had in buckets – funny bones. You can't buy it. Charm and warmth. Most of all sincerity. I miss him greatly.

The last time I saw Sir Ken was just days before he ended up in hospital. But what a gig. It was his last ever show at arguably his favourite theatre The Grand in Blackpool. A freezing Sunday night he'd over sold-out. I shit you not people were sitting on planks of wood! The God's were packed for the Blackpool 'Comedy God' himself. He did something extraordinary that made me certain I'd never see him again. As I greeted the car with Lady Anne driving, as I'd done for two or more decades, he said "film me, don't stop filming me until I tell you to stop." WTF? He'd never said this in twenty-five years. That night I filmed his every move and this glorious rare and precious backstage insight is still on YouTube to this day. What an honour. I don't think anyone has EVER had such 'real' access to the 'real' man…...behind the scenes from beginning to end. Talk about chuffed! This was Ken's parting gift. Indeed, his swansong. That night my dear mate and Doddy's spec act Andy Eastwood was there. Honestly, I think Andy and I were his honorary grandsons. We popped for a pint and fish and chips with <u>plenty</u> of time to spare during his first spot. How funny is that. His interval came down after most show's finale. Both of us knew he was different. An energy like thirty years ago.

Incredible. His last hurrah in the #1 variety theatre in the country. Ken had turned ninety, became a Sir and in my opinion achieved EVERYTHING he wanted…. well, other than marrying Anne which he did two days before passing. Andy and I had known each other from day one. He loved Ken too. Both of us are the same age. We've become great friends together with his stunning and talented wife Helen. They've just had a buba which also is precious. Ken would have been so proud of that baby! I'll never forget that night.

I never saw Ken again. This was the third major blow in weeks. Losing three male role models was tough. I hugged him as I left at 1am and I told him that I loved him. I did love him and still do – beyond words. Three patriarchs had passed. They ain't building heroes like this anymore. On the morning of Sir Ken's passing, I was asked to talk to Nick Ferrari on LBC and various others. I never do interviews but this was a true honour to celebrate my dear friend's life. It was heartbreaking personally, but not a tragedy. I'm a true believer in 'things happen for a reason' and someone somewhere sends angels into your life. Whoever allowed Sir Ken Dodd to profoundly inspire my life has my eternal gratitude. So few people get to meet true genius. I was blessed to learn from his wisdom and knowledge, and profit profoundly from his guidance, support, love and more importantly comic timing. I'm eternally grateful to Sir Ken and Lady Anne.

The day of his funeral was magnificent. Ken had no fear. His faith and tons of love filled his heart until the very end. The gathering afterwards was so filled with love and warmth. I miss Sir Ken EVERY single day. I'll never forget how lucky I was to have him, Lady Anne and the Doddy family in my life. God knows what he'd make of my current predicament. He'd had the odd run in with the Clown Court himself. Funny old world…...but it's far less funny without Dody in it!

## Vegas, Twirlies and End of Showbiz

I can't lie, it was the end of theatre, entertainment and showbiz for me after Doddy died. Nothing was ever as special and 'the game' had changed beyond all recognition. Little or nothing excited me. It was the same old shite. Vegas had spoilt me. I'd seen it all. There was little heart left in the biz which was cluttered with fakes and bullshitters. Production values had gone to pot and producers were happy to rip off punters with substandard cack that they knew insulted their intelligence at double the price. I couldn't stay quiet. No longer did I want to play 'my colleagues' game of back handers for good reviews and nor did I want to interview every shithead offered to me who I'd indulged a hundred times before. I guess after twenty odd years I saw the business for what it was. I was done! I was bored. As we now know too well, it's a mostly vitriolic, vile and vindictive charade attracting seriously unwell, medicated, unstable, bitter and cloak and dagger people willing to destroy others at any cost to aid their own success. Even Vegas had changed. No longer was it 'quality over quantity,' it was 'who could con the biggest mug out of their kid's inheritance,' to fund a new show that would be closed in seconds. Their theory was 'they won't be back so who cares.' Appalling. I feel theatre generally has the same theory now with all of the crap 'drag' pantos cluttering theatres with such inappropriate and classless guff. Enough to make you heave. More and more shit was filling showrooms that would be laughed out of Blackpool – let alone Caesars Palace.

PRs now ran the town buying reviews, stars for posters and even awards – yep $10,000 for 'Best Show' award. Scandalous. Again, most award ceremonies are now million pound generating businesses where the highest bidder gets the gong and best seat. One big con! Pitiful. These sharks don't care so why should I give two shiny shites or want to be part of this sham? Hopeless! My brutal honesty was at the root of VOR's success which in turn created a cesspit of enemies, who would do anything to destroy me, as the industry was so nervous because I was the only authentic investigative journalist and 'critic' brave enough to tell the truth. I was getting too big for my boots. I knew where the bodies were buried and I was stood at ground zero. They needed to shut me up and wipe me out sharpish. Welcome dark forces! Even now I'm amazed how touchy people are. I'm equally shocked that anyone would care about my opinion. It turns out showbiz tarts are fickle, sensitive and can't stand the truth. Put a mirror up to these fruits and it blows their mind. Some will be reading this right now spitting feathers. They paid to be infuriated. They claim to despise me but bought the book. A purchase they'll never reveal – identical to their butt plug and gimp mask at the back of their wife's knicker drawer! They watch me to be outraged. Proper insanity. Sums it all up really! They'll never change. They're ill. I'm all they have. Creepy hey? But boy would I pay a big price when the twatter trolls descended.

On YouTube via my first brand 'Celebrity Radio' I'd become the #1 reviewer online. No one could compete. Not just in London but in Vegas and often on Broadway too. People liked my no-nonsense approach and the algorithms pushed me to the top almost instantly due to my 'under five-minute' rule as most twirlie types have ADHD or worse and can't focus for more than two choruses of 'The Sound of Music' in a straight-jacket. Word was spreading. In Vegas I had my first spat with a hero of mine David Copperfield. I'd backed his nemesis Criss Angel and he was pissed off. I became obsessed with Copperfield as a kid. He was breathtaking on TV but LIVE his show was very good, but in my view not as cool, sexy and high energy as Criss Angel – David's arch enemy. I believed Copperfield to look tired and be bored – who wouldn't be, doing three shows a day and decades of jiggery pokery. Against most critics I championed Criss and gave him 5* at his Luxor Mindfreak opening. He had a ten-year contract with Cirque du Soleil. Everyone was shocked by my genuine endorsement. For a start the Criss Angel production was massive by comparison and his showgirls were stunning. David was much older and his show was clunky and robotic. David had honoured me with three interviews for which I was thrilled but now I was persona non grata – a shithead and dead to him. After my 5* endorsement of Criss he hit the roof and made it known around town that I was not welcome back. I sat in my suite one afternoon at the Tahiti Village and Copperfield phoned me. He could not believe I'd given his only serious magical competition a better review. He was furious Criss quoted me on the poster. This was the point that I realised showbiz is tribal and my quotes and reviews now carried weight and came with influence and consequences. I was costing these people money in their show business.

I'd become very close to Criss and his family. Criss was opening a show at Foxwoods, just outside New York and there was an 'accident' with the drowning/holding breath 'Water Torture' trick and one of his guys had to be saved. I arranged to get the footage and leak it as an exclusive. Criss saved this performer's life! I did my online and PR magic and in 24 hours this twelve second clip appeared on over a thousand web sites on three hundred TV channels around the world and all over in the press from India to Dubai. It's still my most watched clip over on YouTube. As you can imagine Foxwoods were over the Moon! Money can't buy publicity! They flew me out to New York for ten days as a thank you to see the show and I was treated like gold. I had a hoot! This one clip gave them a $1,000,000 worth of publicity for the show that money can't buy. It's all a game. Knowing where to place it and timing is the skill born out of experience. This proves telling the truth, following your heart and being loyal <u>ALWAYS</u> pays off in the end. I'm proud to call Criss a dear friend. Twice in 2022 I stayed at Planet Hollywood to see and work with him. We had a hoot playing Blackjack……thank God it wasn't on the $1,000 table. Such fun. I always say I'm no fun, but this was a ball. Amazing how free voddy and diet cokes makes you empty your pockets. I'm still (and always will) be in awe of talent. Criss Angel's craft, skill and devotion, amazes me. He's an amazing Dad. Huge respect.

The reality is, if you say nice things people love you, if you don't – well, obviously they won't, BUT the smart people will respect you a million times more for being authentic. This is a life choice and career decision based on integrity. I just can't lie. The truth has a HUGE price. In a business of fakes this paid off big time with the audience but created <u>powerful</u> highly connected and wealthy enemies around the world. Honesty has ultimately cost me my freedom. Remember, as I'll explain in book two, I'm not in jail for lying. I was never accused of not telling the truth. People I didn't know and hadn't met 'had to say something!' Compelled to watch and comment right? I didn't ask anyone to watch me. Strange isn't it. The truth hurts! They tried to 'close me down' because I said and did things they did not approve of. <u>All</u> of my 'victims' were from media, radio or theatre exclusively. For many of these people it was the first time someone had put a mirror up to them. The world of showbiz DOES NOT LIKE IT! I believe I was the first (and probably the last) to be an online critic exclusively, successfully as a job not just a part time hobby to get free comps and (ego) wank chorus boys and suck of showgirls. My financial success made the trolls even more jealous, nuts and determined to silence me. The 'influence' terrified them! Why? I'd better write book two! As for offending people, I've never given offence in my life – if dopes choose to take it, that's their problem.

I cannot tell you how empowering it is not to 'beg' for a press ticket. So liberating. I've removed PRs, publicists, managers and theatres from my life. I pay and sleep very well at night. They don't want the veneer to crack and the truth to come out. Lifting the lid on this crooked, creepy, corrupt and crackers industry (along with the establishment who fund them) was a step too far. I had to be banished, hopefully scared into suicide or bankrupted into obscurity. Sadly, it was a mega fail from the media and theatre mobsters. I'M BACK! I've met less than a handful in Radio, theatre and showbiz that I would give my number to, let alone allow one inch across my front gate. I wouldn't let half of the deviants eat out of Doddy's dog bowl, let alone on my nicely polished table. All that dribbling whilst fingering my lazy Susan would put me right off.

I can promise you from the very bottom of my bottom I don't regret a word I have ever broadcast. If you're in this business, you (as am I) are up for critique and there's nothing you can do about it. Sadly, in the post covid hurt feelings 'boohoo' 'I'm off to rehab' world this comes at a huge price, but what a journey getting there. So, by 2019 I'd made it. I was living the dream. I was not a millionaire (and never wanted to be) but I had a three-bed house (not a mansion – pointless), drove a Kia Sportage (more than enough) and professionally achieved my dreams of travelling the world in style and living my best life with no bone heads dragging me down with their 'issues' or 'conditions.' I was surrounded by love, had an amazing family and had more friends than I could shake a stick at! What more could I have hoped for? What could possibly go wrong?

I knew some were so jealous of me and that they'd do anything to destroy me, but who cares – I'd fight back bigger and better and rise above their bait. I never looked in my rear-view mirror, balls to the whack jobs and fruit loops! I was respected by those who mattered to me - the rest can insert a cactus up their jacksy. Again, the greatest achievement of my life and career is the solidarity and mutual respect of those I adore. Why would I care about worthless imbeciles with pea brains on social media? Honestly if these jackasses put their heads together, they'd make a plank. My protective bubble of love kept me well, happy and sane. I believe a testament of your sincerity and success is the level and desperation of your critics and assassins who want you silenced. What is it these people have to hide? Why go to such effort. Curious hey?

As far as I was concerned no opinion mattered other than those around my dining table. I wasn't born with a silver spoon in my gob and my roots and grounding made me the man I am - not clicks, hits, chitter, chatter or filibustering from those who need to be spanked with a scented jock strap. Unlike the social media obsessed world of 'likes' – I couldn't care less. I have no interest in Tik Tok or Insta. I'm all about meaningful words and content - not images of my breakfast. Now more than ever I had chosen to be an outsider AND LOVED IT. Why? Why? Why? – because this elevated me to be unique and having my own party where I only have invited guests. I didn't want to be at someone else's table pretending to fit in with conversation and bon ami driven by a sniff of Columbian marching powder. The root of my 'issues' with our millennial world is hypocrisy. 'Earth Day' is a good example. Vegas turns off every light for 24 hours to pretend to be environmentally friendly – but then switches millions of unnecessary bulbs on for 364 days until they fake it again. Own who you are! Laugh in the face of the environment – like you do 99.9% of the year. It's <u>bullshit</u>. It's a game. It's unedifying and it sums up our pitiful world of fakery and razzle dazzle. I want no part of it thank you. Stop the world, I want to get off! I still blame Simon Cowell. His crap reality shows hypnotised a nation to believe unless you had a disability or sob story, you can't win. Boohoo off!

I have a mum and dad who are my every breath, a sister who I adore and stuck by me forever and wider family and friends who I love to bits. What other POSSIBLE definition of success is there?

Through the ups and downs, hiring and firings, loves and losses and heartbreak and joy – I'd made it to nearly forty years old doing exactly what I wanted to do – when I wanted to do it against all the odds. I truly did it my way at any cost. Not many can say that. So, what would 2020 bring? Fack me with a cricket bat! It was the reckoning. The world stopped and showbiz ended. Family and friends were literally torn apart and the world would become 'them and us.' It was all taken away in one announcement by the crooked liar and cheat Boris Johnson and his woeful government, 'save the NHS and stay at home.' Oy vey, this was it. The end of the world as we know. When you choose to be holier than thou and point fingers at people – remember there are three others pointing back at you! It takes a long time, but the truth will bite you in the ass. These protected pricks HATE that! History has of course totally vindicated our side.

2020 was the start of the most exciting two years of my life. The most success I'd ever encountered and such obscene income I could buy each one of my lawyers a new holiday home in Barbados. YAY!

But first, in October 2019 an anonymous email inciting social media to 'close him down' was sent by a BBC person and published by a man I'd never met or heard of. The consequences of this witch hunt would land me a jail sentence for FIVE AND A HALF years. As a man of 40 years good character – for a non-violent, non-sexual and non-drugs related crime I'd be vilified on national news and sent down for stalking WITHOUT fear, alarm or distress – a conviction NEVER mentioned anywhere in the press or even in court. Could this really be the truth, the whole truth and nothing but the truth? The BBC presented a file of 'evidence' to the corrupt, evil and unspeakably stupid Nottinghamshire Police and I was arrested five times and raided illegally three times without a warrant. My life would never be the same again.

A week before lockdown in March 2020 my entire diary was cancelled. What the actual clucking duck was I going to do? How would I pay my mortgage? When would I see people again?

None of this mattered. I wanted to make my only remaining life's ambition come true. This was something I could never do before because of time, work and travel. No, not 'The Voice of Reason' = I bought a puppy! I win.

So, 'F' YOU COVID, Handcock and your despicable corrupt government and mafia police force! I went and bought my cockapoo called Doddy and for the next twenty-four months my life, career and world was on fire!

It is unbelievable that I finished this book at 5pm on New Year's Eve 2022. How poetic is that?

Find out about Covid, Lockdown, Doddy, the birth of Voice of Reason and how I was kidnapped by the authorities and held hostage by the state in book two – 'LOCKED DOWN : LOCKED UP.'

Thanks for reading my autobiography to 40! You ain't read nothing yet…….

**I love you and there's nothing you can do about it!**
**Alex x**

## The Titles that Didn't Make it!

- Enema of the State
- Hoist by my Own Retard
- Don't Respect Your Elders
- Working Class Hero (Rebel)
- Rebel without a Pause
- Missionary of the Masses
- Respect is Earned NOT Expected
- Not a Shock Jock, not a Rock Jock – Not even Scottish!
- Radio Rebel = You bet your FM Life
- The Truth Hurts
- Resilience! Stand Up to Shitheads
- 'If it Looks Like a Duck and Quacks Like a Duck......'
- Rollercoaster Life! A Circus Full of Clowns
- In my Own Little World
- You Won't Beat the System (But you can try……)
- It's all One BIG Game
- Pain in the Art
- Numpties, Mardy Arses and Chopsy Saboteurs
- The Price of Fame
- Born with a Silver Foot in his Gob
- A Life Dropping Bollocks
- Disc Jockey to Nob Jockey
- BBC – Belfield's Broadcasting Celebration

**Don't miss the other books in the series:**

**Book Two – Locked Down: Locked Up**
The Evil BBC and Corrupt Police Witch Hunt

**Book Three – Surviving the Slammer**
A Screw Loose! : 5.5 Years Pleasuring His Majesty

**Book Four – HMPontins**
Super Jail = Super Fail

**Book Five – HMPortaloo**
A Sure Wank Redemption : All Screwed Up!

**Book Six – HMPointless**
5* Pokey Spa and Asylum
Therapy Horses, Pedicures and Yoga
Murder, Rape, and Suicide